Genre and Generic Change in
English Comedy, 1660–1710

In this study of stage comedy during the late seventeenth century Brian Corman examines one of its most remarkable qualities – its stability – and proposes a new way of looking at generic change.

Corman contends that English comedy remained faithful to the inherited repertory that developed from models provided by Jonson and Fletcher. He traces the variations, permutations, and combinations, comparing plays entering the repertory during three five-year periods, 1670–5, 1690–5, and 1705–10. Working from the very different contributions of R.S. Crane, A.H. Scouten, Robert Hume, and Hans Robert Jauss, he develops a theory of generic change in the comedies. Equal attention is given to plays currently in the canon and those that have long been forgotten by all but specialists.

Corman points out the inadequacies of earlier generic formulations of Restoration comedy and, using the theoretical insights of Crane, Claudio Guillén, and Alastair Fowler, he develops a generic model more appropriate for a conservative, traditional, and inclusive genre like comedy.

Corman not only illuminates the broader patterns of generic continuity and change but also brings a thoroughness and sensitivity to his study of individual authors and their works. The tradition of Jonson and Fletcher, we learn, proved sufficiently rich, challenging, and resilient to maintain a prospering generic institution on the English stage.

BRIAN CORMAN is Director of Graduate Studies, Department of English, University of Toronto.

BRIAN CORMAN

Genre and Generic Change
in English Comedy
1660–1710

UNIVERSITY OF TORONTO PRESS
Toronto Buffalo London

© University of Toronto Press Incorporated 1993
Toronto Buffalo London
Printed in Canada

ISBN 0-8020-2885-3

Printed on acid-free paper

Canadian Cataloguing in Publication Data

Corman, Brian, 1945–
Genre and generic change in English comedy, 1660–1710

Includes bibliographical references and index.
ISBN 0-8020-2885-3

1. English drama (Comedy) – History and criticism.
2. English drama – Restoration, 1660–1700 – History and criticism. I. Title.

PR698.C6C77 1993   822'.4   C92-095719-6

This book has been published with the help of a grant from the Canadian
Federation for the Humanities, using funds provided by the Social Sciences
and Humanities Research Council of Canada.

For Linda

Contents

Preface

The book I intended to write many years ago when I began working on late seventeenth-century drama was to have provided the definitive generic map I then thought essential – and possible. Greater acquaintance with the vast number of plays that would have had to be accommodated and with the theoretical complexities of issues of genre and generic change forced me to alter radically the design of this study. While I had never looked at genre prescriptively, I had expected to provide the precise definitions of generic forms required of a good cartographer. And I was equally confident that a series of diachronic maps would produce a historical atlas of great clarity.

The more I looked at the plays, the more I was convinced of the need for the 'institutional' approach to genre I offer in the first chapter. One of its consequences was the recognition that 'institutional' genres, like other institutions, have histories of their own, histories comprising a wide range of changes, some abrupt, some very slow and gradual. And like other institutions, the drama is not immune from pressures that critics more purely formal or structural would consider external. But though I recognize the importance of 'external' influences on the drama, I refer to them only incidentally, instead focusing intensively on the most traditional components of drama criticism – plot and character. This is not because I consider others irrelevant or inappropriate, but in part because I consider plot and character the most useful and direct means to examine issues of genre and generic change, and in part because others have recently used alternative strategies for mapping change in the plays of the period. Notable among these others are Robert Markley, whose *Two-Edg'd Weapons: Style and Ideology in the Comedies of Etherege, Wycherley and Congreve* examines dramatic language as it adapts in response to historical change; Eric Rothstein and Frances M. Kavenik, whose *The Designs of Carolean Comedy* provides a model of comedy based on the changing needs and desires of the audience; and Rose A. Zimbardo, whose *A Mirror to Nature: Transformations in Drama and Aesthetics 1660–1732* sees changes in the drama as the result of changes in the concept 'imitation of nature.' Each of these studies has contributed significantly to our understanding of late seventeenth-century comedy. I see my own not as an answer to any of them – in fact, they appeared after my project was initially formulated – but rather as a complementary study, one that differs from theirs in its primary focus on genre and, consequently, on the structural elements of comedy. The resulting narrative is perhaps less conclusive since it is less directed by method or thesis. Its tentative quality reflects the complex history of the institutional genre, comedy, as I have charted it over the fifty-year period following the Restoration.

A number of friends and colleagues have offered important assistance in the course of my writing this study. I would like to thank Patricia Brückmann, David Richter, Richard Van Fossen, and Sheldon Zitner for their invaluable help at various stages of composition; the late George Falle, Arthur Friedman, and Sheldon Sacks for earlier aid and encouragement; Jean Christie and Cecilia Martino for preparing the manuscript; Darlene Money for expert copy-editing; and Katherine West for help with proofreading and indexing.

I would also like to acknowledge the considerable support I have had from the Department of English at the University of Toronto and the Division of Humanities at Erindale College. Financial support has come from the University of Toronto and the Social Sciences and Humanities Research Council of Canada. My book has been published with the help of a grant from the Canadian Federation for the Humanities, using funds provided by the Social Sciences and Humanities Research Council of Canada.

My greatest debt is to my family, both for essential encouragement and for having to put up with the trials of research and publication. I regret that my father, Harry Corman, did not live to see it to completion; my gratitude to him, to my mother, Anita Corman, to my wife, Linda, and to my daughter, Sarah, is greater than I can express.

1

The 'Mixt Way' of Comedy

The most important contribution *The London Stage* has made to a critical reassessment of late seventeenth-century drama has been in forcing critics to acknowledge the enormous diversity of dramatic activity in post-Restoration London. It is no longer possible to argue for a monolithic 'Restoration comedy,' 'comedy of manners,' or 'comedy of wit' based on the plays of a few favoured writers, such as Etherege, Wycherley, and Congreve. The pioneering efforts of such critics as A.H. Scouten established the need to look beyond the canon to capture a representative selection of plays; Robert D. Hume's Herculean survey of all the new plays to appear in London between 1660 and 1710 provided definitive support for Scouten's argument.[1]

Critics have been far less successful in reaching a new consensus about either the nature or the development of the reconstituted body of plays they must now contend with. It is the purpose of this study to offer one such explanation of the range of plays that are called comedies and of the changes that genre undergoes in the fifty years after the Restoration. English comedies of this period form a subset of the longest, most continuous generic tradition in Western literature. Stage comedy had emerged with most of its representative characteristics by the time Aristophanes and Menander offered their plays on the Athenian stage. Because of the loss of Aristotle's lectures on comedy, the theory of comedy remains less well developed than the theory of tragedy. And even though it is too late to consolidate generic thinking on comedy to the degree achieved for tragedy, a generic approach remains most fruitful if for no other reason than its incredibly deep roots in the minds of playwrights and critics for more than two thousand years. Since approaches to genre and to generic change are as diverse as the plays I intend to discuss, I begin with a brief discussion of my understanding and use of genre theory and its application to problems in literary history. What follows is an approach to the first fifty years of post-Restoration comedy that accounts for its generic changes. The balance of my study applies that approach to eighteen representative plays.

The greatest temptation for a generic critic of English comedy of the late seventeenth century is to try to recover the theory of genre held by late seventeenth-century playwrights. Claudio Guillén bases part of his defence of genre on its usefulness to artists in providing 'a contemporary model – a "working hypothesis."' He points out that most genres discovered by critics postdate the works themselves: 'A preexistent form can never be simply "taken over" by the writer or transferred to a new work. The task of form-making must be undertaken all over again. The writer must begin once more to match matter to form, and to that end he can only find a very special sort of assistance in the fact that the fitting of matter to form has *already* taken place. To offer this assistance is the function of genre.'[2] Yet recognition of the value of genre for the artist must not imply, as it occasionally does for Guillén or for Gustavo Perez Firmat, that reproduction of the perspective of the artist is the end of literary history or criticism. The business of the literary critic is to provide the most powerful explanation possible for what the artist did, that of the literary historian to explain how the compositional principles of the genre were used in the unique achievement of that artist. Attempts to do so within reconstructed versions of the conceptual framework of the artist are inevitably inadequate.[3]

The title page of Dryden's *Marriage À-la-Mode* provides a familiar example on the level of the most basic of generic distinctions. The play is called 'A Comedy.' Now even if Dryden and his contemporaries distinguished *Marriage À-la-Mode* from *Secret Love* and *The Spanish Friar*, neither of which is labelled a comedy – and I consider this most unlikely – such a distinction is far too subtle for twentieth-century critics, who have uniformly considered these plays tragicomedies. Similarly, *The Indian Queen* and *Tyrannick Love* are both labelled tragedies, though few critics today will accept either label and still fewer consider them two of a kind. Shadwell's *The Libertine* is 'A Tragedy,' while his *Timon of Athens* is 'A Play' – perhaps the most flexible of all late seventeenth-century generic classifications. Similar inconsistencies abound in the works of other playwrights.

Moreover, generic attribution in the seventeenth century – as today – is often honorific. Stephen Orgel has pointed out that Heminge and Condell were 'conferring the dignity of ancient drama on the work of their fellow actor' by distributing Shakespeare's plays among the classical genres in the first folio.[4] The same assumption lies behind Dryden, Shadwell, and Crowne's complaint that in *The Empress of Morocco* Settle 'has debased Tragedy to farce'; it is expressed more strongly still by Rymer in his lament that in writing *Othello* Shakespeare is guilty of 'profaning the name of Tragedy.'[5] A generic approach to comedy that accepted only those plays that meet with the critic's approval might be an interesting document in the history of taste; it would be of little value as literary history.

A literary historian is grateful to have recorded Dryden's sense that his predecessors left him 'scarce an Humour, a Character, or any kind of Plot, which they have not blown upon.'[6] Similarly, his famous exchange with Shadwell about Ben Jonson's place in Restoration comedy provides the essential raw material of literary history:

DRYDEN I declare that I want judgement to imitate him: and shou'd think it a great impudence in my self to attempt it.

SHADWELL I am so far from thinking it impudence to endeavour to imitate him, that it would rather (in my opinion) seem impudence in me not to do it.[7]

Conscious – and for that matter, unconscious – motivation is, of course, of central importance, but it can be misleading; theory and practice are seldom one. Moreover, literary history as perceived by Dryden and Shadwell is no more 'historical' – and therefore pure – than twentieth-century literary history. One need not read much Dryden and Shadwell to realize that their plays are not Jonson (or Shakespeare or Beaumont and Fletcher) clones. It is, as a result, difficult to limit 'legitimate lexicography,' as Clayton Koelb does, to 'the notion the playwright and his audience had' of literary forms. Koelb claims 'we can talk about Old Comedy, Restoration Comedy, Elizabethan Comedy ... What we cannot do is talk about all comedy at all times and all places and say anything sensible.'[8] Koelb is surely right in urging caution in the use of large, synchronic generic terms like 'comedy.' As R.S. Crane warned in 1935, 'these terms are universals; they represent natures which do not change, however differently at different times they may be defined by critics or embodied by artists in particular works; as essences they lend themselves only to general and scientific, not to historical, statement.'[9] The same distinction informs Firmat's approach to genre: 'The real alternative in genology is ... between deductivism and historicism ... This disjunction gives rise to two separate disciplines: theoretical genology, the deductive classification of literary works, and historical genology, the study of genres from the vantage point of their contemporaries.'[10] Yet however useful the distinction in differentiating goals of critical activity, it is no more valid than the distinction between deductive and inductive genres that Firmat rejects most convincingly in his discussion of Todorov on genre.[11] It is no more possible to construct 'historical genre' without reference to a prior, synchronic class of texts than it is to construct a 'theoretical genre' that does not privilege examples from a limited, historically determined subset.

There is an additional problem with the distinction as Koelb applies it. While there are clear practical advantages, advantages of which I avail myself here, to limiting the study of 'comedy' to 'Restoration comedy,' merely confining a study to works written at a given time does not ensure their generic uniformity. Extensive reading in 'Elizabethan comedy,' or 'Restoration comedy' quickly limits a critic's ambition. Even the limited number of extant Greek comedies and tragedies reveals significant differences of form. An extensive reading of seventeenth-century critical theory is sufficient to dispel the notion that critics then were any more of one mind than they are today.[12]

Twentieth-century genre critics cannot depend on seventeenth-century playwrights and critics to provide them with coherent and consistent models. And even if such models were available, subsequent developments would render them inoperative. 'Literary works,' as Paul Hernadi points out, 'are not only read but also written one after another. In a sense, therefore, the diachronic sequence of history determines how much and what kind of theoretical insight is potentially available in a given decade or century. The history of response to *Le Misanthrope* offers a revealing example: 'As Molière's contemporary, the Ideal Critic would applaud or reject the Misanthrope as a comic figure; as Rousseau's, he could hardly help but see him as the unduly ridiculed hero of a "tearful comedy"; as Goethe's, he might even decide to regard him as tragic; and as ours, he would probably align Alceste with such tragicomic misanthropes as Shakespeare's Timon, Lessing's Tellheim, and Ionesco's Berenger in *Rhinoceros*.'[13] *Le Misanthrope* simply is not a 'comedy' for many critics. Objecting to its reclassification is like objecting to H.D.F. Kitto's 'calling some of Euripides' plays melodramas, others tragi-comedies' through 'distinctions based upon analogy with his understanding of Shakespeare's development' because the Greeks did not recognize such distinctions.[14] It is as likely that given our experience, literary and otherwise, they would respond with approval to Kitto's taxonomy. Nor should we be so confident of the state of our historical understanding. Even though I believe that recent criticism of late seventeenth-century drama is more valid historically than most of what passed for historical criticism in the eighteenth and nineteenth centuries, I have no reason to think that twenty-first-century critics will share my judgments.

The attempt to understand genres by recovering the very models that enabled writers to contribute to them, then, has not been realized despite the considerable effort of able critics for many years. The obvious conclusion is that despite impressive incidental insights, the method is fundamentally flawed. Several methodological issues support this conclusion. The most central is the ontological status of genres. Genres offer interpretative strategies for readers (and writers) to help them understand literary works and their constituent parts. They offer theoretical approaches to the most fundamental questions unfamiliar works provoke in readers or audiences: 'What kind of work is this? Where does it fit in the larger context of other works?'[15] As Alastair Fowler puts it, 'genres have to do with identifying and communicating rather than with defining and classifying. We identify the genre to interpret the exemplar.' Or, again, genre theory 'deals with principles of reconstruction and interpretation and (to some extent) evaluation of meaning. It does not deal much with classification.'[16] Genres, then, are best seen as species of works heuristically conceived in terms of artistically selected elements and principles. They are nothing more – or less – than constructs made by writers, readers, audiences, and critics.[17]

Determination of membership in a generic class is, as Guillén points out, 'but one part of a broader process of definition and interpretation.' The genres themselves 'are like coordinates through which the individual poem can be apprehended and understood,' and thus genre theory provides 'a problem-solving model on the level of form.'[18] Thus conceived, genre theory avoids its most common pitfall, prescription. If generic formulations come only after the examination of individual works, they cannot be imposed upon works yet unwritten or unread. In practice, most genre critics continue to enlarge the membership of the class in question, to develop their constructs more fully or test their validity. And the larger and more long-lived the genre, the clearer the futility of prescription. Genres change. Genres mutate. By recognizing the mutability of genres, critics avoid the other major pitfall of genre criticism, its tendency to ahistoricity.

Closing a genre is necessarily an arbitrary act, if also a useful interpretative strategy for critical study. Nonetheless, some genres are more resistant to closure than others, particulary those large and amorphous genres with long histories and large memberships, genres like tragedy, satire, the novel, and, of course, comedy. To close such concepts as comedy requires a determined rigour of exclusion, especially when applied synchronically. Because he is willing to pay the price for such rigour, Elder Olson offers a useful example in his *The Theory of Comedy*. As the title reveals, Olson is after a comprehensive theory, and, following the procedure of Aristotle in *The Poetics*, produces a clear and coherent definition of comedy. He leaves no doubt in his application that his model provides closure; it also provides a powerful analytic tool for those works that fall within its well-defined boundaries. The problem is that many do not. For example, only five of Shakespeare's plays – *The Merry Wives of Windsor*, *The Comedy of Errors, Love's Labour's Lost, A Midsummer Night's Dream*, and *The Taming of the Shrew* – qualify.[19] Now even if the coherence of Olson's formulations produced a better understanding of those works that deviate from its rigid norms (and most great works do), there is an obvious practical problem. To be successful in attempting to close as large and unwieldy a genre with as long a history as comedy requires the willingness of other critics in the field to accept and use the proposed new principle of closure. Olson, at least to date, has proved no more successful than his predecessors in persuading others to accept his definition. A genre critic can, of course, choose not to work with as baggy a generic monster as comedy. Guillén is probably right that at least in theory, 'all genres are potentially useful – and expendable.'[20] But for a genre critic of the drama to dispense with 'comedy' or 'tragedy' is to fly in the face of twenty-five hundred years of critical tradition, to ignore two of the best-known, most useful terms in a lexicon not known for its richness of vocabulary. The alternative is to recognize the nature, strengths, and limitations of these 'institutional' genres and to work with them as they are. They are 'externally defined' genres; that is, they have been constructed without 'an internal definition discoverable by analysis.'[21] Membership is instead determined by comparison and relation. What is lost in precision is compensated for by inclusiveness and responsiveness to historical change. And considerable precision can be regained by breaking down institutional genres into constituent subgroups, what Fowler calls subgenres.[22]

Maintaining the largest institutions of generic drama criticism, comedy and tragedy, makes it possible to work within a long and strong tradition. New generic formulations often assist in producing excellent practical criticism, but new genres rarely last. At the same time, recognizing the institutional nature of comedy and tragedy encourages refinement simultaneously in two directions. The need for and place of more exact formulation should already be evident. A second, crucial advantage is that in recognizing the unwieldy nature of comedy and tragedy as generic concepts, the critic is discouraged from seeing them as rigidly defined, mutually exclusive poles. Such procedures necessarily create 'problems,' plays that resist the dialectical opposition of the prescriptive critic. Since comedy and tragedy themselves are not monolithic forms, one has no reason to expect them to be omnivorously inclusive forms.

It is only in part, then, for practical reasons that comedy and tragedy have remained among the central concepts of most generic approaches to the drama. There are strong theoretical foundations to support past practice. First, any critic who decides to deal with the drama has already accepted a primary generic distinction. Further classification must be limited to the level of species. Second, although comedy and tragedy were once intrinsically known subgenres, with time they have become institutions. Their very institutional nature encourages rather than precludes their use for explaining literary change. Thus an attempt to examine historical change in comedy or tragedy based on a construct of an institutional genre helps genre criticism avoid the tendency to err in the direction of the synchronic. It forces the critic to reject the equivalent to a 'great man' theory of history. However appealing the desire to limit discussion to the 'best' examples of a genre in a given period, a more inclusive account is necessary because of the very selectivity that is an inevitable part of historical analysis. A history of the *best* late seventeenth-century comedy is very different from a history of late seventeenth-century comedy.[23]

Recognition of the need for inclusiveness, then, encourages a systematic approach to genre and change. As Guillén argues, since 'literary genres have always tended, in the European tradition, to constitute *systems*,' an approach of this sort allows the critic a high degree of specificity and historicity within a larger framework designed to reveal the relational nature of literary works and hence their *institutional* unity. Or, as Fowler puts it, 'genres are better understood ... through a study of their mutual relations, which actually affect writers and readers ... These relations are partly diachronic or dynamic (formation, combination, mixture), partly static (similarities, contrasts). But even the synchronic contrasts are not absolute or fixed.'[24]

The drama, then, for this study, is a system of genres emerging from and based on comedy and tragedy. Whether this particular argument explains the genesis of English drama is, finally, of no importance, for although it is possible that in England, before the Reformation, comedy and tragedy were not the primary forms of drama, they have been ever since the time of Shakespeare, even at those times when they have not been produced by playwrights.[25] Although twentieth-century critics, like their seventeenth-century predecessors, have been unable to agree upon a definition of comedy or tragedy, their practice reveals a limited number of shared assumptions about such elements as comic plots and characters. Comic characters, for example, are traditionally seen as worse, morally, than we are, and, hence, a formulation of comic plots such as Olson's ('an imitation of valueless action, in language, performed and not narrated, effecting a katastasis of concern through the absurd') makes precise a common and persistent view of comedy. This is the tradition of much seventeenth-century comic theory, the tradition of such critics as Ben Jonson, Thomas Shadwell, and John Dennis. It was a conservative tradition by the late seventeenth century, but one still very much alive today in, for example, the work of Bergson, Freud, and Eric Bentley. Paul Goodman considers it comedy at its 'purest'; Shaw considers it 'farcical'; in the late seventeenth century it was associated with 'humours.'[26]

Alternatively, the other traditional view of comedy, one that in England is *expressed* for the first time, I believe, by such critics as Dryden and Congreve (though they both continued to accept much in the Jonsonian view), focuses instead on the love-plot tradition of Greek New Comedy. It remains familiar today in Northrop Frye's 'Argument of Comedy,' with his description of the 'comic Oedipus situation' in which 'the maneuvering of a young man toward a young woman' with marriage as 'the tonic chord on which it ends'; in Susanne Langer's 'Comic Rhythm,' where comedy is seen as 'an art form that arises naturally wherever people are gathered to celebrate life, in spring festivals, triumphs, birthdays, weddings, or initiations'; in Sheldon Sacks's 'comic action' in which 'all the techniques of representation from beginning to end lead us to expect that all the "good guys" and the "bad guys" will receive their ethical deserts.'[27] This is the tradition of Shakespeare's best comedies (those Olson had to exclude from his study), and one that late seventeenth-century critics associated most strongly with the 'wit' comedies of John Fletcher. The first group of comedies, those I shall call punitive comedies, depend for their effect on responses to the ludicrous, the ridiculous, or the absurd. The second, those I shall call – for want of a better term – sympathetic, depend similarly – and again traditional terminology is not strong for this kind of comedy – on the agreeable, the amiable, even what Steele called 'a joy too exquisite for laughter.'

A twentieth-century attempt to define those plays that most critics have called comedy would, I think, have to account for both of these – admittedly loosely defined – kinds of comedy. In the absence of an intrinsic definition, I look to the intersection of these two kinds for the institutional centre of dramatic activity in comedy, a particularly practical approach both to the challenge playwrights faced to position themselves in a tradition and to a point Dryden, the most articulate and important critic of the Restoration, must surely have recognized in voicing his preferences for 'the mixt way of Comedy; that which is neither all wit, nor all humour, but the result of both.'[28] Dryden's 'mixt way' offers one approach to the range of ingredients available to comic playwrights. The conventionality of those ingredients led to frequent charges of plagiarism by source hunters like Gerard Langbaine. It also led to convincing defences, like the one offered by Wycherley: 'tho' the Matter that a Writer treats of be not new, the Disposition, Method, or Uses of it may be new; as it is the same Ball which good and bad Gamesters play with, but one forces or places it better than Another, by a different Art, Use, or Disposal of it.'[29] The more thorough the survey of plays, the more accurate Wycherley's description appears. The implication for genre theory cannot be ignored. As Thomas G. Winner formulates it, 'since genre represents both the system of artistic norms (rules or devices available to the artist and his receivers at a given time) and the potential artistic deviations and innovations related to these constructs for a given type of artistic utterance, genres are never static and must be studied both synchronically and diachronically.' Or, as Guillén claims, 'systems will tend, generally speaking, to absorb change and assimilate innovation. On the other hand, assimilation becomes a small step in a larger process of change.'[30]

To visualize the system of drama diachronically would therefore require extending its synchronic, two-dimensional representation into a third dimension representing time. It is possible then, by taking, as it were, a cross-section of that extension (representing the changing system of genres) to isolate and identify that system for any specified period. Comparison of representative cross-sections provides essential data for a generic history of the drama.[31] If that data is taken into account, the historian should be working within a context that ensures against inconclusiveness of evidence, though it also undermines conclusive analysis. The merits of the subsequent analysis will not be limited by an inadequate awareness of the full range of plays current at a specified time; its short-comings, consequently, will be analytic, not contextual.

It can, of course, be objected that these proposed cross-sections are arbitrary or contrived, since they have been selected by the historian. Because of the impracticality, if not impossibility, of treating all of the comedies written between 1660 and 1710, it is indeed necessary to make choices. What is important for this study is that those choices be representative – that is, that they be chosen 'objectively' on grounds other than personal taste. To be credible exemplars of late seventeenth-century comedy, they must not be chosen to fit an already formulated template. What I propose as a basis for analysis are three cross-sections, each of five-year periods, to represent the entire fifty years: 1670–5, 1690–5, 1705–10. This selection is intended to facilitate comparison over the entire period; the particular five-year periods are, admittedly, arbitrary. Because the drama as an active system includes all plays performed during a given period, revivals are included with new productions. They can easily be separated for more sophisticated historical study. I have, of course, used the performance records in *The London Stage* as my primary source of data.

An examination of the comedies performed in the three selected five-year periods provides resounding evidence of the diversity of late seventeenth-century comedy. There is no single mould capable of containing even the new comedies of a single season. Each five-year period will be characterized by reference to six representative comedies that (1) were successful in their original productions and (2) remained in the repertory at least through 1710. Most of the plays held the stage throughout the eighteenth century. The plays are: (1) 1670–5: Betterton's *The Amorous Widow*, Wycherley's *Love in a Wood* and *The Country-Wife*, Buckingham's *The Rehearsal*, Shadwell's *Epsom-Wells*, and Crowne's *The Countrey Wit*; (2) 1690–5: Dryden's *Amphitryon*, Mountfort's *Greenwich-Park*, Durfey's *Love for Money* and *The Marriage-Hater Match'd*, and Congreve's *The Old Batchelour* and *Love for Love*; (3) 1705–10: Vanbrugh's *The Confederacy*, Farquhar's *The Recruiting Officer* and *The Beaux Strategem*, Cibber's *The Double Gallant*, Centlivre's *The Busie Body*, and Charles Shadwell's *The Fair Quaker of Deal*.[32]

Before a discussion of these plays, however, it is important to provide a sense of context for them; that is, to see them as part of a growing and slowly evolving dramatic repertory that included a large number of regularly performed plays. Performance records are, of course, spotty, but *The London Stage* provides me with sufficient evidence to generate the following lists of comedies, divided into four chronological groups.

Of the twelve pre-1660 comedies, three stand out in popularity: Fletcher's *Rule a Wife and Have a Wife* and *Wit without Money*, and Beaumont and Fletcher's *The Scornful Lady*; the others are Fletcher's *The Woman's Prize*; Fletcher and Massinger's *Beggar's Bush*; Jonson's *Volpone, Epicoene, or The Silent Woman, The Alchemist*, and *Bartholomew Fair*; Shakespeare's *The Taming of the Shrew* (often in Lacy's adaptation, *Sauny the Scot*); and Brome's *The Jovial Crew* and *The Northern Lass*.

Twelve comedies from the 1660s are, in two groups of six based on popularity: Sir Robert Howard's *The Committee*, Etherege's *The Comical Revenge*, Dryden's *Sir Martin Mar-all*, Dryden and Davenant's (and Shadwell's) *The Tempest*, Buckingham's *The Chances*, and Etherege's *She wou'd if she cou'd*; Cowley's *Cutter of Coleman-Street*, Tuke's *The Adventures of Five Hours*, Lacy's *The Old Troop*, Shadwell's *The Sullen Lovers*, Dryden's *An Evening's Love*, and Caryll's *Sir Salomon*.

Sixteen more comedies join the repertory between 1675 and 1690, again arranged in two groups: Etherege's *The Man of Mode*, Wycherley's *The Plain-Dealer*, Otway's *The Cheats of Scapin*, Behn's *The Rover* (part one) and *The Emperor of the Moon*, Ravenscroft's *The London Cuckolds*, Tate's *A Duke and no Duke*, Crowne's *Sir Courtly Nice*, and Shadwell's *The Squire of Alsatia*; Durfey's *A Fond Husband*, Otway's *The Souldier's Fortune*, Shadwell's *The Lancashire Witches* and *Bury-Fair*, Crowne's *City Politiques*, Jevon's *The Devil of a Wife*, and Carlile's *The Fortune-Hunters*. In the period 1690–5, parts one and two of Durfey's *Don Quixote* were added to the six plays mentioned above.

Nineteen comedies entered the repertory between 1695 and 1705, in two quite uneven groups; since most of the plays at this time tend to be extremely popular,[33] the distance between success and failure seems much greater. The plays in the first group were Cibber's *Love's Last Shift, Love makes a Man, She wou'd and She wou'd not, The School-Boy*, and *The Careless Husband*; Ravenscroft's *The Anatomist*;Vanbrugh's *The Relapse, Aesop* (part one), *The Provok'd Wife*, and *The Pilgrim*; Farquhar's *The Constant Couple* and *The Stage-Coach*; Congreve's *The Way of the World*; Granville's *The Jew of Venice*; Baker's *Tunbridge-Walks*; Centlivre's *The Gamester*; and Steele's *The Tender Husband*. The second group includes only Vanbrugh's *The Country House* and Steele's *The Funeral*.

Finally, Vanbrugh's *The Mistake* and Cibber's *The Lady's last Stake* should be added to the repertory comedies of 1705–10.

These eighty-one plays provide a good sense of the comic repertory between 1660 and 1710. The most prominent feature of this repertory, again, is its diversity. The sheer number and range of comedies to hold the stage year after year preclude easy or automatic organization or classification. The need for a theoretical framework to facilitate interpretation should be apparent to any critic interested in any approach other than an atomistic one.

One of the most obvious and puzzling features of any repertory is the plays it excludes, and London theatre of the late-seventeenth century offers no exception. Among the earlier dramatists, Chapman, Dekker, Middleton, Marston, Shakespeare, and Shirley are especially noticeable by their absence, as are the late Caroline playwrights, even Davenant and Killigrew. And while two of Brome's plays remain popular, he does not influence post-Restoration dramatists the way Beaumont and Fletcher and Jonson do. Some plays are quite successful in their original productions and even for the next few seasons but never quite achieve repertory status. Examples include Ravenscroft's *The Citizen Turn'd Gentleman*, Rhodes's *Flora's Vagaries*, Duffet's burlesques, Sedley's *The Mulberry-Garden* and *Bellamira*, and Shadwell's *The Humorists* and *The Virtuoso*. Finally, some plays admired by twentieth-century critics aroused minimal interest – or outright hostility – in late seventeenth-century audiences, such as Wycherley's *The Gentleman Dancing-Master*, Dryden's *Mr. Limberham*, Otway's *Friendship in Fashion*, Lee's *The Princess of Cleve*, Southerne's *Sir Anthony Love* and *The Wives Excuse*, Congreve's *The Double-Dealer*, and Burnaby's *The Ladies Visiting-Day*. (Comedies revealing deep disillusionment or cynicism almost inevitably fail in this period.)

The reasons for success or failure on the stage are, of course, varied, and need have little to do with the intrinsic merits of the play. The quality of the initial production could make or break a play (a common theme in prefaces to failed plays), as could the favour or performance of a given actor. Topicality was occasionally sufficient cause for success, but the success was rarely long-lived. The lives of several repertory pieces were prolonged by later alterations; the addition of a song or two by Purcell was on occasion sufficient to revive popularity. Catering to current fashion did not guarantee success, nor did innovation necessarily bring failure. Accurate stage history requires analysis of the various special circumstances surrounding the production of each play as an individual case. Generic history begins, in a sense, where stage history leaves off, with the facts of success and failure – that is, with the repertory as it emerged.

The division of comedy into two basic types, punitive and sympathetic, offers an especially useful model for a body of work with few basic story lines, each type directed essentially toward one of two objects – love and money; courtship provides the outline for most sympathetic comic action, and the pursuit of cuckolding and/or money generates most punitive comic action. But as I have indicated above, the forms rarely remain pure in practice – or even in theory. As the seventeenth-century critics never tired of reminding their audiences, the English stage was characterized by its insistence on variety. Plays with neither subplots nor multiple plots are rare indeed. As a result, in spite of the very conventional nature of late seventeenth-century comedy, playwrights mixed those conventions extensively, using elements from sympathetic and punitive plots in varying degrees to produce an extremely rich and diverse comic theatre capable of accommodating ever-changing thematic demands.

The purest examples come from the playwrights whose comedies formulated the tastes and provided the early comic repertory for the restored theatres – Beaumont and Fletcher, and Jonson. Although Beaumont and Fletcher were the most popular pre-Restoration playwrights on the late seventeenth-century stage, Jonson remained the most respected. Critical thinking about comedy began with Jonson, and when his impact on the development of Beaumont and Fletcher is taken into account, his influence on the Restoration theatre can hardly be overemphasized. It is most clearly seen in two areas, characterization and plot form.

Jonson's theory of comic characterization is based on his highly influential theory of humours, presented most clearly in the early 'comicall satyres.' Asper, in *Every Man out of his Humour*, distinguishes three kinds of humours, beginning with genuine humours, those found

> ... when some one peculiar quality
> Doth so possesse a man, that it doth draw
> All his affects, his spirits, and his powers,
> In their confluctions, all to runne one way,
> This may be truly said to be a Humour.[34]

He also takes into account those whose 'abuse of this word Humour' reduces it to fashionable, meaningless jargon, and those who affect humour – any 'Idiot' who has 'an apish, or phantasticke straine' (ll. 115–16) and chooses to call it his humour.

From this three-part definition follows the purpose of the 'comical satyres,' Asper's indignant desire to 'strip the ragged follies of the time, / Naked as at their birth (ll. 17–18) – though the exposure is not for its own sake. In a calmer moment Asper returns to his medical metaphor of the poet-satirist as physician: 'I would give them pills to purge, / And make 'em fit for faire societies' (ll. 175–6). For Jonson, a 'humour is not simply an abnormal psychological condition; ultimately, it is that evil moral condition that occurs when man's carnal appetite gains ascendancy over reason.'[35] Jonson's goal, as Asper presents it, is to return his humours to their reason, thus alleviating the prevalence of folly about him.

The 'comicall satyres' end with the reformation of the humours into more rational and balanced members of society. This, of course, is not the case for many of the humours in Jonson's later, and greater plays, the plays that entered the repertory after the Restoration. With the partial exception of *Bartholomew Fair*, Jonson's late seventeenth-century successes – *Volpone*, *The Alchemist*, and *Epicoene* – are notably lacking in reform and reintegration. Such humours as Corvino, Corbaccio, Epicure Mammon, Surly, Ananias, Tribulation, Kastril, Morose, John Daw, Amorous La Foole, and the Collegiate Ladies – all prominent models for Restoration playwrights – remain excluded from what happy comic resolution Jonson allows.

The reasons for Jonson's growing reluctance to reform his humours are many and complex. Principal among them, no doubt, was his increasing recognition of the determinism latent in the doctrine of humours, a recognition that led to the later development of his doctrine of vapours.[36] If an individual's behaviour depends upon his humour, and that humour is part of his mental makeup, how is it possible to correct vice and folly? (This became the central crux for later comic theorists, a point I shall return to.) But also important for Jonson's altered treatment of his humours were his ongoing experiments with comic plot form. The writer of the loosely structured, episodic 'comicall satyres' developed into a playwright able to produce what Coleridge considered one of the three most perfect plots ever constructed.[37]

It is the plot form of Jonson's so-called middle period, the period of his greatest achievements as a playwright, that provides the model for what I call punitive comedy. Paul Goodman, like Coleridge, looked at Jonson for 'the purest comic actions' in English, and, in particular, to *The Alchemist* for his analysis of the nature of 'comic intrigue.' His frequently reprinted discussion of the plot of *The Alchemist* is still the best one available. Goodman sees an action as comic when the intrigue of a base character 'can be reversed or even be deflated (come to nothing), and still the character is not destroyed.'[38] In Jonsonian punitive comedy, then, rogues or wits – not mutually exclusive categories – are granted a licence to work outside the normal rules and regulations prescribed by their society, in order, for a limited period, to gull a number of fools (or humours) – sex and/or money being the usual objects. The intrigue is allowed to expand, generally without reversals, until the gulls are successfully cheated; the resulting deflation of the comic intrigue is then usually followed by the revoking of the comic licence and the restoration of the (sometimes restructured) order of society. In *The Alchemist*, the return of Lovewit – an inevitability that in a sense predetermines the time of the withdrawal of the licence – necessitates the return to normalcy, albeit a normalcy that leaves the rogues unpunished and Face – and Lovewit himself – quite well rewarded. In *Volpone*, the rogues overextend their licence and eventually threaten the welfare of some good and innocent people and finally all society. When their gulls are no longer merely self-serving fools, the rogues must be stopped; the revocation of their licence, in this case, includes punishment for their evil actions. In *Epicoene*, Dauphine's intrigue against his uncle Morose through mock-marriage to the title character results in his successful winning of his fortune. When the licence is withdrawn here, it is no longer needed, because Dauphine has recreated normalcy in his own desired image. The rogue, in other words, is allowed the full benefit of his intrigue. Punitive comedy in Jonson's hands, then, was a rich and flexible form, and one that proved seminal in the development of comedy in the seventeenth century.

In a brief 'note' on what he unfortunately calls 'sentimental comedy,' Goodman offers a useful distinction between the punitive comedy of Jonson, a form too intellectual and too calculated to produce anxiety for most audiences, and the far more popular 'mixture of a comic intrigue with a sympathetic love story' I have referred to above as sympathetic comedy, the form that goes back to Greek New Comedy and enters Restoration comedy most directly through the work of Beaumont and Fletcher, mainly through Fletcher's later comedies. 'In sentimental comedy,' according to Goodman, 'the romantic plot persists from the beginning to the end; it is not deflated. The romantic plot is not noncomic in the sense of being merely normal (outside the comic license); the love story excites an independent interest, with feelings of desire, anxiety, fulfilment; it gives the audience something to latch on to. This sympathetic line, with which the audience can identify, is crossed by the malicious and resentful accidents of the comic intrigue – and the whole is an accurate imitation of the insecurities of adolescent sexuality.'[39]

It is unfortunate for later critics that like Shakespeare – and unlike Jonson – Fletcher left no record of his principles of dramatic comedy. There remains no theory of comic character, no discussion of comic plot. His impact, however, on seventeenth-century critics is well captured by Dryden in his familiar evaluation: '[Beaumont and Fletcher] understood and imitated the conversation of Gentlemen much better [than Shakespeare]; whose wilde debaucheries, and quickness of wit in reparties, no Poet before them could paint as they have done. Humour, which *Ben. Johnson* deriv'd from particular persons, they made it not their business to describe: they represented all the passions very lively, but above all, Love.' When Henry Harington's emphasis on Fletcher's 'plot' (in this case, the plot of *The Wild-Goose Chase*) – 'Whene'er we read, we have and have it not, / And, glad to be deceived, finding thy drift / T' excel our guess at every turn and shift' – is added to Dryden's catalogue of Fletcher's strengths, the list is more or less complete. And, as a recent editor of *The Wild-Goose Chase* has noted, there has been little change in focus in three hundred years of criticism: 'Liveliness, wittiness, outspokenness, intricacy of plot – these are the recurrent positive notes of the comments.'[40]

It is *The Wild-Goose Chase*, of course, that has been selected by twentieth-century critics as the most important precursor of late seventeenth-century comedy, anticipating 'by forty years the main trend of the Restoration.' Clifford Leech, who thinks little of the play, proposes that 'the reason for its being frequently noticed in recent years is doubtless that its chief male character is called Mirabel, and there is thus a link with *The Way of the World*.' The tendency to see 'Restoration comedy' as merely the comedy of Etherege, Wycherley, and Congreve is certainly a factor in the elevation of *The Wild-Goose Chase* to a place where even the editors of *The London Stage* claim for it an influence in the Restoration completely unsupported by their calendar of performances.[41] What has been said about *The Wild-Goose Chase*, nonetheless, remains valid for a more general assessment of Fletcher's contribution to the development of English comedy. Rota Lister's description of Fletcher's comedies outlines the sympathetic comic action, just as Goodman has furnished an outline for the punitive comedies: 'The subjects of these comedies, usually involving some kind of amorous intrigue, appear most frequently to have two basic types of motivation and direction: a despiser of love and the opposite sex, either male or female, is brought to heel, or a fool is given his treatment; a clever but down-on-his-luck younger person of either sex, thwarted by the "humours" and tyrannical withholding of his or her rights by an older character, eventually triumphs over the oppressor and converts the "tyrant" to his or her view.'[42] Marriage, as critics have often observed, usually provides the tonic chord.

Sympathetic comedy supplied Fletcher with as rich and flexible a comic form as punitive did Jonson. The plays in the post-1660 repertory offer sufficient examples: the pursuit of the title character by the Elder Loveless in *The Scornful Lady,* of Margarita by Leon and of Michael Perez by Estifania in *Rule a Wife and Have a Wife,* and of Petruchio by Maria and of Rowland by Livia in *The Woman's Prize* give one a good sense of Fletcher's range in treating amorous intrigue. (Oriana's pursuit of Mirabel is a further demonstration.) The triumphs of Young Loveless over Moorecraft in *The Scornful Lady,* of Leon over the Duke of Medina and Estifania over Cacafago in *Rule a Wife,* and even of Valentine over virtually all the other characters in *Wit without Money* indicate the potential of the second kind of intrigue.

Fletcher's love of intrigue, of 'a rare situation,' has also provoked considerable hostile response from critics; his obvious strengths and weaknesses are one. As a 'speculator in human affairs,' he has always been subject to attack from those who view intrigue for its own sake as a sure sign of moral decay. The priority given to the action in his plays implies the subordination of character that has been noted by admirers and detractors alike. The uneasiness his endings evoke in his critics is evidence of the place given to character by Fletcher. Leech defines the general critical issue in his discussion of *The Custom of the Country*: 'If Fletcher were the kind of dramatist to make us concerned about the subsequent lives of his characters, we might wonder a little at the prospects of married happiness for either Leopold or Arnoldo. But of course he is not that kind of dramatist: his characters exist only within the crucial situation that the play presents, and there indeed their responses are often shrewdly observed; when those situations no longer exist, the characters have lost the function that called them into being and cannot be imagined without that function.'[43]

Fletcher's comedy, then, does not reveal the interest in character, especially character for its own sake, that is found in the comedy of Jonson. His interest in intrigue, in the traditional conventions of the New Comedy, however, did require repeated attention to certain types of character, in particular the young lovers ultimately to be mated. As Kathleen Lynch points out, 'Fletcher's best-drawn characters are undoubtedly the young libertines who, from the earliest plays to the latest, throng the pages of his comedy.' Although their brand of 'indolence and prodigality' reflects a fashion quite unlike that of 'the Restoration *beau monde,*' in their impudence, cynicism, and taste for witty speech and for unscrupulous intrigue, Fletcher's gallants predict, in a general way, the heroes of Restoration comedy.'[44]

The comedies of Jonson or Fletcher are, of course, no more a single, monolithic form than those of any other playwright worthy of attention. Fletcher's plays abound in humours, and Jonson is not averse to witty young men and women. Fletcher's plays contain punitive actions and Jonson's, occasionally, sympathetic actions. And by the time of the Restoration theatre, the influence of Jonson and Fletcher was tempered by the development of such Caroline playwrights as Brome and Shirley, who 'represent the amalgamation which was taking place before the Restoration, between the various "humor" themes of Jonson and the intrigue-romance of Fletcher; the domestic comedies of Massinger and Middleton blending in later.'[45] Numerous French and Spanish playwrights, most notably Molière, must also be added to the mix that, in fact, produced the comedy of the late seventeenth century – and these are merely the dramatic influences. But influences aside, Jonson and Fletcher remain useful as models for the two central kinds of comedy current after the Restoration, and models the playwrights themselves turned to. In their familiar exchange about the appropriate form for comedy, Dryden and Shadwell set the terms for much of the subsequent debate by agreeing to situate comedy along a Jonson-Fletcher axis; humour and wit, judgment and fancy are central terms in their dialectic. Neither could have believed that these categories were mutually exclusive absolutes; neither remained within the confines of one or the other in practice. And when he presents his own formula for comedy, his 'mixt way,' Dryden quite candidly abandons ideology for the pragmatic concerns of sound dramaturgy. He will have 'neither so little of humour as *Fletcher* shews, nor so little of love and wit, as *Johnson:* neither all cheat, with which the best Playes of the one are fill'd, nor all adventure, which is the common practice of the other.'[46] The best of both comic worlds, he discovered, was the most likely way to please his audience. The development of comedy in the late seventeenth century can be traced in the development, both in theory and practice, of the comic models of Jonson and Fletcher in their various combinations and permutations. The following chapters attempt to trace these transformations through the examination of the representative comedies described above.

2

Six Representative Comedies,
1670–1675

The most visible and vocal follower of Jonson in the Restoration was, of course, Thomas Shadwell. Shadwell's theory of humours is presented most concisely and clearly in the epilogue to *The Humorists:*

> A Humor is the Byas of the Mind,
> By which with violence 'tis one way inclin'd:
> It makes our Actions lean on one side still,
> And in all Changes that way bends the Will.
>
> ...
>
> The Mighty Prince of Poets, Learned BEN,
> Who alone div'd into the Minds of Men:
> Saw all their wanderings, all their follies knew,
> And all their vain fantastick passions drew,
> In Images so lively and so true;
> That there each Humorist himself might view.[1]

In spite of the self-conscious nod toward Jonson, Shadwell alters Jonson's theory of humours significantly. While following him in using the comedy of humours as a vehicle to attack vice and folly, Shadwell changes the humour itself into a rhetorical device in a very different pedagogical process: the character on stage is now there to provide a mirror for the audience in order to provoke the self-recognition necessary to effect the purgation of the offending humour. It is the audience, not the characters on stage, who are to be driven out of their humours. Jonas Barish's observation that in *The Sullen Lovers* Shadwell 'does not engage [his humours] in an action that will expose them *to themselves*'[2] applies to the Shadwell canon in general, with a few exceptions in the later plays. Like most of his contemporaries, he does not attempt to educate his fools, cure them of their folly, or integrate them into an improved or more inclusive society. Fools and gulls remain fools and gulls, seldom the wiser for their comic exposure. Whatever the process, they invariably provide negative examples on the Restoration stage.

Epsom-Wells was among Shadwell's more successful comedies, and though a better play than most of his earlier pieces, it is nonetheless representative in its treatment of humours. Of the humours, Summers singles out the London-hating magistrate Clodpate as a 'particular source of unfailing delight to Shadwell's audiences,' a view confirmed by Colley Cibber's praise for Underhill's portrayal of 'the course, rustick Humour of Justice *Clodpate*,' as 'a delightful Brute.'[3] What delight Clodpate offers tends to come at his own expense, as his hatred of London, a product of having been 'beaten, clapt, and cheated there,'[4] leaves him vulnerable prey to the 'silly, affected Whore' Mrs Jilt, who is able to marry him merely by pretending to share his loathing of London. Clodpate learned nothing from his initial London experience as a young man, the source of his later antipathy, and his current experience teaches him only to consider Epsom, and like resorts of fashionable Londoners, as mere extensions of the 'Sodom' he had rejected earlier. Shadwell allows him to buy his way out of what proves to be only a mock-marriage, but his final declaration shows that his experience has left him unchanged: ''Sdeath and Hell, if ever I come so near *London* agen, I'le commit Treason, and have my head and quarters set upon the Bridge' (5.1. p 180). A nineteenth-century admirer of Shadwell – a rare creature indeed – was surely anticipating later developments in comic humours when he likened Clodpate to Squire Western.[5]

The remaining principal humours in *Epsom-Wells* – the matched pair of citizen couples, the Biskets and the Fribbles – are so obviously presented as mirror images of each other – the 'quiet, humble, civil Cuckold' Bisket with his 'impertinent, imperious strumpet' of a wife and the 'surly Cuckold' Fribble with his 'humble, submitting ... very Whore' of a wife – that they reflect in their conception more of Fletcher than of Jonson. Shadwell's attention to symmetry here, as well as in the love plot, recalls the sense in which, in Fletcher, 'the very contrasts between the characters' appear 'the sine qua non' of a play like *Wit without Money*.[6] There is, however, nothing of Fletcher – and little of Jonson – in Shadwell's working out of the design of his citizen plot. Rather, when Bisket and Fribble catch their wives in flagrante delicto with the coward-bullies Kick and Cuff, they anticipate the farcical sex comedy of the next decade, though the way in which the citizens resolve the dilemma created by their cuckolding reveals them as true Shadwellian humours in the end:

FRIB. Well, I'le pass it by for once; but I'le not fail to sue *Cuff* upon an Action
of Assault and Battery.
BISK. And I'le sue *Kick* too. If we order our business wisely and impannel a
good substantial Jury, of all married men, they'll give us vast damages.
FRIB. I have known a man recover 4 or 500 *l.*
in such a Case, and his Wife not one jot the worse.
BISK. No, not a bit.   (5.1.p179)

In constructing his plot, Shadwell is no more true to his master than he is with his characters. As James Sutherland points out, 'What is most un-Jonsonian in Shadwell, and what – writing when he did – he obviously felt bound to supply, was the sexual intrigue which the contemporary audience expected.'[7] Given Shadwell's admiration of the comedies of Etherege, and given the likelihood that Summers, Borgman, Nicoll, Lynch, and Alssid are right in seeing *She wou'd if she cou'd*, the play Shadwell called in 1671 'the best Comedy that has been written since the Restoration of the Stage,' as a likely source for *Epsom-Wells* in particular and Shadwellian comedy in general, it is difficult to see Shadwell's inclination toward 'sexual intrigue' as an unwilling nod in the direction of the taste of his audience.[8]

The gulling of Justice Clodpate and the cuckolding of the citizens are joined by two other sets of intrigues, the courtships of two witty young couples, Rains and Lucia, and Bevil and Carolina, and the dissolution of the precarious marriage of the Woodlys. In the courtship intrigue, Shadwell follows the typical format of most post-Menandrine comedy. Shadwell's lovers, like Etherege's Courtall and Ariana, and Freeman and Gatty, engage in a familiar love game; love at first sight is followed by the wit contest that confirms each combatant as a suitable match for his or her chosen. When the (in this case minimal) obstacles are removed, the matches are more or less assured. Shadwell's reluctance to make explicit the unions of the lovers has provoked the following response from one of his best critics: 'Unlike the women in the earlier comedies, [Lucia and Carolina] do not get married by the last act. They hold off the ceremony, demanding a time of trial during which the rakes must prove their loyalty by good behavior. And, even though Bevil humorously insists that their marriages are inevitable ("for one Fortnights conversing with us will lay such a scandal upon 'em, they'll be glad to repair to Marriage"), one suspects that the rakes will never reform and that there will be no weddings.'[9] I, however, can see no more reason to doubt the likelihood of these marriages than of those in *She wou'd if she cou'd*, Shadwell's likely model and a play that has not elicited similar critical doubt. Nor do I think Shadwell encourages such questions about events after his play concludes: here, too, he follows in Fletcher's footsteps. Lucia and Carolina are no more in need of our concern than Fletcher's Leopold or Arnaldo – or, for that matter, Etherege's Harriet and Dorimant.

Alssid's concern about the ending of *Epsom-Wells* would seem more appropriate if expressed over a play like *The Way of the World*, where Congreve gives considerable attention to ensuring that his ending projects answers about his characters' futures. But Shadwell, like Etherege, goes only far enough to assure his audience that his young lovers are genuinely in love and of reasonably equal social and intellectual stature. Perhaps it is the presence of the Woodly intrigue that encourages a kind of concern that is finally inappropriate. The Woodlys, like Doralice and Rhodophil in Dryden's *Marriage À-la-Mode*, which was first produced the preceding season, offer an example of a marital discord action, Shadwell going a step further than Dryden in allowing his unhappy couple to separate permanently in the end. (He does not go as far as Dryden in examining the psychology of their kind of unhappiness.) Their inverted proviso scene with some lively and effective comic business provides a sense of closure that should discourage us from envisaging either a future of debauchery or a happy second marriage for either of the Woodlys.

Despite Shadwell's Jonsonian persona, *Epsom-Wells* is not a conservative play for 1672. His young lovers are very much in the Etherege mould, and if *She wou'd if she cou'd* provides a model, Shadwell's Rains, in turn, can be seen as a further step in the direction of Etherege's Dorimant.[10] The treatment of cuckolding of the citizens, similarly, is at once traditional, from a long line of pre-Restoration citizen comedies, and innovative, especially in its explicitness and spiritedness, which point toward the acme of late seventeenth-century sex farce roughly ten years later in such plays as Ravenscroft's *The London Cuckolds* and Dryden's *Mr. Limberham*. The same can be said of the Woodly action, which treats the unhappy marriage in a way that anticipates Southerne's *The Wives Excuse* and Vanbrugh's *The Provoked Wife*. And finally, the Clodpate intrigue takes the country bumpkin justice closer, if not to Squire Western, then to his less distant ancestors, from Shadwell's own Sir Jeffrey Shacklehead in *The Lancashire Witches* to Farquhar's Justice Ballance in *The Recruiting Officer*.

Although Shadwell, quite rightly, has never been considered to be a writer who devoted much effort to careful revision of his texts, in *Epsom-Wells* he has taken care to provide a structure that holds together his disparate intrigues remarkably well. In his analysis of the unity of 'multiple-plot drama,'[11] Richard Levin distinguishes four 'modes of integration' available to a playwright. These correspond to the four causes of Aristotle. The first and 'least artistic' – because it requires 'much less creative effort than the rest' – is the material cause, part of 'the *donnée* of the action,' a constant, static 'building-block' for 'more complicated structural effects,' but itself of minimal complexity and interest (8). In this mode, 'a connection is made between individuals from different plots by means of some conventional relationship' (5), usually one of kinship or geography. Material unity is achieved most effectively in *Epsom-Wells* by the fact that all the characters, as visitors to the spa, are involved in the same basic round of activity, focusing especially on the daily visit to the Wells with which the play opens. Shadwell is thus able to introduce his characters in a single place where they might reasonably be expected to meet and mix, very much in the tradition of *Bartholomew Fair*, though because the social range is more limited, this social world is even more unified. He adds to that closeness by identifying Carolina and Lucia as cousins to Woodly (and accordingly assigning them lodgings next to the Woodlys) and by having Mrs Woodly's maid, Peg, prove to be Mrs Jilt's sister.

Levin's second mode of integration, equivalent to Aristotle's efficient cause, 'is in fact what we ordinarily speak of as a "causal" connection, in which a character or event from one line of action directly affects the other.' It is a more difficult connection to construct because it 'must be built into the plot sequences rendered on stage,' and it is 'a more meaningful way to combine plots, because their mutual interaction knits them more closely together and makes them, quite literally, part of the same dramatic universe' (8). Most writers of broad comedy and farce are especially gifted in manipulating this kind of unity, and Shadwell is no exception. All the intrigues involve varying degrees of love, sex, or money, and there is considerable overlap from intrigue to intrigue. Clodpate courts Carolina and Lucia before turning to Mrs Jilt; Kick and Cuff also pursue the sisters, and Woodly is in love with Carolina. Bevil cuckolds Woodly, and Rains plans to do the same. Rains, moreover, has affairs in progress with Mrs Bisket and Mrs Jilt. Cuff and Kick cheat Clodpate of £100 and his horse before tying him up with a sheet over his head to be mistaken for a ghost. Rains and Bevil meet Lucia and Carolina when the ladies request their aid in freeing them from the unwanted attention of Kick and Cuff.

And the budding relationships between the heroes and heroines are almost destroyed by the intrigues of each of the Woodlys, hers motivated by her concern for Bevil and his by his concern for Carolina. At the level of the causal mode, then, *Epsom-Wells* is indeed a very tightly structured work.

But, as Levin points out, both the material and the causal modes ultimately must contribute to 'more complex and more important modes of integration' (9), a third mode, corresponding to Aristotle's formal cause, which 'includes all the logical – or more accurately, analogical – relationships obtaining between the plots.' The formal mode is rendered in the action (like the efficient), but remains constant throughout (like the material), in effect a 'spatial integration of plots' (10). This mode is generally the focal point of critical studies of multiple-plot plays, and has prompted the better analyses of *Epsom-Wells*. Michael Alssid's analysis of the play as a 'holiday of love' provides a useful example of analysis in the formal mode:

The public world of the Wells is a world closer to 'nature' than London; it is a place to which visitors flock to enjoy for a brief while a release from the humdrum commitments of life, a place where they can bowl, drink, and love in imitation of the idle rich. As Lucia, one of the bright young lovers of the comedy, remarks in Act IV, the 'freedom of *Epsom* allows almost nothing to be scandalous.' *Freedom* is a key word, for the idea of freedom in love and in marriage binds together the high and the two low plots. The three plots, with their abundant contrasting characters and situations, accentuate and proliferate the meaning of freedom. Epsom is, symbolically, the site of freedom, where people unmask and where truths are revealed.[12]

The problem with analysis in the formal mode is that the ingenious critic finds little opposition in the pursuit of a desired unity: the extremes here range from the mere compilation of miscellaneous parallel details to the ignoring of inconvenient details in pursuit of a universal theme. Such dangers can be averted, Levin argues, by the critic who recognizes the need to go beyond the formal to the affective modes of integration, corresponding to Aristotle's final cause; it is in this mode that the various parallels and connections are best seen in relationship to each other (where such relationships exist), and that the unique character of the particular play is best seen behind the presence of the universal theme. It is here that Shadwell's use of the most basic form of unifying multiple plots, the 'direct contrast plot,' (21–54) reveals the special achievement of *Epsom-Wells*. The four intrigues of *Epsom-Wells* break down into pairs of courtship and cuckolding plots, each with a high and a low member. Thus, *Epsom-Wells* offers a double contrast, first the Bevil–Carolina–Rains–Lucia courtship with the Clodpate–Carolina–Lucia–Jilt series of courtships, the one leading to the promise of marriage, the other to a mock-marriage that dissolves into nothingness; and second, the Woodly–Mrs Woodly–Bevil cuckolding with the Bisket–Mrs Bisket–Kick and the Fribble–Mrs Fribble–Cuff cuckoldings, the former ending in an amicable 'divorce,' the latter in an equally amicable set of reconciliations. Similarly, the two higher intrigues contrast marriage and divorce among the sophisticated London gentry while the lower plots contrast the matrimonial misfortunes of city and country gulls.

Appropriate hierarchies of characters and values are maintained throughout, most notably in the attempts by male characters in all the intrigues to marry or seduce the women in the successful courtship intrigue, Carolina and Lucia, and in the similar attempt by female characters in all the intrigues to marry or seduce the men in the successful courtship intrigue, Bevil and Rains. The young lovers thus embody the appropriate combination of class and social status to provide a constant set of comic values to apply throughout the play. Yet the very nature of the comic intrigues prevents these values from providing a moral context of any genuine seriousness. Any of the intrigues could have been constructed to do so, but Shadwell systematically defuses the potentially serious by allowing relatively happy endings, however unrealistic or unconvincing, for all four intrigues. The result is a play in which the various intrigues are so well balanced against one another that, in the generic system proposed above, *Epsom-Wells* is a mainstream comedy, an even mix of Fletcher and Jonson, the very kind of comedy Dryden formulated four years earlier.

Through a very different method of unifying multiple plots, Wycherley also achieves a 'mixt way of Comedy' in *Love in a Wood*. The next most common unifying device after direct contrast, Levin argues, is the 'three-level hierarchy,' plays containing a third, usually lower, group of characters in a relatively independent intrigue. His general description of the form, though intended to account for Renaissance drama – Levin's models are *The Second Maiden's Tragedy* and *The Changeling* – seems as if it were written to include Wycherley's first play – and certainly offers strong evidence for the backward-looking, apprentice-piece nature of the play. After noting that the third or lower plot takes place at a different 'level of emotional tone or sensibility,' Levin points to the differing 'modes of sensibility' that distinguish the remaining two plots. These plays are built upon a 'hierarchy of descending magnitude and seriousness ... a main plot consisting of characters deliberately elevated above the others, usually in heroic or romantic terms; a subplot of more ordinary people viewed from a more realistic and often ironic or satiric perspective; and a third group debased to the level of low comedy' (55–6; see 55–108).

In constructing his three-level play entirely within a comic framework, Wycherley is following not his source, Calderón's *Mañanas de abril y mayo*, but what A.H. Scouten characterizes as 'Etherege's pattern of interlocking parts' in his first play, *The Comical Revenge*.[13] In his briefer treatment of *Love in a Wood*, Scouten nowhere suggests that Wycherley aspires to the all-encompassing breadth of *The Comical Revenge*, one of the two most successful comedies of the preceding decade (the other was *Sir Martin Mar-all*).[14] Etherege's play, for Scouten, is 'an ambitious exercise ... an effort to show all levels of London society ... to cram a Balzacian *comédie humaine* into five acts. The achievement was impossible, but this is not to say that Etherege lacked control over his material. The reader will find four distinct plots, but he will find them tightly interwoven with reduplicating episodes and imagery.'[15]

The difference between the plays is not in Wycherley's inattention to unity. *Love in a Wood* contains a plot with three distinct levels of courtship intrigue, Valentine and Christina (Wycherley's lovers, like Etherege's and Calderón's, are separated because of the hero's participation in a duel); Lydia and Ranger; and Lady Flippant and Sir Simon Addleplot, Gripe and Lucy, Dapperwit and Martha. In the material and efficient modes, moreover, Wycherley has connected his characters with great care: Vincent, as friend to both Valentine and Ranger, serves conveniently in both their intrigues; his house is also but five doors from Christina's. Lady Flippant maintains friendships with both Lydia and Christina and is thus able to introduce Lydia into Christina's house when she fears being found in the park by Ranger. As a result, when Ranger follows her, he finds Christina, and falls in love with her. Dapperwit, as a hanger-on of the genuine wits, Ranger and Vincent, links the middle and low plots by such acts as bringing Ranger to see his mistress, Lucy. Similarly, Dapperwit approaches the masked Lydia in the park, as Ranger does Lady Flippant. Wycherley, like Shadwell, works within the unities of time and place, albeit loosely defined, and again, like Shadwell, makes use of a specific geographic place, in this case St James's Park, to provide a probable occasion for bringing all his characters together.

Nor is there an absence of unity in the formal mode. Several critics have pointed to the wordplay of the title as a key to its thematic unity, noting, as Katharine Rogers puts it, that 'it is not hostile fortune that keeps the lovers apart, but Ranger's compulsive inconstancy, Valentine's senseless and selfish jealousy, and a generally self-seeking and mercenary attitude toward sexual relationships.'[16] In all of the first three modes, then, Wycherley is at least Etherege's equal. In fact, he goes much further. All his intrigues, even the punitive ones, are courtship intrigues, and the London in which they take place comes across as a small world indeed. Wycherley breaks from Etherege's model, too, in not following the tradition of presenting his high plot in verse, a choice that has garnered repeated praise from critics.[17]

Yet all Wycherley's carefully constructed unity remains 'ingenious but mechanical,'[18] since it is not, in the end, in the service of a coherent, synthesizing, final effect. *The Comical Revenge*, as Scouten suggests, attempts a Balzacian treatment of its society, which places it very much in the tradition of Renaissance three-level plays. Etherege's version also points to the influence of Spanish comedy in the 1660's after the enormous initial success of Tuke's *The Adventures of Five Hours*. But Wycherley has transformed his Spanish source entirely, making it into a distinctly London comedy.[19] By denying the high plot its elevated tone and sensibility, and by bringing the low plot within reach of the middle, Wycherley placed the levels of his comic intrigues too close together to represent a *comédie humaine* but not close enough to contain a single, tightly knit little world such as he achieved in his next comedy, *The Gentleman Dancing-Master*.

Love in a Wood is thus an object lesson in the need for the highest level of unity in plot construction; no amount of careful work in the lesser modes can overcome its absence. It is also interesting as a transition piece in the history of multiple-plot plays. With the passing of the 1660s vogue for a high-toned, Spanish-influenced comedy of love and honour, such as *The Adventures of Five Hours*, Dryden's *The Rival Ladies*, Porter's *The Carnival*, etc, the higher plots of *comic* multiple-plot plays are gradually reduced to the level of the middle plot in *Love in a Wood*. Wycherley's critics have complained most about the high plot of *Love in a Wood*; Valentine, in particular, is (rightly) deemed unworthy of Christina.[20] Valentine offers a paradigm for the weakness of the work as a whole: to succeed in the play his jealousy must be seen in the context of an exalted sense of honour if Christina's portrait of him as 'a brave man ... worthy the love of a Princess; ... good as Angels'[21] is to be given any credibility. Instead it seems merely a perverse and misguided humour, the antecedent of Congreve's more successful Vainlove, as we shall see in the discussion of *The Old Batchelour* in chapter 3.

That Valentine should seem a humours character is not terribly surprising in a play in which the genuine humours characters are its greatest triumphs. What was true for Shadwell is still more significantly true for Wycherley – that his 'gallery of well-defined characters, and the astringency of the commentary they provide on London life, remind us that Ben Jonson was his master.'[22] Ranger and Lydia have occasional moments of brilliance, but it is Gripe and Dapperwit, Sir Simon Addleplot and Lady Flippant who are the most effective characters in *Love in a Wood*. These are the characters who serve as focuses for 'the moral awareness which was to distinguish Wycherley among his contemporaries,'[23] a moral awareness that left him, and not Shadwell, as the heir to Jonson's comic mantle – a fact obscured by the tendency of twentieth-century critics to co-opt Wycherley in such camps as the comedy of manners and comedy of wit. Nowhere is this clearer than in the evaluation of the tough, but generally fair-minded contemporary, Gerard Langbaine. Langbaine considers Shadwell an accomplished writer of 'Excellent Comedies' as well as a personal friend. He prefers his comedies to those of Dryden, defending him from Dryden's attacks, which he likens to Aristophanes' attacks on Socrates, and taking no small pleasure in Shadwell's ultimate triumph 'in wearing the *Bays*.' But when it comes to placing him in the company of the 'Great Man' Jonson, Langbaine tactfully draws the line: 'That Mr. *Shadwell* has propos'd B. *Johnson* for his Model, I am very certain of; and those who will read the Preface to the *Humorists*, may be sufficiently satisfied what a value he has for that Great Man; but how far he has succeeded in his Design, I shall leave to the Reader's Examination.' Langbaine considers *Epsom-Wells* 'so diverting' and 'so true a Comedy' that he notes, without comment, 'that the *Sieur De Saint Euvremont*, speaking of our *English* Comedies in his *Essays*, has ranked this Play with *Ben Johnson's Bartholomew Fair*, as two of our most diverting Comedies.' It is no contemner of Shadwell's efforts at comedy, then, who describes Wycherley, not his personal friend, as 'a Gentleman, whom I may boldly reckon amongst the Poets of the First Rank: no Man that I know, except the Excellent *Johnson*, having outdone him in Comedy; in which alone he has imploy'd his Pen, but with that Success, that few have before, or will hereafter match him.'[24] Langbaine's judgment seems a just one, too, in the context of my discussion of comic form, for nowhere does Shadwell provide as vigorous and uncompromising a punitive comic action as the one Wycherley builds around Horner in *The Country-Wife*.

Because of the similarity of their opening scenes, and because Horner indulges in a feigned physical disability, *The Country-Wife* is frequently compared to *Volpone*, and, most particularly, Horner to Jonson's eponymous rogue-hero. For example, for Louis Kronenberger, Horner 'is to sex what Volpone is to gold; and, as with Volpone, the game itself means as much as the rewards ... Horner, even more than Volpone, lacks conventional vanity; he is willing to seem impotent as a smart gambler is to seem a dub or a crack diplomatist to seem a duffer.'[25] And because both characters have provoked strong negative responses from critics, who often portray them as villains, it seems inevitable that the two be compared. But since *The Country-Wife*, unlike *Volpone*, remains safely within a comic framework throughout – compare the fates of Volpone and Horner – Virginia Ogden Birdsall is surely right to suggest that closer analogues can be found in Jonson's work. Her own suggestion is *The Alchemist*. More specifically, she finds in Face 'a closer Jonsonian ancestor, in terms of spiritual kinship' as well as 'the audacious cleverness and the comic and creative resiliency which they share.'[26] Birdsall limits her comparison to these two characters, but the similarities extend well beyond individual character to overall plot structure. When Dr Quack reports 'throughout the whole Town' that Horner's misfortunes in France have left him 'as bad as an *Eunuch*' (1.1.6), the nature of his comic licence is established. In typical Jonsonian fashion, his gulls almost instantly bring their wives to him, and his scheme is so successful that by act 4, scene 3, he is utterly drained, suffering from physical exhaustion. But even this comic humiliation does not end his intrigue: it continues to build to its climactic confrontation when Margery Pinchwife, in her simple innocence, almost reveals to the gulls their duping – in this case cuckolding.

Here the appropriateness of the comparison to *The Alchemist* ends. Horner is not cast off to the galleys or the hospital of the *Incurabili*, nor is he rushed off to 'scape the dock.' Even Face, who goes virtually unpunished, must return to his servant's position and Jeremy as a sign of the restoration of social order. But Horner remains not only unpunished, but absolutely unchanged. Pinchwife will no doubt return to the country, taking the unfortunate Margery with him. But Horner never pursued her in the first place; Pinchwife's cuckolding is entirely of his own doing – he corrupts Margery by mistreating her, arousing her interest in Horner, teaching her to lie and scheme, carrying her letter, and finally bringing the lady herself to Horner's bed. Sir Jaspar and Old Lady Squeamish are satisfied and the status quo remains firmly in place in the end. Horner can, with pride, put a final rhetorical question to Quack: 'Well Doctor is not this a good design that carryes a man on unsuspected, and brings him off safe' (5.4.378–9). Like the humours characters, but unlike Jonson's greatest rogues, Horner remains unchanged in the end, thus revealing the major difference between the Jonsonian punitive intrigue and its Restoration imitators. Jonson's view of comedy, and perhaps his view of morality, required that the licence be revoked in the end, for a restored normalcy had to prevail over the social – and moral – anarchy of the rogues. But Horner's world is the normal world. Since it remains unchanged by the granting of the licence, it would remain unchanged if the licence were revoked. And, more significantly, the social or moral need for revocation is eliminated.

Thus, Wycherley points back to still another Jonsonian analogue, the play Dryden singled out from the works of 'the most learned and judicious Writer which any Theater ever had' to honour with the examen that also serves as part of his polemical program for the English comedy of the (immediate) future, *Epicoene, or The Silent Woman*. Dryden prefers *Epicoene* because 'there is more wit and acuteness of Fancy in it then in any of *Ben. Johnson's* [other plays]. Besides that, he has here describ'd the conversation of Gentlemen in the persons of *True-Wit*, and his Friends, with more gayety, ayre and freedom, then in the rest of his comedies,'[27] no doubt that source of the critical commonplace that of all Jonson's characters, Dauphine, Clerimont, and Truewit would be most at home on the Restoration stage. Jonson's wits share, too, with their Restoration counterparts a proclivity for sexual intrigue. The candid discussion of women in the fourth act of *Epicoene* is a model for the countless exchanges among truewits after the Restoration:

TRV. Speake, art thou in loue in earnest?
DAV. Yes by my troth am I: 'twere ill dissembling before thee.
TRV. With which of 'hem, I pray thee?
DAV. With all the collegiates.
CLE. Out on thee. Wee'll keepe you at home, beleeve it, i' the stable, and you be such a stallion.
TRV. No. I like him well. Men should loue wisely, and all women: some one for the face, and let her please the eye; another for the skin, and let her please the touch; a third for the voice, and let her please the eare; and where the objects mixe, let the senses so too.[28]

Though Horner is Dauphine's stallion turned gelding, he and his friends Harcourt and Dorilant are of the same breed of witty young gentlemen as

Jonson's trio, albeit several generations their junior. (In *Epicoene*, it is Morose who proclaims himself 'no man ... Vtterly vnabled in nature, by reason of *frigidity*, to performe the duties, or any the least office of a husband' (5.4.44–7), provoking a response from the collegiates not unlike the one Horner receives from women who 'love the sport' (1.1.152–3.) And Jonson's collegiates, to give them their due, are no less aggressively willing than Lady Fidget and 'the whole knot of the virtuous gang' (5.2.89–90). Wycherley is more graphic and open in his portrayal of sexual licence, but the difference is one of degree only. Jonson, at least in this play, is no more anxious than Wycherley or Shadwell to punish his wits for succumbing to the temptation of promiscuous, foolish, handsome women.

Where Shadwell, whose *Epsom-Wells* is one of his more successful plays, could no more equal his master in wit than he could in plot construction, Wycherley, at least in *The Country-Wife*, is up to the Jonsonian mark in both these areas. Not that Wycherley limits himself to the punitive intrigues surrounding Horner. Like Shadwell, he includes a sympathetic plot, the courtship of Harcourt and Alithea.

It is difficult to disagree with James Sutherland's contention that *The Country-Wife* 'is the best-constructed of all Wycherley's plays; indeed, it is a masterpiece of easy, natural, and self-explanatory movement.'[29] The play is structured around three intrigues, each consisting of two men and a woman: Sir Jaspar–Lady Fidget–Horner, Pinchwife–Margery–Horner, and Sparkish–Alithea–Harcourt. Wycherley links his intrigues at the material and efficient levels by having Pinchwife appear in London to arrange the wedding of his sister, Alithea, to Sparkish; by having Harcourt and Sparkish in the same general social circle as Horner (Pinchwife is a member of this group, too); and by having Margery disguise herself as Alithea to consummate her relationship with Horner. All these characters, in other words, are of the same world, Wycherley having conflated entirely the hierarchies of *Love in a Wood*.

The bulk of Wycherley criticism has been devoted to demonstrating the formal, thematic unity of *The Country-Wife*. Critics may not agree with the particulars of that unity, but the sheer weight of the varying hypotheses offers a strong indication that it is there to be found: 'Positively and negatively, through statement and example, *The Country-Wife* is centrally concerned with providing a definition of masculinity'; 'the theme of jealousy gives a deeper unity to the play'; 'his theme is the selfishness which pervaded sexual relationships in his society'; 'it is an imitation ... of a single model, Juvenal's *Sixth Satire*'; 'it is a play that sets out to attack a society that accepted marital contracts based on interest rather than love,

and it shows the deception, hypocrisy, indifference and cruelty that flow
from such contracts'; 'the tight structure depends on the ironic satire. The
fundamental design is the exposure of inverted values: the sham set
against the reality.'[30] The plot is held together by a series of 'direct contrasts,' most fundamentally between the sympathetic and punitive
intrigues with their alternative views of love and lust – what Holland calls
a 'right-way–wrong-way structure' resulting in, as R. Edgley puts it, the
'triumphs of wit and sense over folly and stupidity.'[31]

The two recurring and related critical cruxes surrounding *The Country-
Wife* – how to respond to Alithea and Horner – result from the difficulty
inherent in Wycherley's particular blend of Jonsonian and Fletcherian elements, a difficulty, it should be clear, he overcomes almost entirely and
quite triumphantly. (These cruxes do not seem to have distressed Restoration audiences and quite often have been of no trouble to twentieth-century audiences.)[32] Virtually everyone recognizes that Alithea is a sympathetic character. Her loyalty to Sparkish, though he is transparently
unworthy of her (Hume calls her behaviour 'block-headed loyalty to an
obnoxious fool'), therefore requires some explanation, especially for those
critics like Righter, who, offended by Horner (a 'wholly negative ... agent
of destruction'), look to Alithea and Harcourt for a 'positive ... centre of
the comedy.'[33] But Hume is surely right to argue that 'if Harcourt and
Alithea are supposed to represent a high moral norm in the play and make
us view Horner with disapprobation, then Wycherley made a mess of
things.'[34] Like most rogue-heroes in punitive comedy, Horner is an attractive and clever character who, though no moral paragon himself, tends to
apply his skills and talents only to those worse than he is. (It is important
to remember that Horner chooses to play the eunuch, as he tells the doctor, to 'distinguish love from good breeding.' His target is only the woman
who 'loves the sport' (1.1.151–3).) And Horner is a particularly successful
rogue-hero, worthy of a high place in the Jonsonian line. As a result, he
overshadows those characters like Alithea who are bound to the rules of
conventional morality. Alithea and Harcourt suffer, in other words, a mild
case of what might be called Celia-Bonario syndrome, the dullness – even
unattractiveness – that good characters suffer from contact with especially
effective and vital rogues.

But Alithea's comparative dullness does not explain that her stubborn
refusal to drop Sparkish. Chadwick suggests that her behaviour simply
reflects the reality of Restoration society as represented by Halifax's
Advice to a Daughter – that most women did not marry for love.[35]
Though accurate as social history, this view, too, does not really apply to

Alithea. As her name suggests, she represents a higher principle than the worldly-wise Halifax recommends to his daughter. When Sparkish finally rejects her, her response is not simply one of relief but rather 'How was I deceiv'd in a man!' (5.3.71), a question that has been troubling the other characters and the audience for four and a half acts. The moral she draws from her own experience – 'now I wish, that if there be any over-wise woman of the Town, who like me would marry a fool, for fortune, liberty, or title, first that her husband may love Play, and be a Cully to all the Town, but her, and suffer none but fortune to be mistress of his purse, then if for liberty, that he may send her into the Country under the conduct of some housewifely mother-in-law; and if for title, may the world give 'em none but that of Cuckold' (5.3.77–83) – certainly indicates that she has learned something that should make her marriage to Harcourt a happier one,[36] but her tenacious defence of and loyalty to Sparkish as an extension of her own personal honour requires still more explanation. The extent to which Alithea represents the 'right way' points to her honour as a device of thematic contrast with the more vocal display of honour from Lady Fidget and her circle. The excessive quality of Alithea's claim to honour, finally, I think, comes from the extent to which the Harcourt-Alithea plot is a remnant, greatly devolved, of the elevated high plot still found in *Love in a Wood*. It is the world of romance, particularly as represented by the Restoration heroic play, that Alithea's honour faintly echoes. Compare, for example, her early response to Harcourt's attentions with the similarly puzzling response of loyalty to Boabdelin that Almahide offers Almanzor in the first part of *The Conquest of Granada*:

> ALMANZ. I bring a claim which does his right remove:
> You're his by promise, but you're mine by Love.
> 'Tis all but Ceremony which is past:
> The knot's to tie which is to make you fast.
> Fate gave not to *Boabdelin* that pow'r:
> He woo'd you, but as my Ambassadour.
> ALMAH. Our Souls are ty'd by Vows above.
> ALMANZ. He sign'd but his: but I will seal my love.
> I love you better; with more Zeale than he.
> ALMAH. This day –
> I gave my faith to him, he his to me.
>
> ...
>
> What 'ere my secret inclinations be,
> To this, since honor ties me, I agree.   (3.1.386–96; 5.1.355–6)

ALITH. The writings are drawn, Sir, settlements made; 'tis too late, Sir, and past
all revocation.
HAR. Then so is my death.
ALITH. I wou'd not be unjust to him.
HAR. Then why to me so?
ALITH. I have no obligation to you.
HAR. My love.
ALITH. I had his before ... but in short, Sir, to end our dispute, I must marry
him, my reputation wou'd suffer in the World else.

...

I wish my Gallant had his person and understanding: – (Nay if my honour –
Aside)   (2.1.212–19, 229–31, 281–3)

Though there is no reason to question the sincerity of Alithea's claim,
particularly as it is reinforced in the aside, its inappropriate key can at
least be explained by its origin. Similarly, one of the strongest pieces of
evidence cited by critics unfavourable to Horner is 'the occasion when he
is forced by his amatory entanglements to belie Alithea,' the result being,
as Rogers characterizes it, 'what his contemporaries would condemn as a
shameful lie.'[37] Alithea is indeed shocked, but Horner's response reveals
that he, too, operates by the gentleman's code of honour (as appropriately
reduced to the scale of punitive comedy):

ALITH. What mean you Sir, I always took you for a man of Honour?
HOR. Ay, so much a man of Honour, that I must save my Mistriss, I thank you,
come what will on't. (*Aside*)   (5.4.239–41)

That Alithea lies to her brother soon after (when Margery is revealed), to
protect Horner and Margery, suggests that she, too, understands and
accepts the code.
   The union of Jonson and Fletcher is rarely an easy one. Because the
punitive intrigues dominate *The Country-Wife* so thoroughly, they over-
power the sympathetic intrigue, particularly in its representation of a sincere, occasionally elevated, model of marriage for love. A generic model of
Restoration drama cannot explain away the oft-perceived critical difficulties in a play like *The Country-Wife*, but it can offer a guide to more accurate interpretation and understanding.

Burlesque, like satire, poses special problems for a model based on Jonsonian and Fletcherian comedy, since, for the most part, it is neither. Much

of the pleasure offered by Buckingham's *The Rehearsal* derives from references to the contemporary theatrical and political world of the 1660s and early 1670s. Its subsequent success depended significantly on the continuing presence in the repertory of plays like *The Conquest of Granada* and on the constant revision to and updating of the text by the gifted actor-playwrights who succeeded Lacy as Bayes, particularly Cibber and Garrick. An audience with some awareness of such personalities as Dryden and the Howards – or Pope and Quin – was, as well, requisite for its repertory status.[38] Sheridan Baker understandably laments that despite an 'hilarious vitality that makes *The Critic* ... trivial by contrast ... directors ... find *The Rehearsal* too remote to risk'; the directors are nonetheless right.[39]

Appreciation of *The Rehearsal*, then, depends upon the recognition of a substantial number of its targets. In its form and to some extent its impact, Buckingham's play nevertheless resembles more conventional contemporary comedy. When Smith and Johnson agree to accompany playwright Bayes to the dress rehearsal of his new play, the situation becomes very much like that of the standard, Jonsonian punitive comedy. In this case, the rehearsal is equivalent to the world under comic licence with Smith and Johnson in the roles of licencees. Though they lack the wit and charm of Jonson's rogues and many of their Restoration offspring, Smith and especially Johnson nonetheless represent a standard of urbane judgment able to encourage and preside over the exposure of Bayes's latest folly. (The Smith-Johnson-Bayes trio resembles Wycherley's trios of Dorilant-Horner-Sparkish and Vincent-Ranger-Dapperwit.) They are of course, hardly the active agents of a genuine punitive comedy, since Bayes needs only an audience to witness his deflation: even the equivalent of the removal of the licence is self-imposed when Bayes withdraws his play as revenge on the players for abandoning his rehearsal in favour of their dinner.

The complexity of *The Rehearsal* comes from Bayes's poorly constructed, splintered, highly episodic, nonsensical play-within-a-play; Buckingham's play, with its straightforward skeletal rehearsal plot, is simplicity itself by contrast. Smith, Johnson, and the Players are all rather bland figures used to set off Bayes and his play. The ridiculous playwright reveals his humour of what Baker calls 'mad authorial egotism' in his obsessive desire to 'do nothing here that ever was done before,'[40] a humour that makes him typical of the victims of punitive comedy in the 1670s. Bayes, of course, remains confirmed in his folly right to his final burst of bathetic defiance against a society unwilling to acknowledge his genius: 'The Town! why, what care I for the Town? I gad, the Town has us'd me as scurvily, as the Players have done: but I'l be reveng'd on them too, for I'l Lampoon 'em all: And since they will not admit of my Plays, they shall know what a Satyrist I am. And so farewel to this Stage, I gad, for ever' (5.1.408–13).

Baker's attempt to rescue *The Rehearsal* from the 'historical particulars' so necessary to understand it, that is, his attempt to see it as a punitive comedy rather than a burlesque, is a valiant one, if finally unsuccessful. For Baker, Buckingham's powerful depiction of his central character creates a 'comedy of blind conceit' that ultimately 'transcends the personal satire in which it originates.' That transcendence launches *The Rehearsal* into 'the necessary orbit of any great literature,' the depiction 'of something permanently true about human nature.'[41] Though Baker points to a hundred years of stage success in support of his argument, he overlooks the constant revision that was necessary to maintain that success. When *The Critic* effectively replaced Buckingham's much-revised burlesque in the repertory, it may well be that the triumph was that of an inferior. But Sheridan's play was fresh and timely, Buckingham's dated and tired. Sheridan developed Garrick's satiric focus on theatrical convention along with providing topical political and literary allusions for the Georgian audience. And despite Sheridan's popularity for two centuries, *The Critic* is hardly a repertory piece today.

The Rehearsal contains much first-rate comedy, and comedy, moreover, as representative of its time as the numerous references to historical particulars that finally led to its removal from the repertory. But because it depends on familiarity with its many allusions – and their context – for satisfactory understanding (Bayes remains more a means to an end than an end in himself), its burlesque character, finally, removes it from the province of the standard broad range of late seventeenth-century comedy that is nonetheless the prerequisite for its presence on the stage.

Far more typical of the comedy of the 1670s are the two remaining plays in this group, both distinctly inferior to the best work of Wycherley, Shadwell, and Buckingham, yet both clearly above average for the period – Betterton's *The Amorous Widow* and Crowne's *The Countrey Wit*. Both playwrights borrow extensively from Molière, as did Wycherley in *The Country-Wife*, yet both reveal the more pervasive influences of Jonson and Fletcher. Molière's influence, as usual, is limited to 'comic matter, farcical plots, and theatrically effective situations.' Betterton's extensive borrowing leads John Wilcox to consider *The Amorous Widow* 'the first major translation of Molière'; the result, he finds, is nonetheless 'a masterpiece of plagiaristic economy, producing a great distortion with little change.'[42]

Wilcox objects to *The Amorous Widow* because Betterton has 'reduced' Molière's *George Dandin*, a 'thoughtful comedy of manners,' to 'a farcical underplot' in 'a commonplace comedy in the conventional style of the Restoration.'[43] His description is accurate, for Betterton has yoked *George Dandin* to Thomas Corneille's *Le Baron d'Albikrac*[44] and used both to prepare the way for a distinctly native, English play. Betterton's play lacks the tight material and efficient unity of *Epsom-Wells* or *The Country-Wife*, but he does not ignore such matters entirely: since Lady Laycock and Lady Pride are close relations (sisters?), Lady Laycock lodges at the house of the Prides' son-in-law, Barnaby Brittle; Cunningham's servant, Clodpole, carries letters to Mrs Brittle for Lovemore, who, in helping his friend Cunningham court Philadelphia, becomes one of the objects of Lady Laycock's affections; the Prides are invited to Lady Laycock's dance; and all the characters are brought together at the end. Unity in the formal mode, however, is not so easy to find. As Wilcox points out, Cunningham's intrigue to win Lady Laycock's permission to marry her niece, Philadelphia, through the presentation of a false suitor, his falconer Merryman, for the aunt's hand (the same device Mirabell uses in *The Way of the World*, though without Cunningham's success) seems arbitrarily bound to Mrs Brittle's intrigue to cuckold her husband with Lovemore. Cunningham and Mrs Brittle both successfully outwit the characters who attempt to block their intrigues, Lady Laycock and Barnaby Brittle respectively, and, in the process, each is reformed from a libertine to a more conventionally moral person.

It is difficult, however, to see any higher motivation in Betterton's choice of *George Dandin* and *Le Baron d'Albikrac* than his ability to unite the two into a highly entertaining and stageworthy piece, though the two plots do offer the familiar Restoration contrast between a happy marriage for love and an unhappy marriage for money and social status. Molière's play is an interesting mixture of farce and mild social satire against unequal marriages, which focuses from start to finish on the title character. His opening soliloquy presents his predicament and his awareness of his helplessness in the face of it with a clarity that shapes the following drama:

Ah! qu'une femme Demoiselle est une étrange affaire, et que mon mariage est

une leçon bien parlante à tous les paysans qui veulent s'élever au-dessus de
leur condition, et s'allier, comme j'ai fait, à la maison d'un gentilhomme! La
noblesse de soi est bonne, c'est une chose considérable, assurément; mais elle
est accompagnée de tant de mauvaises circonstances, qu'il est très bon de ne s'y
point frotter. Je suis devenu là-dessus savant à mes dépens, et connais le style
des nobles lorsqu'ils nous font, nous autres, entrer dans leur famille. L'alliance
qu'ils font est petite avec nos personnes. C'est notre bien seul qu'ils épousent,
et j'aurais bien mieux fait, tout riche que je suis, de m'allier en bonne et franche
paysannerie, que de prendre une femme qui se tient au-dessus de moi, s'of-
fense de porter mon nom, et pense qu'avec tout mon bien je n'ai pas assez
acheté la qualité de son mari. George Dandin, George Dandin, vous avez fait
une sottise la plus grande du monde. Ma maison m'est effroyable maintenant,
et je n'y rentre point sans y trouver quelque chagrin.[45]

Betterton does not introduce Barnaby Brittle until the middle of the
second act, and we first hear of the Brittles from Lovemore as he looks for
someone to carry a letter to Mrs Brittle for him. Brittle appears shortly
thereafter, first by himself receiving Lovemore, who inquires of him if
Lady Laycock is at home, then with his wife, who quarrels with him when
he tells her not to leave the house. He loses the argument, of course, and
at that point Betterton has him close act two with a truncated version of
Dandin's soliloquy above: 'This 'tis for a Tradesman to marry a Gentlewoman. A Curse on such Gentility! What shall I do? I shall be damnably
plagu'd with her Father and Mother. Well, next Month I must take up in
Bedlam; a Judgment, which every Citizen deserves, that marries above his
Quality.'[46]

In his discussion of *George Dandin*, Lionel Gossman shows how
Molière sets up a three-level social hierarchy within the single intrigue by
representing Clitandre, the lover of Angélique, Dandin's wife, as 'Monsieur le vicomte de chose ... ce jeune courtisan' (1.2.p291), and thus as far
above her proud parents, the de Sotenvilles, as they are above Dandin.[47]
Clitandre is a witty courtier, but somewhat cold and distant, not as sympathetic or attractive a figure as Betterton's young wit Lovemore, a rake
whose involvement in Cunningham's intrigue in the main plot makes him
a more important character than his counterpart in *George Dandin*. His
presence in the Brittle subplot does set up a similar hierarchy, but not one
so totally determined by class structure. Lovemore is superior to the
Prides in wit and sophistication, not in class, so that their folly becomes
more completely one of pride than of the false sense of place revealed by
Clitandre's perspective of the de Sotenvilles: for him they are 'not Soten-

ville, but *Sot-en-ville*.'[48] The Prides are indeed the objects of Betterton's comic disapproval, but their folly is not generalized to the extent that 'concepts of social hierarchy and rank are being criticized, concepts that Molière never dreamed of questioning.'[49] In *George Dandin* the questions of social hierarchy are more central than they are in *The Amorous Widow*, where a falconer impersonates a viscount without raising any issues of social hierarchy, though Molière's main purpose is no more revolutionary than Betterton's.

As his initial soliloquy reveals, Dandin's problem is his own. 'The satire is directed, as elsewhere in Molière, not against a social system, but against individuals who have only their own stupidity to blame.'[50] Dandin winds up more or less where he started, as Molière also ends his play with a Dandin soliloquy: 'Ah! je le quitte maintenant, et je n'y vois plus de remède. Lorsqu'on a, comme moi, épousé une méchante femme, le meilleur parti qu'on puisse prendre, c'est de s'aller jeter dans l'eau la tête la première (3.8.p328). Although some highly respected Molière critics have taken this passage seriously – that is, have projected Dandin's suicide – Joan Crow is surely right to argue that 'Molière is here ending his play on a very old if bitter joke,' the perfect 'anticlimax for an anti-hero.'[51] And Betterton cuts this scene entirely, instead ending his play, as he began it, with the main plot: the marriages of Philadelphia and Cunningham, Jeffrey and Prudence, and Clodpole and Damaris are still settled. Thus Brittle's dilemma is lost in the end in the general round of happiness surrounding the three pairs of lovers, and he remains a far less sympathetic figure than George Dandin. And while he has probably, like Dandin, learned little if anything, his wife has learned a great deal and, as the play ends, is a very different woman from the 'wanton wife' who gave the play its subtitle.

Betterton's reduction of Dandin from central character and anti-hero to a secondary character and typical citizen husband, a change facilitated by his decision to set the play in London rather than in the country (*Le Baron d'Albikrac* is set in Paris), points to his place in the tradition of English citizen comedy as modified by Fletcher, the source of the majority of cuckolding intrigues in later seventeenth-century comedy. One of the most noteworthy characteristics of post-Restoration dramatists is the way in which they turned their backs on the more hard-nosed citizen comedy of Jonson, Middleton, and Dekker. (Their Caroline predecessors anticipated them in this turn.) If Brian Gibbons is right to use as a model for citizen comedy Chapman, Marston, and Jonson's *Eastward Ho!* with its satire on citizens, usurers, and gallants to the point of 'self-parody of the genre's typical styles of comedy and language,'[52] then he offers a splendid model, too, for what was rejected by playwrights after the Restoration. The focus on tradesmen and apprentices, complete with Puritan proverbs for how to succeed in business and improve your social standing; on prodigal gallants whose folly has lost them their fortunes and thus makes them targets for ridicule; and on citizen-usurers who are often successful in spite of their immoral dealings – all with a 'critical and satiric design' that excludes 'material appropriate to romance, fairy-tale, sentimental legend or patriotic chronicle'[53] – distinguishes these plays from those of Betterton, Shadwell, Wycherley, Buckingham, and Crowne.

It is only as modified by Fletcher that city comedy evolved as an important influence for most playwrights.[54] For, as Alexander Leggatt explains, it was Fletcher who took 'plot materials from both the private and public traditions, softening the satire of the one and draining away the morality of the other' to produce a comedy that emphasized 'entertainment, provided by witty dialogue, clever intrigue, and an overall air of playful fantasy.' It is the Fletcherian synthesis that provides 'the elements of citizen comedy that seem to have the greatest power of survival after 1610 ... the London setting, the intrigue, and the interest in one particular class, the idle young men about town.' Lost in the process is 'the predominantly middle-class social milieu' and the resulting 'common factor in these plays, an interest in practical social issues: how to get money, and how to spend it; how to get a wife, and how to keep her.' Courtship and romance are noticeably absent from citizen comedy, and 'young lovers, when present at all, have to make their way in a world of hard bargaining, and it is the bargaining more than the love that commands our attention.'[55]

The world of citizen comedy before Fletcher is indeed a long way from the world of *The Amorous Widow*. This is especially clear in the latter's main plot, borrowed from Thomas Corneille – the courtship of Cunningham and Philadelphia through the intrigue that overcomes the barrier to their marriage offered by Lady Laycock. As with Molière, Betterton incorporates 'large stretches' of 'speech-for-speech translation.'[56] And again, he makes significant changes while altering little. For example, in Corneille's play, there is a real Baron d'Albikrac, an impoverished Breton, who has been encouraged to come to Paris to marry the heroine's widowed aunt and thus enable the young lovers, Oronte and Angélique, to marry. It is only when Oronte's friend Léandre tires of holding off Angélique's aunt in lieu of the baron that the plot is hatched:

LISE. Ah, si votre Breton était prêt d'arriver!

> ORON. L'argent comptant le charme, il viendra nous trouver,
> Et craignant qu'on ne songe à presser les affaires,
> Il m'envoie un pouvoir passé devant notaire;
> Mais de plus de dix jours il ne saurait partir.
> LISE. Et Léandre pour rien ne voudra consentir ...
> LÉAN. Non; mais, à mon défaut employez La Montagne;
> Qu'il fasse quelques jours le baron de Bretagne,
> On ne le connaît point.[57]

As a result, the deception of the aunt is tempered by the knowledge that the real baron will eventually make his appearance to satisfy her hunger for a husband. In *The Amorous Widow*, however, there is no real Viscount Sans-terre; the deception is consequently a crueller one. Or, more accurately, Lady Laycock is treated as a humours character and blocking parent who, as such, deserves no better treatment than she gets. She learns nothing from her pursuit of every eligible man in the play, and Betterton leaves her quite uncertain about her future at the end: she has yet to learn of Merryman's true identity and nothing better or more suitable awaits her. Like Barnaby Brittle and the Prides, like the humours characters described in the plays above, and like her nearest antecedent counterparts, Lady Cockwood, in Etherege's *She wou'd if she cou'd* (1668), and Lady Loveall, in Killigrew's *The Parson's Wedding* (1664), Lady Laycock is not treated gently. Betterton thus sweetens the bitter satire of Molière while putting more bite into Corneille's gentler comedy; the result, to his credit, is a well-homogenized blend.

The Amorous Widow has been singled out in recent criticism as 'the play which ... was to have the effect of opening the eyes of the dramatists to the possibilities of cynical sex comedy.'[58] It is a curious candidate for such an honour. The lovers in the main plot are conventional almost to the point of dullness, especially Philadelphia, and what rakishness Cunningham may have had in the past has been reformed by his love. Lady Laycock, despite her name, is after a husband, not a lover (Lady Cockwood was far more licentious), and both Cunningham and Lovemore anticipate Mirabell in their determination not 'downright personally to debauch her.' Cunningham's servant, Jeffrey, refuses to carry Lovemore's letter to Mrs Brittle because he does not 'care to meddle in a Cause, where there's a Process of Cuckoldom going forward' (2.1.p27), and he is allowed his 'principles.' The only real sex intrigue is between Lovemore and Mrs Brittle, and not only does it remain unconsummated, but Mrs Brittle, when she learns from Cunningham the real nature of Lovemore's interest in her, undergoes an interesting transformation:

CUN. My Friend never wants a Mistress (I'll say that for him) in any Place, if he has but an Opportunity, which he seldom wants. I have often wonder'd at his Luck.
MRS BRITT. Say you so? I find he makes it his Business to ensnare and deceive women at this rate.
   (*Aside*: I'm glad I know it in time, whilst I have Power to make my Retreat. I had like to have been finely caught. Well, Husband, seeing so many join'd in Happiness, if you'll promise never to be jealous, I'll promise from this Moment never to give you Cause, and endeavour to make you as happy as I can.   (5.1.p86)

Hume may well be right to hold out *The Amorous Widow* as 'a prototype for the comedy of the 1670s' with its 'romantic plot [,] cuckoldry (not quite consummated in this instance), satire on cits and pretenders to gentility, borrowing from Molière, and a good bit of farce.' But he is also right that 'the combination of romance action and satire can be traced right back to *The English Monsieur*, *The Committee*, and Cowley's *Cutter*.'[59] All are variants of the Jonsonian and Fletcherian conventions that combine and permutate throughout the period. Perhaps the one genuinely original contribution made by *The Amorous Widow* is in involving a young town wit in a cuckolding intrigue. Betterton's choice to do so may have been determined by nothing more than an easy way to link his two intrigues, and the cuckolding, to repeat, remains unsuccessful. Yet it becomes absolutely formulaic in a very few years, and, within two years, is followed by *Epsom-Wells*, a play much more appropriately seen as 'cynical sex comedy.' It is ironic that Molière should provide the source for the first Restoration-style cuckolding intrigue, that Betterton should encourage the development of sex comedy in a play that is relatively pure and moral, and that Shadwell, despite his blanket of moral satire, should produce in *The Humorists* and *Epsom-Wells* some of the earliest examples of the sex comedy that was to become so prevalent in the 1670s.

The Countrey Wit, like *The Amorous Widow*, has had its twentieth-century reputation based on the discovery in it of qualities clearly found in later drama. But where Betterton's play is credited with a licentiousness beyond what is found in its text, Crowne's is seen to prefigure the heightened moral sensibilities of the following generation. The focal point for such readings is the reform of the rakish hero Ramble, who, among his several nods at libertinism, paraphrases from Crowne's patron (at this time) Rochester's famous poem, 'A Satyr against Reason and Mankind': '*The order of Nature?* the order of Coxcombs! the order of Nature is to follow my appetite: am I to eat at noon, because it is noon, or because I am a hungry? to eat because a clock strikes, were to feed a clock, or the sun, and not my self: let dull grave rogues observe distinction of seasons, eat because the sun shines, and when he departs lye drown'd some nine hours in their own flegm; I will pay no such homage to the sun, and time, which are things below me: I am a superiour being to them, and will make 'em attend my pleasure.' [60]

In seconding the view of Smith, Hume summarizes the critical consensus – if such a phrase can be applied to a play that has not received a great deal of critical attention – on Crowne's play: 'J.H. Smith rightly sees [Ramble] as part of the move toward Dorimant, and simultaneously as a premonitory symptom of the moral sentimentalism so prominent in a later play like *The Squire of Alsatia* (1688) – which is to say that Shadwell and Cibber did not invent the penitent rake. Crowne uses sex and basks in morality and seems not a whit uncomfortable.'[61]

Both elements are indeed clearly present. Ramble anticipates Dorimant not only in echoing the fashionable, avant-garde pronouncements of the daring Rochester, but in his active pursuit of large numbers of women. Crowne used Molière's *Le Sicilien ou l'Amour peintre* as his source for Ramble's attempt to seduce old Lord Drybone's young mistress Betty Frisque,[62] but with some significant changes. Molière's Adraste (Ramble) is in love with the Sicilian Dom Pèdre's (Lord Drybone's) Greek slave Isidore (Betty Frisque), and after an unsuccessful late-night serenade, learns that Dom Pèdre has hired the painter, Damon, to do a portrait of Isidore. Adraste prevails upon Damon to provide an introductory letter that allows him to appear in Damon's place and thus gain access to Isidore. This is the material Crowne borrowed. In *Le Sicilien*, Adraste is genuinely in love with Isidore, manages to whisk her away from Dom Pèdre's house by trickery, and will marry her shortly thereafter. Ramble, however, is in love with Christina and his main design is to marry her. As he later tells Christina, Betty Frisque is merely the diversion of the moment, an attractive young woman he should but could not resist: 'Oh, forgive me, I acknowledge my faults with grief and penitence; I am amazed how it was possible for me to think of any thing but you, but hopes of love, are like the prospect of a fair street a great way off, and you cannot blame a poor thirsty traveller, if he takes a sip here and there by the way –' (*Kneels.*) (5.2.439–44).

Libertine pronouncements and penitent genuflection, then, all do seem part of Ramble's character. But both the Rochester paraphrase and the above reformation contain similar shifts of tone midway; each turns into the more exuberant, self-confident voice of the earliest and most innocent of Restoration rakes, the character type Robert Jordan has called 'the extravagant rake.' This rake is characterized by his 'wildness,' by the 'frantic intensity with which he applies himself to the life of the moment,' and by the predominance of 'manner' over 'deeds,' of talk over action.[63] Ramble is initially described by Christina's father, Sir Thomas Rash, in terms that mistake words for deeds: 'He has not been come from France above three months, and here he has debauch'd four women, and fought five duels; not a keeper in the town can preserve his doe from him' (1.1.234–7). Even Christina's witty maid, Isabella, succumbs to the rhetoric of extravagance: 'To be plain, he is false to you, and I dare swear you make but one of the fifty in the catalogue of women he makes love to' (1.1.282–4). But Christina is a level-headed, sensible young woman, and her immediate response makes Crowne's point very well: 'All is not truth that is reported; he may love the conversation of women, out of the ayriness and gayetie of his temper, and yet have no ill design' (1.1.252–4). Like many another comic heroine, Christina is quite prepared to accept the notion of the occasional mistress. (Etherege's Harriet provides the most familiar example when she replies in response to Dorimant's vow to 'sacrifice' to her 'all the interest' he has 'in other Women': 'Hold – Though I wish you devout, I would not have you turn Fanatick.')[64]

Ramble runs into difficulty with Christina, and almost loses her, only when she is led to believe he has trifled with her honour. He is, however, as he declares, innocent. Sir Thomas has overheard parts of Ramble's late-night attempt to meet Betty Frisque and inferred incorrectly that his daughter is the subject of Ramble and Lord Drybone's discussions. Her temporary rejection is thus very much like Sophia Western's of Tom Jones, and similarly can be overcome when the truth is revealed about the alleged crime against her honour. Like his brother extravagant rakes, most notably Dryden's Bellamy and Wildblood (*An Evening's Love*) and Celadon (*Secret Love*), Etherege's Sir Frederick Frollick (*The Comical Revenge*), and Behn's Willmore (*The Rover*), Ramble ends his extravagant career by viewing it as youthful indiscretion to be cast off in favour of a new maturity represented by his forthcoming marriage to Christina.

Crowne's extravagant rake, then, is a long way from Molière's passionate young lover. And the result of his impersonation of a gentleman-amateur limner differs, too, from that of Adraste's marriage intrigue. Ramble is eventually ordered out by Lord Drybone to be pleasantly surprised by Betty's offer to meet him outside to 'go and sit for an hour in any place, you shall think convenient' (4.4.277–8). But just as Ramble arrives safely at his lodgings with Betty, he is greeted first by two vizards, then by Sir Mannerly's aunt, Lady Faddle, who has followed the 'artist' from Lord Drybone's that he might satisfy her importunate request: 'Put me in any posture you please, sweet sir, and let me taste plentifully of your skill' (4.5.49–50). Finally, after his servant, Merry, saves Ramble from Lady Faddle, Sir Thomas Rash appears, first to denounce him for dishonouring his daughter, and then to offer her to him in marriage. He is followed by Christina herself, who has come to disown him publicly, since she has yet to learn of the misunderstanding described above. Betty's response to this, like Mrs Brittle's to Lovemore at the end of *The Amorous Widow*, is to dismiss Ramble from her service permanently: 'So so, Mr. Ramble, you are a very fine man, some women come to you for their pictures, and others for promise of marriage; I have heard all passages; this is you that lov'd, admir'd, adored me above all creatures in the world ... well, I thank you, you have done me a kindness, I shall endure my confinement a little better after this: nay, I shall thank my old Lord, for keeping me out of the temptations of such false dissembling insinuating men.' (4.5.228–39).

Jordan makes two other points about the extravagant rake that are especially relevant to Ramble and *The Countrey Wit*. He argues that one of the functions of these characters is in filling 'a carnival role,' that is,' He is a one-man *mardi gras* and provides the appropriate therapeutic release for the audience irrespective of whether or not he is put in a carnival setting. In him customary restraints are thrown off with a wild exuberance and an unashamed joy, and if he does finally dwindle into a husband this could be said to mark the passing of carnival and the acceptance of responsibility.'[65] In the terms of this study, what Jordan is describing is still another way in which Restoration comic writers achieved 'the mixt way of Comedy,' in this case by transferring the licence granted the rogue in punitive comedy to the lover of sympathetic comedy: revocation and marriage thus occur simultaneously in the end. The result is an especially joyful type of comedy, since the manic energy of the punitive rogue is finally absorbed by the order of society, with the heroine offering more than adequate compensation for the loss of his licence for extravagance.

The extravagant rake, like the rogue, is often a sympathetic, even admirable figure, but rarely one set up for emulation. Jordan's other point helps explain why. In spite of the aesthetic difficulties created by our doing so, we can see the extravagant rake as a humours character, since, as

Dennis puts it, 'Joy when it is great is a Passion, Jollity and Gayety perhaps may be said to be Humours.'[66] Extravagance is thus a young man's humour, and, as such, offers a rare example of a humour that is corrected in the comedy of the 1670s. But it is corrected only after the imposition of what might be considered the comic analogue of poetic justice. The extravagant rake invariably overreaches himself and suffers a consequent humiliation. When Betty Frisque abandons him, Ramble reflects appropriately: 'So, so, forsaken, and hated by every one, all afflictions come together; I am justly serv'd for my liquorish, greedy, insatiable, ridiculous temper; that like Adam, could not be contented in Paradise, but must be tasting all sorts of fruit, lawful or unlawful, though I had pleasures enow in Christinas love to satisfy a demy-god, and more than any meer creature could merit.' (4.5.240–6). Ramble had earlier suffered a similar humiliation when he followed the masked Isabella, Christina's servant, to an unknown 'most delicate young lady' who 'has been sick for [him] these six months' (3.1.23–5). The woman, of course, proved to be Christina, and he was roundly denounced by her as a 'prodigy of impudence' for his efforts. His fifth-act repentance results from the last of a series of exposures that finally drive him from his youthful humour. The hero as humour thus offers Crowne still another way of combining the familiar conventions of his comic tradition.

The Countrey Wit also abounds in more familiar types of humours characters. Ramble's courtship of Christina provides the centre of the play, but his other adventures, most notably his pursuit of Betty Frisque, are the more typical matters of punitive comedy. And as punitive comedy requires gulls, gulls require humours. In order to win Christina, Ramble must overcome the objections of her father, Sir Thomas Rash, whose impetuosity leads him to behave as rashly as Squire Western. He has, it seems, the same generous nature, however, as Sophia's good-hearted father. Ramble must also defeat his rival, the title character, Sir Mannerly Shallow, Lady Faddle's nephew, whose country wit leaves him vulnerable to being cheated by Sir Thomas's porter and namesake, Rash, and his apple-woman wife. In fairness to the Rashes, however, it might be more accurate to say that he insists on believing Rash to be Sir Thomas in spite of the porter's protests, and that the resulting marriage of Sir Mannerly to Rash's daughter, Winnifred, offers still another example of the self-gulling of the humours character. Sir Mannerly is a Justice Clodpate in the making, for all he learns from his London experience is that the city is a dangerous and wicked place: 'So, I have come up to London to a very fine purpose; I ha lost my mistriss, lost my money, am married to an Applewomans daughter, and must keep a beggar-womans bastard, whereas I thought to have liv'd in London, and never seen the countrey more: I will now go down into the countrey, and spend all my time in rayling against London: I will never see London more, so much as in a map, I will burn my map of London that hangs in my parlour' (5.2.551–8).

The other offshoot of what is essentially a single-plot play with two subsidiary, related intrigues, is the courtship of Lady Faddle by Ramble's man, Merry, an intrigue very much like Merryman's courtship of Lady Laycock except that Merry's interest is not in diverting the lady from his master – Ramble later happily takes advantage of this incidental benefit – but in marrying her to make his fortune, which he does. Her amorous humour allows her to be gulled easily, and though she gains a husband, she gains little in the way of self-knowledge or wisdom.[67] Both of these subordinate intrigues serve as foils for Ramble's courtship of Christina, and thus unify the play in the formal mode as well as the material and efficient.

The Countrey Wit, then, looks back to its predecessors, particularly the extravagant rake plays of the 1660s, far more than it anticipates developments of the 1690s. Nor should this be surprising in Crowne's first comedy. With a play like *Sir Courtly Nice* (1685), Crowne might well have contributed to cleaning up the sex comedy of the 1670s and 1680s. But there is no reason to read back into *The Countrey Wit* characteristics or effects of later comedies. Virtually everything in Crowne's comic apprentice piece is to be found in the plays of his post-Restoration predecessors, even in the other five plays from the period 1670–5 discussed in this chapter. If there are 'advances' to be found in these plays, they are in increased explicit sexuality, especially in cuckolding intrigues (*Epsom-Wells, The Countrey Wit*) and in the emergence of the less innocent kinds of rakes represented by Lovemore, Woodly, Harcourt, and Horner, none of whom match Ramble, or even Ranger, in qualities of extravagance. Crowne is noticeably conservative in both of these areas, a point that becomes more evident with the examination of the next group of comedies, those of the period 1690–5.

3

Six Representative Comedies,
1690–1695

Like most first comedies, including *Love in a Wood* and *The Countrey Wit*, Congreve's *The Old Batchelour* serves more to summarize its dramatic tradition than to advance it. Johnson describes it as 'one of those comedies which may be made by a mind vigorous and acute, and furnished with comick characters by the perusal of other poets, without much actual commerce with mankind,' and Southerne confirms this impression in his account of the early revisions of Congreve's original manuscript:

He began his Play the old Bachelor haveing little Acquaintance withe the traders in that way, his Cozens recommended him to a friend of theirs [probably Southerne], who was very usefull to him in the whole course of his play. He engagd Mr Dryden in its favour, who upon reading it sayd he never saw such a first play in his life, but the Author not being acquainted with the stage or the town, it woud be pity to have it miscarry for want of a little Assistance: the stuff was rich indeed, it wanted only the fashionable cutt of the town. To help that Mr Dryden, Mr Arthur Manwayring, and Mr Southerne red it with great care, and Mr Dryden putt it in the order it was playd.[1]

But in the nearly twenty-year gap that separates *The Old Batchelour* from the plays discussed in chapter 2, a gap of a full generation, significant changes occurred in the conventions of dramatic comedy. The comedy Congreve inherited was quite different from what Wycherley and Crowne had found in the early 1670s. This is again evident in the theory and practice of humour, already altered from its classic Jonsonian formulation by such writers as Shadwell. By 1668, Dryden, like Shadwell, had recognized the deterministic nature of humours theory, but his response was a rejection outright of the need for comedy to do the impossible, that is, to correct vice and folly. Instead, he defines humour, at least in its English context, as 'some extravagant habit, passion, or affection; particular (as I said before) to some one person: by the oddness of which, he is immediately distinguish'd from the rest of men; which being lively and naturally represented, most frequently begets that malicious pleasure in the Audience which is testified by laughter.'[2] Where for Shadwell, humour had to be general to allow the audience to recognize itself, Dryden provides his audience with an object for malicious ridicule. Given his Hobbesian perspective, Dryden need not concern himself with whether the humour is capable of change.

Dryden's solution failed to win many followers, however influential his practice, since its abandonment of the poet's moral function outraged traditionalists and its assumptions about audience response distressed the growing numbers of readers and theatre-goers who saw themselves as far more benevolent by nature. John Dennis represents the former group in his attack on Jonson's Morose – the character Dryden defends immediately after the above quotation – for the 'Singularity' of his character, 'which is too extravagant for Instruction, and fit, in my opinion, only for Farce.' Comedy, Dennis insists, exposes those follies 'which some part of an Audience may be suppos'd Infected; and to which all may be suppos'd Obnoxious.'[3]

Dennis' objections occur in a letter to Congreve, requesting his thoughts on the matter. In his response, 'Concerning Humour in Comedy,' Congreve tactfully differs from Dennis, preferring Dryden's concept of humour while safely eliminating the cause for moral opprobrium. Morose is ridiculous, Congreve argues, because of his excess, not because of his singularity; hence there is nothing inherently low or farcical about singularity. It is, in fact, essential to his definition of humour as *a singular and unavoidable manner of doing, or saying any thing, Peculiar and Natural to one Man only; by which his Speech and Actions are distinguish'd from those of other Men.'* Congreve distinguishes 'humour' from the other raw material of comedy often mistaken for it, notably 'affectation' and 'habit,' and places it in a privileged position, claiming – after Sir William Temple – that it is 'almost of English growth,' a logical extension of 'the great Freedom, Privilege, and Liberty which the Common People of *England* enjoy.'[4] Congreve, no more than Dryden, rules out ridicule (his practice bears this out), but the resulting instruction or delight must, as Stuart Tave points out, 'take a form different from a satire against specific follies.' And it takes only an additional step for one to realize that if 'every man has his singular natural humour, then every humour is universally

significant.' As Tave recognizes, Congreve does not draw out all the implications of his theoretical position, but it is a position, nonetheless, that
undermines completely the traditional theory of humours as its eighteenth-century development so clearly demonstrates.[5] (I shall return to
this point later.) Congreve's practice, like his theory, reveals some breaks
with traditional comic characterization, but the breaks are neither consistent nor absolute. In this respect, he is very much a transitional figure.[6]

Dryden, it should be recalled, downplayed the instruction to be derived
from a comedy built around satirizing specific follies in favour of a comedy of 'divertisement and delight,' since the latter is 'the chief end' of
comedy. The pleasure to be derived from the malicious laughter evoked by
the Jonsonian humour, it follows, is inferior to the 'more noble' response,
even 'if not always to laughter,' derived from a comedy of wit. The
resulting emphasis on 'repartie' as 'the greatest Grace of comedy' necessarily favoured what I have been calling sympathetic comedy, that is, the
Fletcherian tradition. Dryden recognized that theory and practice vary,
and even his theory, of course, calls for 'the mixt way.'[7] By the 1690s,
Dryden's disciple, Congreve, had assimilated the theoretical implications
of Dryden's comic theory in his revised notion of the humour, one that
could allow for the more noble response Dryden prefers in comedy. Congreve's comedies remain very much in 'the mixt way,' but the nature of
that mixture has altered once more, this time in directions that lead to a
transformation so radical that its Jonsonian origin is lost.[8] But in the conservative world of the theatre even radical change is slow and gradual, so
much so that it is often accomplished before it is noticed.

The Old Batchelour, to repeat, has never been taken for a very original
play. Malcolm Elwin is surely right that 'the painstaking Langbaine would
have revelled in a perfect paradise of plagiarism had Congreve's comedy
appeared before his valuable critical work in 1691.'[9] Fletcher, Dryden,
Otway, Wycherley, Molière, Jonson, Shadwell, Crowne, Durfey, and
Ravenscroft are some of the sources Congreve mined in constructing his
first play. With hindsight, it is perhaps surprising that Congreve's most
original contributions in *The Old Batchelour* should be in his treatment of
humours characters. It can be no accident, for example, that the play is
named for Heartwell, Congreve's curious combination of Wycherley's
Pinchwife and Manly.[10] Betterton had the role of the original Heartwell at
a time when he was also playing Manly, and Congreve's old bachelor is
the very character critics have often wished – and even insisted – that
Wycherley created.

Like Manly, Heartwell is best known for his plain dealing: 'My Talent is chiefly that of speaking truth, which I don't expect should ever recommend me to People of Quality – I thank Heaven I have very honestly purchas'd the hatred of all the great Families in Town.'[11] A witty, Jonsonian satyr, Heartwell, like Manly, disturbs many of the people around him by 'snarling odious Truths' (1.1.180–1). But his plain dealing is balanced against those aspects of his character resembling Pinchwife: he is an aging bachelor with a well-earned reputation for misogyny who knows the town. His putative marriage to Silvia, however, results not simply from a desire to possess alone what he lusts after, but also from a more sincere and humane response to what he takes to be genuine innocence, all expressed in the incomparable idiom of the self-conscious plain dealer: 'Oh Manhood, where art thou! What am I come to? A Womans Toy; at these years! Death, a bearded Baby for a Girl to dandle. O dotage, dotage! That ever that noble passion *Lust*, should ebb to this degree – No reflux of vigorous Blood: But milky Love, supplies the empty Channels; and prompts me to the softness of a Child – A meer Infant and would suck. Can you love me *Silvia*? speak' (3.2.45–52). Heartwell can even anticipate the punishment he most fears will result from his folly: he will be 'the Jest of the Town' (3.1.79), the punishment most appropriate for one who makes a show of laughing at similar follies in others. Heartwell is sufficiently part of his society to care about such things: his plain dealing never reaches the bitter, self-isolating misanthropy of Wycherley's Manly. The young wits have their laugh at his expense, but Bellmour will not let it go beyond that: 'Look you,' he explains to Silvia's maid, Lucy, '*Heartwell* is my Friend; and tho' he be blind, I must not see him fall into the Snare, and unwittingly marry a Whore' (5.1.60–2).

By 'lightening the texture of langauge while complicating motive and plot,' Congreve alters the pattern of the Jonsonian humour. The result is a character whose 'faults no doubt warrant the affliction into which they lead him, though his virtues are such that they also warrant his release from it.'[12] Heartwell is more clearly a humour than Manly, yet far more sympathetic than Pinchwife. Heartwell resembles Shadwell's Clodpate, too, in many ways. Like Heartwell the aging Clodpate is easily tricked into marrying a younger 'whore,' and, like Heartwell, when he finds out the truth about his new wife, he is saved from his misfortune by a false marriage. But where Clodpate is taken in by the 'silly, affected' Mrs Jilt, the sister of Mrs Woodly's maid Peg, who merely has to humour him to win him on the rebound from his rejection by Carolina, Heartwell falls for the artful lure of Vainlove's 'forsaken Mistress,' Silvia, who portrays vulnerable innocence splendidly in winning over the old bachelor. Clodpate is married by Woodly's man in disguise, as part of the servants' plot to relieve him of some of his estate. Heartwell is married by Bellmour (as Sparkish was by Harcourt in *The Country-Wife*), who has displaced Silvia's original scheme with one more in his friend's best interest. When Clodpate discovers the truth, he must pay to recover his freedom; once it is recovered, he departs abruptly, cursing the town. When Heartwell discovers the truth, he must endure the ridicule of the young wits, but soon after they restore to him his freedom. He quickly resumes his old place in his society:

HEART. ... For my part, I have once escap'd – And when I wed again, may she be – Ugly, as an old Bawd. –
VAIN. – Ill-natur'd, as an old Maid. –
BELL. Wanton, as a Young-widow. –
SHARP. And jealous as a barren Wife.
HEART. Agreed.   (5.2.158–64)

Congreve does not sentimentalize Heartwell, as later playwrights would; like Clodpate he remains unchanged in the end. And, rather than being driven out of his humour – how could he be, given Congreve's theory of humours? – he has been rescued from acting in contradiction of it. What in Clodpate's case was an action almost entirely punitive has become in Heartwell's case a kindness. The humour, itself, has not been altered significantly; the representation, however, is much fuller and the response far more complex.

Congreve uses similar complexity in his treatment of Fondlewife, another stock character type, the old Puritan alderman with a beautiful, young wife. Vainlove accurately encapsulates him for Bellmour as 'a kind of Mungril Zealot, sometimes very precise and peevish: But I have seen him pleasant enough in his way; much addicted to Jealousie, but more to Fondness: So that as he is often Jealous without a Cause, he's as often satisfied without Reason' (1.1.105–10). From the beginning, then, the edges have been softened around a type traditionally victimized in punitive intrigue brought about by hypocritical Puritan values and resulting in cuckolding. Fondlewife inherits his jealous nature from earlier, older husbands and keepers such as Pinchwife and Lord Drybone, as well as from city husbands threatened by the more fashionable young men about town such as Barnaby Brittle and Sir Jaspar Fidget. Like Sir Jaspar, Fondlewife is a man of business who must leave his wife in order to pursue his profit, and again like Sir Jaspar, he seeks safe masculine company to watch over his wife in his absence, in this case the Puritan preacher Tribulation Comfort, who, when impersonated by Bellmour, proves as unfortunate a choice for Fondlewife as Horner was for Sir Jaspar.

Where Congreve breaks with these predecessors is, as Maximillian Novak points out, in treating Fondlewife 'with a certain degree of compassion, or rather, while making him comic, he also makes him human.'[13] In his initial appearance on stage, Fondlewife must choose between watching over his wife and £500; he, of course, finally chooses the money, but not before delivering the following soliloquy:

And in the mean time, I will reason with my self – Tell me *Isaac*, why art thee Jealous? Why art thee distrustful of the Wife of thy Bosom? – Because she is young and vigorous, and I am Old and impotent – Then why didst thee marry *Isaac*? –Because she was beautiful and tempting, and because I was obstinate and doating; so that my inclination was (and is still) greater than my power – And will not that which tempted thee, also tempt others, who will tempt her *Isaac*? – I fear it much – But does not thy Wife love thee, nay doat upon thee? – Yes – Why then! – Ay, but to say truth, She's fonder of me, than she has reason to be; and in the way of Trade, we still suspect the smoothest Dealers of the deepest designs – And that she has some designs deeper than thou canst reach, th' hast experimented *Isaac* – But Mum.   (4.1.49–63)

His candid self-examination reveals little in his character to admire: he is as suspicious as his fellow businessman Sir Jaspar and as ill-equipped to be a husband as Pinchwife, though less brutal. The subsequent 'Nykin'– 'Cocky' dialogues in baby talk with his wife make him appear at least as ridiculous as either of Wycherley's cuckolds; the echo of Antonio in Otway's *Venice Preserv'd* hardly generates sympathy for him. What it does do, however, is reduce the possibility of a one-dimensional response to Fondlewife. Like Heartwell, Fondlewife emerges from a flattened caricature into a three-dimensional human being. He is no less a 'Mungril Zealot' at the end than he was at the beginning. His confrontation with Bellmour, whom he has caught partially undressed in his wife's chamber, ends in the verification of Vainlove's original descriptions as Fondlewife chooses not to 'believe [his] own Eyes' (4.4.263), and instead accepts Bellmour's fanciful explanation as punctuated by Laetitia's tears. (Unlike Mrs Brittle, Laetitia Fondlewife remains unchanged by her experience.)[14] But Congreve's presentation of Fondlewife, particularly in soliloquy, has forced a mixed response to his situation: ridicule is tempered by what Novak calls 'pathos'[15] to the exclusion of the unmixed scorn of punitive comedy.

Congreve's young wits, Bellmour and Vainlove, are similarly modified

versions of character types of the previous generation. The exuberant
Rochesterian libertinism of Crowne's Ramble or the more calculating
sexual hedonism of Wycherley's Horner give way to the milder, more
retired epicureanism of Congreve's heroes. Bellmour still resembles the
extravagant rake of the earlier plays, but his extravagance is clearly an
effort:

Why what a Cormorant in Love am I! who not contented with the slavery of
honourable Love in one place, and the pleasure of enjoying some half a score Mistresses of my own acquiring; must yet take *Vainlove's* Business upon my hands,
because it lay too heavy upon his: So am not only forc'd to lie with other
Mens Wives for 'em, but must also undertake the harder Task, of obliging their
Mistresses – I must take up, or I shall never hold out; Flesh and Blood cannot
bear it always.[16]   (1.1.137–45)

Where Crowne's Ramble apologizes for his uncontrollable appetite,
Bellmour's concern is the strain and exhaustion caused by doing other
men's work for them. The moral dimension of his activity is not an issue
here, as it was in *The Amorous Widow*, nor need it be an issue, since Bellmour's commitment to Belinda is clear from the opening scene. Rather,
again as in the case of Dorimant in *The Man of Mode*, Bellmour's behaviour is presented as normal, that is, not requiring discussion. Kenneth
Muir understandably describes him as a character who 'might have
appeared in almost any comedy of manners.'[17] As he is an ordinary young
wit, this is no doubt true, but he is nonetheless a figure of a more precise
time than Muir's description indicates. It is telling, for example, that
unlike the heroines of the comedies of the 1670s discussed above, Belinda
remains unaware of and uninterested in Bellmour's love affairs and mistresses. His pursuit of Laetitia Fondlewife remains uncomplicated by a
need to keep it from Belinda's suspicions. Bellmour is a standard type, but
a type that evolved and changed throughout the late seventeenth century.
His friend Vainlove, however, is a far more singular figure. While the
extravagant rake could, in a sense, be understood as a humour, Vainlove
can be understood in virtually no other way. Described by Congreve as
early as the first quarto as 'capricious in his Love,'[18] Vainlove harbours an
attitude toward love and women that surely qualifies him as a humour
even by Congreve's strict definition. Vainlove is intelligent, witty, and
attractive – so much so that Harold Love takes his confident disdain as a
sign of a genuinely 'superior status'[19] – but what Aubrey Williams calls
'his squeamish overnicety toward woman, along with excessive self-

esteem'[20] surely undermines his position in any hierarchical representation of the characters in *The Old Batchelour*. The following exchange between Vainlove and Sharper is occasioned by Vainlove's credulous acceptance of Lucy's counterfeit letter from Araminta acknowledging her love for Vainlove. It reveals how severely Congreve criticizes his humorous wit, especially as the exchange culminates in Sharper's turning his unpleasant animal metaphor back at him by referring to him as a 'Mungril,' the very name Vainlove himself had earlier used to describe Fondlewife:

SHARP. Lost! Pray Heaven thou hast not lost thy Wits. Here, here, she's thy own Man, sign'd and seal'd too – To her Man –A delicious Mellon pure and consenting ripe, and only waits thy Cutting up – She has been breeding Love to thee all this while, and just now she is deliver'd of it.

VAIN. 'Tis an untimely Fruit, and she has miscarried of her Love.

SHARP. Never leave this damn'd illnatur'd whimsey *Frank?* Thou hast a sickly peevish Appetite; only chew Love and cannot digest it.

VAIN. Yes, when I feed my self – But I hate to be cram'd – By Heav'n there's not a Woman, will give a Man the pleasure of a chase: My sport is always balkt or cut short – I stumble ore the Game I would pursue – 'Tis dull and unnatural to have a Hare run full in the Hounds Mouth; and would distaste the keenest Hunter – I would have overtaken, not have met my Game.

SHARP. However I hope you don't mean to forsake it, that will be but a kind of Mungril Curs trick.   (4.1.163–82)

Wycherley's Valentine, in *Love in a Wood*, comes across as a character from a heroic play caught in the world of punitive comedy; as a result he seems not only out of place, but unworthy of his beloved, Christina. In Vainlove, Congreve has further naturalized the heroic lover into a comic world by transforming the high-toned niceties of his predecessors into a comic humour.[21] Like Valentine, Vainlove can seem not only unworthy of Araminta but incapable of the genuine commitment required for a successful marriage. Bellmour and Belinda announce their wedding at the end of the play, but Vainlove can only 'hope' for 'so great a Blessing' (5.2.171). And, as Bellmour recognizes, Araminta 'dares not consent, for fear he shou'd recant' (5.2.175–6). Vainlove is, characteristically, true to his humour to the end; his relationship with Araminta, as a result, remains at the same impasse it was at the beginning. In Vainlove, then, Congreve again alters a stock character type by mixing Jonson and Fletcher anew. Vainlove, in turn, fathered a line of humorous lovers that continued to be redefined in the eighteenth century, leading to such versions of the pee-vish and overly nice young lover as Goldsmith's Charles Marlow.

Not that all Congreve's humours in *The Old Batchelour* alter estab-lished types. Few could be more traditional than Sir Joseph Wittol and his 'back,' Captain Bluffe, characters modelled, as Thomas Davies pointed out, on Jonson's Bobadil and Master Stephen,[22] and dating back as far as char-acter types themselves. In these cases, Congreve is quite content to pro-vide two-dimensional characters, since no constructive purpose could come of mixing sympathy with the ridicule directed at them. Bluffe is a somewhat less rough version of Shadwell's Kick and Cuff: he has no more success with the rich heiress than they do, and he is also denied the oppor-tunity for cuckolding given instead to Bellmour; in the end, he is unwit-tingly married off to the maid, Lucy. Sir Joseph, in turn, serves as the universal gull, a character even Bluffe is able to bully and manipulate. His one bold stroke, rising to Setter's bait and trying to displace Vainlove in Araminta's affections with a quick elopement, results in his marriage to Silvia. Such marriages are appropriate punishments for fools – Crowne's Sir Mannerly Shallow underwent a similar punishment – and little con-cern is given to the consequences, a poetic justice, in other words, that could not survive the imposition of the more rigorous, moralistic critical theory of the eighteenth century. But Silvia and Sir Joseph are not viewed in the same complex perspectives given to Heartwell and Fondlewife.

The large number of characters in *The Old Batchelour* reflects the com-plexity of its plot; Congreve followed the pattern established by Etherege and Wycherley in starting with a multiple-plot play and simplifying thereafter. But where they began with three-level hierarchies, Congreve contracts his plot to a single social milieu, albeit one extended to the point of fragmentation. Elwin's complaint that *The Old Batchelour* 'has not the slightest semblance of unity' is understandable, if overstated. Muir's claim that 'the only serious weakness in the play is one of structure' is closer to the mark.[23] But Congreve surely cannot be faulted for inattention to the material and efficient modes of unity. Belinda and Araminta are cousins, and in the same social circle as Bellmour, Vainlove, Heartwell, and Sharper. Vainlove, Bellmour, Heartwell, and Sir Joseph are all connected to Silvia, who in turn uses Araminta to gain revenge on Vainlove. Sharper takes a turn in the park with Belinda, and helps Setter trick Sir Joseph and Bluffe, both of whom are interested in Araminta. Belinda takes special pleasure in accepting Bellmour's offer of 'an Opportunity ... to revenge your self upon *Heartwell*, for affronting your Squirrel' (5.1.395–6) (Mar-gery writes to Horner of her fear that Pinchwife will kill her squirrel

(4.3.279).) Sir Joseph has his money on deposit with Fondlewife, and when he comes to collect it, finds himself accused of attempting to ravish a kiss from Laetitia 'by main force' (4.4.54). And, when nearly all the characters are gathered at Silvia's house in the final scene, Sir Joseph and Heartwell discover their fates simultaneously when Silvia unmasks.

Nor does Congreve neglect to unify his plot in the formal mode, at least according to most recent critics of *The Old Batchelour*: 'the theme of deception .. underlies the entire play'; 'each character is created from a single factor, his reaction to the central problem of appearance contradicting nature'; 'Congreve seems to exploit, in the most teasing fashion, the age-old idea of mankind as "actors" who "play a part" on the world-stage'; 'it has meaningful, if sometimes distasteful, answers to give to the problem of how the individual is to live in this world successfully'; 'Congreve presents the stock characters of Restoration comedy – the rake, the fop, the railing satirist satirized, the impotent cuckold – as stages of a single life's progress.'[24] However tight its thematic unity, however, *The Old Batchelour*, as Clifford Leech observes, 'is remarkable ... for the variety within its structure.'[25] More often than not that variety is subordinated to a series of 'direct contrasts' or parallels, such as those between Vainlove, Bellmour, and Heartwell, and Araminta, Belinda, and Silvia as lovers, between Heartwell and Fondlewife (complete with similar soliloquies) and Sir Joseph as victims, and between Sharper's gulling of Sir Joseph for money and Bellmour's of Fondlewife for sex. The variety is not, finally, contained within a coherent structure, and, as numerous critics have objected, the parts cannot be seen as subordinate to an inclusive, higher unity. Both Bellmour's fourth-act excursion to the Fondlewifes and Sharper's second-act encounter with Sir Joseph and Bluffe – especially in their localized presentation – seem digressive; their presence works against a final, higher unity.

One of the consequences of the growing obsolescence of such complex multiple plots as the 'three-level plot' by the 1690s is that multiple-plot plays such as *The Old Batchelour* suffer from being in an almost untenable, transitional position. The various plots are no longer sufficiently diverse to require the kind of artificial, analogical unity frequently found in Renaissance drama, but neither are they structured tightly enough to render the issue obsolete. But where Congreve fails to achieve a certain kind of unity in *The Old Batchelour*, perhaps for the very same reasons, he succeeds wonderfully in balancing the comic traditions he inherited. Humours characters and sympathetic characters, punitive intrigues and love intrigues coexist in a symbiotic relationship rarely, if ever, attained by other post-Restoration playwrights. Etherege – and occasionally Dryden – share Congreve's sense of balance, but neither so thoroughly integrates the Jonsonian and the Fletcherian. In Congreve, 'the mixt way of comedy' is most triumphantly realized.

One of Dryden's greatest theatrical successes – second only to *The Spanish Friar* in eighteenth-century performances – and his most popular comedy, was his adaptation of the Amphitryon legend after Molière, Plautus, and Thomas Heywood.[26] Despite considerable borrowing, especially from Molière, Dryden's play, like Betterton's and Crowne's Molière adaptations, is no mere translation. Even Langbaine, who considered Dryden's 'Genius ... to incline to Tragedy and Satyr, rather than Comedy,' and who thought Dryden resembled 'Vulgar Painters, who can tolerably copy after a good Original, but either have not judgment, or will not take the pains themselves to design any thing of value,' acknowledged that, in the case of *Amphitryon*, 'what he has borrowed, he has improv'd throughout; and *Molliere* is as much exceeded by Mr. *Dryden*, as *Rotrou* is outdone by *Molliere*.'[27] Earl Miner rightly calls the play 'one of the unrecognized masterpieces of English comedy, quite unlike anything else in its age, before, or since in England.'[28] It is, I think because the Amphitryon story, complete with its represented gods and goddesses on stage, is so unlike other Restoration comedy that it has been neglected by twentieth-century critics.

Original and unusual as it is, however, *Amphitryon* still shares a number of features with other plays of its time. It is unique in the Dryden canon, among other reasons, as the only comedy among Dryden's post-revolution plays – and his first since *Mr. Limberham*. Yet Frank Harper Moore recognizes that *Amphitryon* is representative of Dryden's later drama in reflecting his movement toward the natural and the satirical in comedy, at the expense of the artificial, be it heroic, platonic, or farcical;[29] comparison with *An Evening's Love* or *The Assignation* confirms Moore's judgment. It is a movement, however, not unique to Dryden, and not one in which he was at the forefront.

Dryden's Jupiter is certainly a more earthy character than his models in Plautus or Molière, but his world is nonetheless still one of gods, generals, and servants, that is, a variant of the old three-level hierarchy. Greek mythology thus offers Dryden a way to work within a favoured structure, utilized especially effectively in the multiple-plot tragicomedies, while simultaneously diminishing the distance between his plots. A generation earlier, Dryden felt compelled to defend his 'indecorum' in allowing Celadon and Florimell to treat 'too lightly of their marriage in the presence of the Queen' in *Secret Love*.[30] By 1690 he felt able to mix freely even levels of being. *Amphitryon* consists of three basic intrigues: in the main plot Jupiter seduces Alcmena in the person of Amphitryon, and in the others, Mercury pursues Alcmena's maid, Phaedra, in the person of Sosia while trying to avoid the attentions of Sosia's wife, Bromia. Jupiter is, of course, king of the gods, Amphitryon a heroic soldier, and Alcmena his beautiful and virtuous wife – here are all the ingredients of a heroic love triangle. Mercury, the god of wit; the coward, Sosia; and his neglected wife offer the raw material for a second love triangle, though a most unheroic one. And Mercury; the greedy judge, Gripus; and the unprincipled but beautiful Phaedra provide still a third triangle, again comic.

The plots are very tightly unified. Mercury is Jupiter's son, as is Phoebus, who appears in the opening scene; Amphitryon's household consists of the two married couples and Phaedra, who is being courted by Alcmena's uncle, Gripus. The multiple Amphitryons and Sosias create such a confusion of identities that all the characters are involved with all the others, though often unwittingly. Resolution is, in fact, possible only when Jupiter appears in a machine to offer an explanation to the bewildered mortals.

The parallels between the high and low intrigues are many, basic, and obvious. When Jupiter forces Mercury to play Sosia to his Amphitryon, his encounter with Alcmena is naturally contrasted with Mercury's with Bromia. And Jupiter's love scenes with Alcmena are similarly contrasted with Mercury's with Phaedra. The responses of the victimized husbands, too, are clearly paralleled; as John Loftis points out, 'Sosia's aversion to his wife and his reluctance to perform his husbandly duties, as well as his suspicion of Mercury, provides a contrast to the ardours and suspicions of his master Amphitryon.'[31]

In analysing Dryden's use of his sources, Allen suggests that 'one of the reasons [Dryden] chose Molière's *Amphitryon* for an adaptation was that he found in it material for the kind of contrast between two groups of characters that he had been making for years in his own tragicomedies.'[32] And, as the various source studies have shown, Dryden accentuates the contrasts far more than his sources, making them central to his dramatic structure. But the effect is very different from that of *Secret Love* or *Marriage À-la-Mode* or even *Don Sebastian*, for instead of maintaining clear divisions among the levels of characters, Dryden's careful differentiation here finally helps to level the distinctions between them. Dryden has often been condemned for rendering Molière, as one critic puts it, 'vulgar' and 'low' by producing a play that is 'distinctly immoral' and offensive to 'both the taste and the feelings.'[33] Since Dryden's major changes to the play are the addition of Phaedra, Gripus, the songs, some topical satire, and considerable earthiness, slapstick, and even vulgarity, as well as the general downgrading of the gods, it is easy to see why such views are prominent, especially from critics whose admiration for Molière leads them to demand from Dryden a far greater fidelity to his source. But these various nods in the direction of the increasingly popular farce tradition serve Dryden well. Even the heightened exchanges between Jupiter and Alcmena – they at times seem transplants from the heroic play – cannot spare either the main plot or even the king of the gods himself from being caught up in the low comedy of a cuckolding. Jupiter realizes quite early, when Phaedra threatens to displace him in Alcmena's bed, that although he has initiated the action, he cannot maintain full control of it: 'Now I cou'd call my Thunder to revenge me, / But that were to confess my self a God, / And then I lost my Love!'[34]

Jupiter, then, is reduced to a ruthless and powerful rake, a libertine whose 'Hobbism' is opposed to 'normal human decency.' Both Miner and Loftis find the thematic centre of the play in the representation of the gods. For Miner, they are 'repulsive. Such sensual forces of inscrutable will and power intervene and make a mess of human life.' Loftis sees Jupiter as 'despotic' in his 'self-indulgent intrusion ... into the affairs of [his] inferiors'; his actions reveal the 'vulnerability of common folk to the abuse of power.'[35] Jupiter's divine disregard for human morality in what for him is, as Mercury suspects, 'some Petticoat Affair' (1.1.12), tends to support the evaluation of his witty and cynical son: 'Here's Omnipotence with a Vengeance, to make a Man a Cuckold, and yet not do him wrong. Then I find, Father *Jupiter*, that when you made Fate, you had the wit to contrive a Holy-day for your self now and then. For you Kings never Enact a Law, but you have a kind of an Eye to your own Prerogative' (1.1.113–18).

Dryden establishes this perspective on the main action in the opening lines, and it colours everything thereafter. Jupiter's passionate lovemaking in the very next scene, and Alcmena's pious response complete with prayer to Juno to 'pour all [her] Blessings / On this Auspicious Night' (1.2.122–3) are consistently undercut by the cynical ironies upon which the entire intrigue is premised. A worried Jupiter-Amphitryon, for example, urges Alcmena to alter her prayer: '*Juno* may grudge: for she may fear a Rival, / In those bright Eyes; but *Jupiter* will grant, / And doubly bless this Night' (1.2.124–6). Even Alcmena's famous apostrophe to the gods after a glorious night of lovemaking with her 'husband' is under-cut by the situation:

> ALCM. Ye niggard Gods! you make our Lives too long:
> You fill 'em with Diseases, Wants and Woes,
> And only dash 'em with a little Love;
> Sprinkled by Fits, and with a sparing Hand:
> Count all our Joys, from Childhood ev'n to Age,
> They wou'd but make a day of ev'ry year:
> Take back you sev'nty years, (the stint of Life)
> Or else be kind, and cram the Quintessence
> Of Seav'nty years, into sweet Seav'nty days:
> For all the rest is flat, insipid Being.   (2.2.50–9)

These lines, straight out of the heroic play, have been transposed to con-tribute to an effect most unheroic. Dryden has so thoroughly undermined the conventions of decorum that in the end little difference remains between the characters; even the best characters are tarred by the farcical brush, as the decent Amphitryon rejects his wife and the virtuous Alc-mena is led to identify Jupiter rather than her husband as the real Amphi-tryon in the fifth-act confrontation. And by levelling the distinctions in his original hierarchy, Dryden achieves an effect not unlike Congreve in *The Old Batchelour* in his multiple plot within a limited social milieu. The social hierarchy is so intertwined that it, too, is contracted within a narrow frame. Dryden was one of the last playwrights – and the greatest after the Restoration – to use inventively the multiple-plot tradition of Renaissance drama. But in the case of *Amphitryon*, like many of his contemporaries in the 1690s, he has given up the more highly analogical or symbolical unity of the earlier tragicomedies in favour of a simpler, clearer, and hence more 'natural' kind of unity.

Dryden's use of character types was, of course, severely limited by his choice of plot. There was little in the way of comic tradition in represent-ing the ancient gods, and significant limitation imposed by their position. There is also limited opportunity for the development of humours. Jupiter, nonetheless, shares many of the traits of the Hobbist libertine, and those traits enter strongly into any response to him. And like many libertines, especially married ones, in the comedies of the 1690s – Southerne's Frien-dall in *The Wives Excuse* is an extreme example – Jupiter is not an attrac-tive figure. Mercury, who does much of the dog work for his father,[36] and engages in a witty parody of a love-game complete with mock-proviso scene, is far more attractive in his honest if cynical response to life. Perhaps Mercury and Phaedra should be seen as an early example of the tendency in eighteenth-century comedy to limit the wit, especially in courtship, of the relatively immoral Restoration lovers to the servant class. Mercury is very much of the line of clever rogues from punitive comedy, though his major victim, the real Sosia, is not a fully unsympathetic figure as the cowardly soldier who backs down in the face of a beating.

Far more conventional are the neglected wife, Bromia, and the greedy judge, Gripus, a deserving victim of the punishment of the rogue, Mercury. But the greatest change, and again one found, too, in *The Old Batchelour*, is in the treatment of Amphitryon and Alcmena, the cuckold and his wife. Amphitryon is a brave general and good man who in no way deserves what he gets. When Jupiter acknowledges his true identity, he promises his victims that the birth of Hercules will compensate them for their wrongs: 'Great, like his Sire, and like his Mother, fair: / Wrongs to redress, and Tyrants to disseize; / Born for a World, that wants a *Hercules*' (5.1.414–16). Here, again, the heroic language is undercut by the situation, and it is difficult to prefer the response of the crowd to that of Mercury:

OMNES. We all Congratulate *Amphitryon*.
MERC. Keep your Congratulations to your selves, Gentlemen: 'Tis a nice point, let me tell you that; and the less that is said of it, the better. Upon the whole matter, if *Amphitryon* takes the favour of *Jupiter* in patience, as from a God, he's a good Heathen.   (5.1.422–7)

It is Amphitryon, not Jupiter, who is deserving of the sympathies of the audience, as, of course, is his wife Alcmena, who is no more guilty of a willing adultery than Otway's Monimia. Miner is not alone in seeing that their situation 'approaches the seriousness of tragedy.'[37] Their dignity certainly removes them from the class of standard Restoration cuckolds and cuckold-making wives. In producing a farcical comedy with tragic overtones complete with gods and goddesses, Dryden stretched the boundaries of the comedy of his time almost beyond recognition; the result is certainly worthy of its recent praise.

Far less innovative, though similarly transitional, is William Mountfort's last and finest play, *Greenwich-Park* (April 1691). Mountfort seems to have been influenced most by plays in which he acted in the few years immediately preceding *Greenwich-Park*, notably James Carlile's *The For-tune-Hunters* (c March 1689), but also plays by Shadwell, Durfey, and Southerne. One of his greatest acting triumphs, it is worth noting, was as Willmore in Behn's *The Rover*. Like most actor-playwrights, he wrote with his own strengths as an actor in mind, as well as his fellow actors, especially his wife's, as the roles of Young Reveller and Florella reveal.

Young Reveller is a curious amalgam of post-Restoration comic male leads. He is described in the 'Dramatis Personae' as 'a wild young Fel-low,'[38] and given his good nature, youthful manic energy, wit, and good looks, he seems at first very much like the extravagant rakes of the preced-ing generation. But, where they were characterized by a preponderance of words over deeds, Young Reveller is quite the reverse: he indulges remarkably little in the philosophy of the rake, while he is far more accomplished in the practice. He follows the pattern of Etherege's Dorimant in his involvement with three women during the play – an old mistress, a new mistress, and a future wife. But where Dorimant is dis-criminating in his choice of women, Reveller shares with Crowne's Ram-ble an almost insatiable appetite for women in general and the tendency to chase any attractive woman who comes his way. He lacks the distance as well as the discernment of the practiced libertine, as his relationship with Dorinda makes clear. According to her initial description (2.2.pp15–16), their relationship began with Reveller's attempt to seduce her at first sight. But as the relationship develops, Dorinda is able to manipulate his almost uncontrollable passions with remarkable ease. She encourages him with loving looks and talk (her 'prosperous Art'), only to deny him those favours he most desires. The effect, as his soliloquy reveals, is to trans-form simple lust into more complex emotions: 'What the Devil ails me! or does the Devil govern me! my Blood's quite alter'd, and those loose desires, which never lik'd but for Conveniency, are chang'd to real Passion; my wanton Drunkenness turn'd to a sober Admiration, and I begin to fear I'm growing a downright dull, insipid, constant Lover! oh for some kind she to allay this mighty Fever, that I may snub this damn'd honest Inclina-tion, before it gets the better of me' (3.1.p27). Fortunately, he is saved for the moment by the convenient entrance of his old mistress Mrs Raison, the grocer's wife, who has been keeping him of late. But as he arrives for his dinner engagement with Dorinda, his soliloquy shows him on the verge of falling into the same trap as Congreve's Heartwell, an error com-pounded in Reveller's case by the need to sacrifice his witty heiress, Flo-rella: 'I am Punctuall to my time, 'tis just one by the Sun-dyall, if this Lady should convince me, she is honest, and has a fortune, I might be fool enough to Love her in good earnest; and that would be a Rascally trick to *Florella*; she has Youth, Wit, Beauty, and money; this has Youth, more wit, and Beauty, and may have more mony: I but *Florella* was my first Mistriss; well, but this is my first Love, I only like the other as yet, Pox on't I'le not trouble my self with the Puncto of the matter, Let the Stars take their Course and fortune use her Pleasure.' (4.3.p44). Since Dorinda has decided 'upon second thoughts' that she would gain 'more security and satisfaction in *Reveller* as a Lover then a husband' (4.4.p45), she spares him from falling further victim of his love for her. And once he possesses her, he proves as unfaithful as any extravagant rake or contemplative libertine; she catches him chasing others the moment he leaves her apartment and is reduced to stock indignation: 'Ungrateful Villain! Was the Prize so poor, it could not merit one Night's Constancy ...' (5.3.p56).

Such behaviour is not, of course, characteristic of the extravagant rake. Nor is being kept, especially by the wife of a friend. In a far more casual affair with a friend's wife, Shadwell's far from extravagant Bevil appeared somewhat sordid, and that was in the far more promiscuous ambience of *Epsom-Wells*. His relationship with Kate Raison is a source of considerable embarrassment – even guilt – for Young Reveller. Lord Worthy's expression of surprised disapproval evinces an explanatory confession:

L. WOR. ... as thy Father says, *George*, I wonder thou canst have the heart
to Cuckold so honest a Friend to the Bottle, as *Raison*.
Y. REV. Faith, my Lord, I'll be ingenuous with you; 'tis an Intrigue of a pretty
long standing, and tho' it be somewhat scandalous to receive more Favours
from Women than one, my necessity has oblig'd me to comply; for ever since
your Travels she has been my Father.   (2.3.p18)

The ingenuous answer is almost as out of place as the earnest question in a cuckolding intrigue. How unlike Nemours' response to Bellamore's disbelief at his desire to cuckold his friend and admirer, the Prince of Cleve: 'I sav'd his Life, Sweet-heart, when he was assaulted by a mistake in the dark, and shall he grudge me a little Fooling with his Wife, for so serious an Obligation?'[39] Nemours is, of course, an extreme and unusually hostile representation of a cuckolding rake, of the type Hume calls the 'vicious rake.'[40] Far closer in spirit is Bevil's defence of his affair with Mrs Woodly in *Epsom-Wells*:

RAINES. Art not thou a Villain to Cuckold this honest fellow, and thy friend *Ned*?
BEV. Gad it's impossible to be a man of honour in these Cases. But my intrigue

with her began before my Friendship with him, and so I made a friend of my
Cuckold, and not a Cuckold of my friend.   (1.1.p109)

For Shadwell, the issue is real, at least as a violation of honour, but it is not
an issue to be faced. Bevil's dismissal of the moral implication of his
actions with a 'School distinction' tells much about acceptable attitudes for
comic heroes in the 1670s. I suspect that violent responses such as Lee's
were necessary to clear the way for Mountfort's assimilation of the tradition of the rake, complete with nostalgia for the 'Golden Days' of the
'court wits' of the Restoration, within the emerging moral code of the
1690s.

Ultimately, Lord Worthy accepts Reveller's affair with Mrs Raison
('Thy old man has us'd thee scurvily' [2.3.p18]), but only because Reveller, too, recognizes that the behaviour his father's severity has forced on
him is sordid. All of this is represented in a manner almost as light-
hearted as Shadwell's for undue emphasis on Reveller's sordidness would
lessen his stock as the play's most attractive character. But the values
implicit in Reveller's exchange with Worthy reveal a marked change from
those applied to Reveller's predecessors of the 1660s and 1670s.

It is perhaps because of his ingenuousness that Reveller, unlike such
predecessors as Crowne's Ramble, is spared the usual comic punishment
of the extravagant rake; even Dorimant receives more severe treatment
for his minor misdemeanors.[41] Reveller's father's ill-treatment relieves
him of responsibility for his affair with Mrs Raison, and Lord Worthy's
'Breach of Friendship' in not trusting him with knowledge of Dorinda,
along with her disloyalty in wronging Worthy 'with the only Man she
knew [his] Friend' (5.3.p57), similarly clears him of any wrongdoing with
Dorinda. The heightened morality of such explanations displaces the
comic poetic justice of the earlier plays just as it virtually eliminates the
carnival function of a character like Young Reveller. By holding him to the
morality of everyday life, Mountfort closes the gap between the rake and
his society. The comic licence has been rendered redundant along with the
need for repentance. Young Reveller is no more the man of sense of early
eighteenth-century comedy than the extravagant rake of Carolean
comedy. In him, Mountfort has constructed a character suited to the
demands of the 1690s, and one that continued to attract actors and audiences for fifty years after the death of the actor-playwright who created
the role.[42]

The extravagant rake is not the only character type to undergo change
in *Greenwich-Park*. Virtually all the others are also accommodated to the

post-Carolean demands of Mountfort's play. Hume points out that gentle-men-heroes in late seventeenth-century comedies tend to be of 'two basic types, the "ordinary rakish gentleman" and the *honnête homme*. Very often a comedy will have one of each, hero and friend. The *honnête homme* type does not become really common until the nineties.'[43] Lord Worthy is the first of this type in the plays discussed thus far, though hardly the first of the type: Lord Bellamy in *Bury-Fair* (1689) seems a likely model for Lord Worthy, especially since Mountfort was a great success in the lead role of Wildish in Shadwell's comedy. In the earlier plays with more than one male lead, the men tend to be far more similar, that is, more rakish than *honnête* – for example, Cunningham and Lovemore, Bevil and Rains, Harcourt and Horner, Bellmour and Vainlove. Lord Worthy, on the other hand, expounds a sententious moral purity in matters of love and honour. What is incongruous about his position is his involvement with Dorinda as her seducer-keeper, an involvement that places him in the position of playing Lord Drybone to Reveller's Ramble since, traditionally, attractive young women like Dorinda and Betty Frisque were kept only by impotent old men. Lord Worthy is indeed, as it were, cuckolded by Reveller – though unknowingly – but the result in this case is his revenge on Dorinda, a humiliating dismissal, and the concomitant moral to be drawn from Lord Worthy's exemplary public declaration: 'Ladies, Sir *Thomas* and Gentlemen; I desired your good Company to see me take leave of an old Acquaintance, being resolv'd to live a sober, discreet Life, and bend my whole thoughts towards this kind Lady [Violante], I have bid adieu to the only Mistress I had' (5.3.p58).

Lord Worthy's public repudiation of Dorinda serves as expiation for what Dryden called 'our crying sin of *keeping*,'[44] though not before he almost compounds his crime by drawing on her. (Young Reveller interposes, until he regains his sense in a scene that prefigures Steele's more well-known condemnation of justice and honour by the sword.) But while the characters in the play seem untroubled by the moral implications of Lord Worthy's behaviour, it is difficult to share Violante's generous response: 'Well, my Lord, you have behav'd your self so like a Man of Honour in this discovery of your Mistress, that it shall no way turn to your prejudice in my esteem' (5.2.p56). In his discussion of Shadwell's *The Squire of Alsatia*, a play in which Mountfort scored one of his great, early successes as Belfond Junior, Hume refers to the uneasy mix of 'the courtiers' morality of its story and the exemplary-didactic method of Steele.' He is surprised, in particular, by Shadwell's 'placid acceptance of Belfond jun.'s moral code in a play so markedly didactic.'[45] *Greenwich-*

Park suffers perhaps still more from the same uneasy mix, in that the moral code the play seems to recommend is represented most actively and eloquently by Lord Worthy himself. Dorinda may have been his only mistress, but his relationship with her nonetheless is sufficient to undermine his moral authority. The transition from a theatre informed by a highly conventional and artificial social code to one dominated by an equally conventional though not so artificial moral code, and one much closer to that of its audience, is revealed in all its structural awkwardness in a play like *Greenwich-Park*.

Martin W. Walsh finds much of the significance of Mountfort's comedy in its early manifestation of 'the growth of sympathy for the merchant class.'[46] Social hierarchies are broken to a greater degree than in any of the plays discussed above. Florella and Violante, as Dorinda informs Young Reveller, come from a rather unsavoury background even for the bourgeoisie: 'Their Father was Lord-Mayor of *London*, their Mother I hear was a Court-Laundress, & being given to blab betray'd the Intrigue of a great Man to his Wife, and was Casheir'd, but having Purchas'd an Interest for former Service, got *Hazard* Knighted, and marryed him' (4.2.p39). These facts are never denied, even when Dorinda taunts Florella and Violante with them later in the play. And Florella sees no need to apologize for their background – and newly acquired money and status – as she makes clear in her candid attempt to persuade Violante to consider Lord Worthy: '... You must have somebody, and why not him; he's a pretty Gentleman, and besides a Lord, and that you know goes a great way with a Merchants Daughter; most of our young Nobility by the Extravagance of their Fathers are left very inconsiderable in their Fortunes; so their quality being necessitated for money, and our Citizens Ambitious of Honour, many a Title has been kept up by the Pride of a Tradesman, who never values what he gives for a Nobleman to his Son in Law' (4.2.pp34–5). Steele's Mr Sealand, in *The Conscious Lovers* (1722), is far more aggressive and far more patriotic in his defence of the still new prominence of the merchant class, but his point remains the same as Florella's: young aristocrats marry merchants' daughters for their money. Florella and Violante resemble the witty, beautiful young heroines of the comedies of the 1670s in every way except for their birth, but here Mountfort chooses significantly to break with tradition.

The more fluid social structure has implications for the humours characters, too, especially the 'jolly Citizens.' The most interesting example is that of the grocer Raison, a 'citizen cuckold,' who, as Paul W. Miller puts it, 'is given some lines of dialogue suggesting that he is actually a man of sense.'[47] Miller, if anything, understates his case. Raison and his drugster-friend Sasaphras are the regular drinking companions of Reveller's father, Sir Thomas (who talks the part of the rake, albeit the aging rake, far more convincingly than his son) because he prefers 'the Honour of the City' to 'the Life of a t'other end of the Town, thorowpac'd Rakehell' (1.3.p9). Sir Thomas 'displays more of the characteristic vices of the Cit than Raison and Sasaphras put together,'[48] so he may not be the most reliable judge of their characters, but Mountfort removes any uncertainty by having Lord Worthy call them 'the honestest *Plebeians* I ever met with' (2.3.p18).

The play opens with Raison denying his wife's renewed request for a coach, thus establishing a stock cuckolding situation. His complaints about her desires being inappropriate for a citizen's wife are countered by hers against his drinking and scowring. Both agree, quite rightly, that 'the times are alter'd' (1.1.p2). Mrs Raison, predictably, departs in defiance, and Raison is left to deliver in soliloquy lines reminiscent of Barnaby Brittle's in *The Amorous Widow* – or, more accurately, lines that recall those of Betterton's source, *George Dandin*:

What will become of me? Beat her I can't, hate her I can't, turn her away I dare not. If I could complain of her, I must not, for my own Reputation suffers in't; besides, she has such a bloody crew of Relations, that would murder me, if I should do any of these things: A Pox of all Fools that marry poor Gentlewomen, for you wed them the whole Family, and entail a Plague upon your Posterity. Well I'll go up to Sir *Tho. Reveller*, invite him to Dinner, with two or three more, and drink her out of my head. The Daughter of a Knight, with a pox! the Honourable Sir *Francis Haughty*, Brother to the Viscount *Blusterer*, Baron of *Rockey Hills* in *Scotland*! Well, take warning all by me

>   I *Robert Raison* Grocer,
>   *To have and to hold*, and so, Sir,
>   Took the Daughter of a Knight from *Covent Garden*,
>   I Worth 10000*l* she not one Farthing.   (1.1.p.3)

Raison never departs from his philosophy of accepting his lot with as much good cheer as possible. As he tells Sir Thomas, he may be a cuckold, but he would nonetheless 'rather be a private Plague' to himself than 'a Publick Jest to the World.' He is, after all, the author of his own fate: 'If we Marry Gentlewomen, they'l play us Gentlewomens Tricks; we Citizens marry them for Love, and they take us for Interest: I wonder at the Impudence of any Tradesman, to think to keep a Gentlewoman to himself' (1.3.p7). Sir Thomas's '*Seneca* the 2*d*' is indeed a far cry from earlier citizen husbands of gentle wives in his thoughtful and loving response to his wife's misbehaviour. It is the gentry, not the citizens, who prefer 'Interest' to 'Love' here, so that Raison, who is even free of jealousy, is clearly differentiated from such predecessors as Sir Jaspar Fidget, Barnaby Brittle, Bisket, and Fribble. His propensity to drink and willingness to take a beating rather than fight make him ridiculous at times, but that ridicule is always balanced and, finally, outweighed by his generous, amiable humour. Emblematic of this complex response is the scene in which the drunken Raison, Sasaphras, and Sir Thomas surprise Young Reveller at his lodging with Mrs Raison. Reveller has Mrs Raison withdraw while he tries to get rid of his unwanted guests, but Sir Thomas insists on seeing who is in his bedroom. Everyone knows the truth of the matter, but Raison agrees to help keep Sir Thomas out, and though very drunk, he stands by his word:

RAIS. Sir, I have given him the Word of a Citizen to stand by him, and my *Puncto* will not allow me to violate the Honour of my Corporation.
SIR THO. Why, you Cuckoldy Dog, it may be your own Wife for ought you know.
RAIS. I care not if it were my Mother, and he were getting an Heir to disinherit me, he shall not be interrupted; and tho' I am as it were dead Drunk, yet I will stand by him, I say I will stand by him. (*Falls down.*)   (3.3.p32)

And Raison keeps his word until he passes out. The inversion of conventional values aside, Mountfort has developed the cuckold-about-to-discover-his-wife-in-bed scene in interesting new directions from such 1670s antecedents as *The Country-Wife* and *Epsom-Wells* – or, for that matter, *The Old Batchelour*. Where Sir Jaspar, Bisket, and Fribble are contemptible to ridiculous, Raison cannot be dismissed simply as a deserving comic victim. In this sense Mountfort anticipates the gradual transformation of the comedy of cuckolding that ultimately produces the discovery scene in *The School for Scandal*.

When Mrs Raison is confronted with Young Reveller's forthcoming marriage to Florella, she finds herself urged by Raison to accept the inevitable – and, like Mrs Brittle, she reforms:

RAIS. Come Wife, you had as good live honest, since you find you can't help it.
MRS RAIS. Why, let him go; here Husband, take what you never had till now, my Heart, your Generosity and good Temper, how ever I have abus'd it, I'll strive to deserve it.
RAIS. Why better late than never *Kate*.   (5.3.p59)

Her proto-sentimental conversion may not be more convincing than Mrs Brittle's or Betty Frisque's fear-inspired promises of faithfulness – Walsh considers her reclamation as 'not very convincingly' presented[49] – but the fact that it comes after a long period of nearly open adultery lends it a poignance and credibility not often found in earlier reforms – or, for that matter, in later more tear-provoking reforms such as Mrs Clerimont's in Steele's *The Tender Husband* (1705). There is little point in projecting a future for the Raisons, but unlike Barnaby Brittle or Lord Drybone, Raison is a character deserving of a happy ending.

In Raison, Mountfort softens the representation of citizens in comedy; he treats the gentry with a corresponding severity. The genuine fools in the play are Sir William Thoughtless, the unnamed beaux, and Bully Bounce – most, that is, of the representatives of the town. Gildon considered Congreve's Bluffe to be 'an Imitation' of Mountfort's Bounce,[50] but where Congreve places Bluffe and Sir Joseph firmly in the tradition of city gulls, Mountfort is more interested in the folly of people of fashion and position. Mountfort's nod in the direction of the Jacobean city comedy of Jonson, Marston, and Chapman in his ridicule of the mindless insolence and cowardice of Sir William and Bounce and the empty affectation of the beaux allows him to balance his more amiable humours with those of the more traditional, punitive breed.[51]

The plot of *Greenwich-Park*, like its characters, is especially noteworthy for the degree to which it conforms to the tendency of comedies in the 1690s to break down social hierarchies. It consists of a unit of three related courtships combined with two love triangles. The courtships of Florella and Young Reveller, and Violante and Lord Worthy follow 'the increasingly common formula of a witty couple ... balanced against a more serious one'[52] while that of the widower Sir Thomas and the widow Lady Hazard is a far less common element. Both triangles feature Young Reveller as the disruptive influence: Raison-Mrs Raison-Reveller and Lord Worthy-Dorinda-Reveller. All these intrigues and plot elements are tightly unified. The young women are sisters, the young men are good friends, and their parents are actively part of the plot. Sir Thomas prefers the company of citizens – hence the courtship of a lord mayor's widow – and Raison is his landlord. Reveller and Lord Worthy both enjoy relationships with women from more than one level of intrigue. Florella and Mrs Raison both keep a jealous eye on Reveller, their surveillance culminating in their simultaneous breeches-courtships of Dorinda. Lord Worthy and Mrs Raison, too, meet similar fates as keepers. The thematic unity provided by the inversion of town and city explains the presence of Sir

William, Bounce, and the beaux, all of whom otherwise would seem digressive elements.

James Sutherland considers *Greenwich-Park* 'a mixture of all the modes'[53] of late seventeenth-century comedy, a description that could well be applied to most of the comedies of the period. But while in the terms of this study, it remains a play clearly of 'the mixt way,' Mountfort has sufficiently softened both the wit and the humour, that is, both the sympathetic and the punitive, so that he points the way to the more thoroughly homogenized blend of the eighteenth century.

Still another of Mountfort's acting triumphs came in Thomas Durfey's *Love for Money, or, The Boarding School*, a play that first appeared on the London stage just a few months before *Greenwich-Park*; it is likely that it encouraged Mountfort the playwright in his use of Jacobean city comedy and in certain of his alterations of comic conventions. His own role, Jack Amorous, belongs with Young Reveller to the extravagant-rake tradition. Following Shadwell's lead, however, Durfey is still more emphatic in his condemnation of libertine behaviour. Like Reveller, Jack Amorous is completely without self-restraint in his relationships with women. He confesses to his friend Will Merriton his 'passionate Inclinations for that delicious Creature Woman, whose sweet dear bewithing [sic] Sex *I* still cannot repent adoring, tho it has been the utter ruin of my Fortunes.'[54] Amorous is described as 'a witty Extravagant of the Town, generous and well-natur'd, but so extreamly given to Women, that he keeps a Jilt, and has spent his Estate upon her';[55] that is, he is a Reveller who has willingly fallen into the hands of a hard-nosed Dorinda – the play's title is the motto of his mistress, Betty Jiltall – and is only too happy to remain there. 'I own my self an Extravagant,' he tells Merriton, 'but no Cully' (1.1.p2), only to find out that Merriton was right to warn him that his extravagances had already blinded him to his cullydom.

Where Mountfort distributed rakish traits and those of the *honnête homme* somewhat evenly between Reveller and Lord Worthy, Durfey makes Amorous both the extravagant and the keeper; Merriton is as pure in his behaviour as he is in his sententious language, a Bevil Junior in the making. He is 'a witty modest well-bred Gentleman, tho' of small fortune, a great lover of Learning, and skill'd in Philosophy, Poetry and Music,'[56] clearly at some distance from the familiar Restoration comic hero. John Harrington Smith's description of the simple contrast between the two male leads is only too accurate: 'D'Urfey expresses all the virtues that he could call to mind in Young Merriton and Mirtilla, the pair of true lovers,

and the more for the edification of his audience includes a contrasting pair,
the libertine Jack Amorous and the mercenary Betty Jiltall, who in the end
learn that their lack of principle does not pay.'[57]

Proto-sentimental elements – even melodramatic elements – have long
been recognized in Durfey's work. Kathleen Lynch considered Durfey's
contribution to the development of sentimental comedy quite simply 'the
sentimental heroine in some of her most characteristic poses,'; Mirtilla,
'the most fully portrayed of D'Urfey's heroines,' exhibits 'all the most
important relationships peculiar to sentimental drama.' Mirtilla is indeed
'modest and decorous,' respectful and obedient to her elders, serious and
committed to love and marriage, and 'prodigal in "all the Tenderness of
soft Affection."'[58] And as a long-lost orphan-heiress, she is even more
like Steele's Indiana than her lover, Merriton, is like Bevil Junior. When
R.S. Forsythe adds 'the villainous guardian, the good young man with a
good father,' and an ending in which 'the villain is discomfited and virtue
triumphs' to the long-lost heroine, he lends considerable credibility to his
case for Durfey as an important forerunner of sentimentalism.[59] But
while many of the elements of later drama are indeed present (Sutherland even likens the play to one of Kelly's or Cumberland's),[60] the overall
effect is quite different from that of a typical mid-eighteenth-century
play.

Love for Money, like many of Durfey's comedies, looks backward to
Jacobean comedy as much as it looks forward to Georgian. C.B. Graham's
list of Durfey's allusions to Ben Jonson's plays and use of characterization
by 'episodic humour-study' is one of few attempts to show that the Jonsonian tradition lived on in plays like *Love for Money*. But, since Durfey has
not attracted much interest from critics, it is not surprising that there has
been minimal discussion of his relationship to earlier playwrights.[61] The
anonymous author of *Wit for Money: or, Poet Stutter*, a 1691 satiric attack
on Durfey, for, among other things, plagiarism, considered Behn's *The
City Heiress* (1682) to be the principal source for *Love for Money*. What
Durfey's antagonist did not realize was that *The City Heiress* is itself a
play made up of elements from plays by Middleton and, to a lesser degree,
Massinger.[62] What Durfey recycled from Behn is largely what she got
from Middleton's *A Trick to Catch the Old One*, that is, the intrigue in
which a nephew who has lost his estate to an usurious uncle disguises a
courtesan as a rich heiress to convince the uncle that he has bright prospects and thus that he should receive better treatment from the uncle.
Middleton's intrigue is mainly that of the young man who must use his
wits to make his way in the world. As a recent editor puts it, 'the subject-
matter of *A Trick* is avarice, the power of money, and the gullibility of

men who pursue it, and Middleton gives depth to his theme by showing a whole society motivated by greed.'[63] Trick or be tricked would seem to be the watchword of Middleton's comic world, a world almost entirely free of sympathetic characters, and, necessarily, of sympathetic plots. Witgood's triumph over his uncle Lucre and their triumph over Lucre's rival, Hoard, is that of a superior and more attractive rogue over his inferiors and, as is often the case, his elders. Like Jonson's Dauphine, Witgood manages to redefine his position in society by the time his intrigue is deflated, and he claims a more prosperous position in the reintegrated society of the play's end.

Behn puts Middleton's intrigue to quite different purposes. In a play still very much in the wake of the Popish Plot, she turns the uncle into the seditious city-knight Sir Timothy Treat-all, who has disinherited his nephew, Tom Wilding, in part for loyalty to the government. He complains to Wilding's friends, 'Men both of Birth and Fortune,' of their corruption of his nephew: 'Yes, he had [some Virtues], but I know not, you have bewitch'd him amongst ye. (*weeping*.) Before he fell to Toryism, he was a sober, civil Youth, and had some Religion in him, wou'd read ye Prayers Night and Morning with a laudable Voice, and cry *Amen* to 'em; 'twou'd have done one's Heart good to have heard him – wore decent Clothes, was drunk but on Sundays and Holidays; and then I had Hopes of him. (*Still weeping*).'[64] Sir Timothy's combination of greed, hypocrisy, and Puritan politics and religion are opposed to Wilding's generosity, decency, and the loyal politics of a Church of England man; they force a moral distinction between segments of society in Behn's London. Sir Timothy is tricked into marrying Wilding's disguised cast mistress, rather than courtesan, but there is a real heiress, too, who is reserved for Wilding, thus adding an essentially sympathetic element to the punitive intrigue, and thus further polarizing the characters. With Behn's addition of the farcical courtship of Lady Galliard, a rich widow who loves Wilding, by Wilding's friend, Sir Charles Meriwill, *The City Heiress* is quite remote from the more purely punitive comedy of Middleton.

And Durfey is no more slavish in his use of Behn than she was in using Middleton. It is Jack Amorous who, largely through his own fault, has lost his estate to his uncle, Sir Rowland Rakehill, 'a covetous mercenary vicious swearing atheisticall Old Fellow ... who by cheating an Infant Orphan to whom he was Guardian, possessed an Estate of 3000*l* a Year.'[65] The seditious Puritan has given way to the infamous Chelsea knight; Merriton assures Amorous that 'there is not such another drunken, aroring [sic], wicked, debauch'd old Dog in the whole Parish' (1.1.p2). In moving the action out of the City and placing the villainous uncle among the gentry, Durfey joins Mountfort in turning old class stereotypes on their head.

And in separating the hero from the nephew, Durfey is able to lend a new perspective to a traditional punitive intrigue, for Jack Amorous's trick to catch his uncle is none of his own device. Rather, it is suggested to him by his friend's father, Old Merriton, as a way to divert Amorous' attentions from Mirtilla, the genuine heiress ignorant of her status. She had been placed in the boarding school years earlier by Old Merriton to protect her from her treacherous guardian, Sir Rowland. Amorous recognizes Old Merriton's design, though not the reason behind it, but goes along, since he can hardly turn down an opportunity to regain his fortune. The instigator and moving force behind the intrigue against Sir Rowland, then, is not his nephew but the man he considers his old accomplice in crime, Old Merriton, characterized as 'an honest, Religious, conscientious Gentleman.'[66] The use of a benevolent father-figure as *animateur* reveals Durfey transforming the inherited conventions of punitive comedy and pointing the way toward Sheridan's Sir Oliver Surface and Rowley. The dissolute Amorous is so incensed by his discovery of Betty Jiltall's unfaithfulness that he immediately tricks her into turning over her settlement before the plot against Sir Rowland is complete, thus encouraging her to betray him to his uncle, marry Sir Rowland, and ensure his disinheritance. Only Old Merriton's discovery of the genuine heiress and the consequent arrest of Sir Rowland makes inevitable the defeat of the villainous characters. The befuddled Amorous, reduced to exclaiming 'My little pretty Tit of the Boarding-School, by all that's good, this subtle old Fellow, I find, has fool'd me damnably' (5.3.p53), is left to the generous provision of the Merritons.

It is the boarding school that provides the point of contact between the related intrigues initiated by Old Merriton and those taking place in the household of Lady Addleplot and her uxorious second husband, Deputy Nincompoop, whom she refers to as 'a fribbling Cit that I have married, and affronted my own Quality to do him honour' (2.1.p18). The Jacobite Lady Addleplot is 'a Lusty flaunting imperious Lady, a high-flown Stickler against the Government, and always railing at it, in talking of Politicks.'[67] She has surrounded herself with the likes of the 'Papist' Lady Stroddle and the 'French Fop' Le Prat, as well as her kept lover, Captain Bouncer, the alias of the 'impudent lying Town Sharper, of infamous Birth and no Merit' Nedd Bragg,[68] in an indulgence of politics and sexuality that recalls Jonson's Lady Would-bee. It is her plan to marry her captain to Nincompoop's daughter, Molly, a plan that is undermined by Old Zachary

Bragg, 'an ignorant Old blunt peevish Granadeer of King *William's* Army,'[69] who inadvertently reveals his son Nedd's true identity – without regret, it should be added, for he shares neither his son's pretentious aspirations, nor his adopted seditious politics. Durfey turns the political values of *The City Heiress* inside out in the process of reconstructing its social values for the 1690s. But his technique, unlike Mountfort's, entails a return to the traditional form of political satire in the drama – punitive comedy.

Young Bragg is not the only swain to aspire to Miss Molly's hand. Her music master at the boarding school, Semibrief, has made use of his time with her to tutor his charge in his desirability as a husband. And Lady Addleplot's daughter, Jenny, is similarly courted by the dancing master, Coupee. Their success defeats Young Bragg while deflating the pride of Lady Addleplot, who considered her daughter in a class apart from Nincompoop's, as she made clear earlier in an exclamation almost worthy of Lady Wishfort: 'The t'other Dowdy indeed I always imagin'd indocible; but that Sir *Arthur's* Offspring, a Child born of my own Body, Bone of my Bone, Flesh of my Flesh, Vitals of my Vitals, that she should degenerate, I am amaz'd at it!' (4.2.p36). Durfey confirms his desire to level Lady Addleplot's distinction in characterizing Molly and Jenny as 'two tawdry hoyden over-grown Rompes of the Boarding-School.'[70] In the end, Lady Addleplot is confronted with the fundamental similarity between her daughter and Nincompoop's, and is then forced 'to drink Prosperity to the King and Government' (5.3.p56); the conventional pattern of punitive comedy is maintained to the end.

Perhaps the most unpredictable intrigue in *Love for Money*, and another reminiscent of Jacobean comedy, is Young Merriton's testing of Mirtilla's loyalty after his father has informed her of her true identity. Merriton's soliloquy makes it quite clear that he expects her to dismiss his concern over appearing to marry her for her money; his real concern is to reinforce his supremacy over her despite their altered circumstances: 'I should be a fool indeed, if I should lose thee for all my seeming sullenness, I know she's fast, therefore play this game, that hereafter she mayn't twit me with her benefits' (5.3.p49). So strong, however, has the desire been to see this couple as 'sentimental' that Forsythe notes Merriton's 'quite serious scruples,' adding that 'no hero of genuine Restoration comedy would have ever thought of making any bones about such a deed.'[71] Given Durfey's presentation of Merriton as an extremely straight-and-narrow young man, Forsythe's view is an understandable projection: Merriton's behaviour is incongruous at this late point in the play. Durfey was either

unwilling or unable to create a hero who remains uninvolved in a traditional comic intrigue.

Another area in which *Love for Money* reveals a transitional character
is with regard to the use of the boarding-school setting, a use making it
for Nicoll 'one of the first of our Restoration plays to exhibit an interest in
"local colour."'[72] In the preface, Durfey denies that he spent a summer
researching his subject at a boarding school only to repay his hosts in
satire, a practice that seems far too contemporary for a writer like Durfey.
The focus on place in *Love for Money* seems more in the Jonson-Shadwell
line of precise London settings, though Durfey provides much less in the
way of detail than Shadwell. Durfey's research does not extend beyond
the occasional jokebook commonplace about the passion of boarding-
school girls for bread and butter. 'Local colour' is subordinated to more
general social issues or farcical, comic business.

Sutherland observes that throughout his career as a playwright, Durfey
'took considerable pains over the construction of his plays,' noting, too,
that their plots 'were borrowed frequently from the earlier drama.'[73] In
the Prologue to *A Fond Husband* (1677), Durfey lamented the inattention
to effective plotting in contemporary comedy – that is, the apparent
supremacy of Dryden's view of comedy on the Restoration stage:

> If plot and bus'ness comical and new,
> Could please the criticks that sit here to view,
> The poet might have thought this play would do.
> But in this age design no praise can get.
> You cry it conversation wants, and wit;
> As if the obvious rules of comedy,
> Were only dull *grimace* and *repartée*.[74]

The above discussion should indicate that *Love for Money* is a very
busy play. It is also a play that reveals considerable attention to the
mechanics of plot construction. If Durfey is guilty of barrenness of invention, it is surely not at the levels of material and efficient unity. Old Merriton and Sir Rowland were involved in the defrauding of the orphan
Mirtilla; Jack Amorous and Young Merriton are close friends. Old Merriton proposes Amorous' plot, and as a result, Betty Jiltall is installed in the
boarding school as Mirtilla – along with the real Mirtilla and Molly and
Jenny. Lady Addleplot's favorite Frenchman, Le Prat, rivals Amorous for
Jiltall, with important success. Semibrief must outwit Young Bragg for
Molly; Coupee introduces Young Merriton into the boarding school as a

fellow dancing master, and both masters are protected from Lady Addleplot by Old Merriton. Like most successful writers of farce, Durfey was a
gifted arranger of intricate plot elements.

The problem with a play like *Love for Money* is that Durfey's attention
to a unified plot rarely extends to the formal or final modes. The contrast
between the pairs of lovers is effective, if obvious, but there is little else to
lend substance to the relationship between the various intrigues. Durfey
touches a number of issues, but pursues few of them. Like Mountfort, for
example, he makes his avaricious guardian a member of the gentry, but
little emerges from that choice. Young Merriton's test of Mirtilla could be
interesting in the context of an extended treatment of the war of the sexes,
but seems completely out of character, given their sententious relationship
as earnest young lovers in the first four acts. Similarly, explaining the
relationship of Lady Addleplot's Jacobite circle to the rest of the play is a
greater challenge than explaining the relationship of the Would-bees to
the main plot of *Volpone*, as is evidenced by the uneasy moments of contact at the boarding school where Mirtilla seems hopelessly misplaced in a
world of farce and satire.

Love for Money, then, resembles its contemporary plays in sharing in
the joint tradition of Jonson and Fletcher, but with a playwright like Durfey, each tradition is being altered fundamentally. As punitive comedy
becomes farcical and sympathetic comedy exemplary, the changes extend
beyond the more typical variations in conventions. And since Durfey's
farce looks back to Jacobean city comedy, it is ill-suited for union with a
more forward-looking love intrigue. It is only when the punitive elements
have been softened by the newer approaches to humours that the two are
successfully reintegrated, a development I shall return to in chapter 4.

Durfey's next comedy, *The Marriage-Hater Match'd*, is even busier than
Love for Money and considerably more disjointed. Again, the main plot,
Sir Philip Freewit's betrayal of Phaebe, whom he had promised to marry,
her subsequent service to him as a page, and their eventual marriage after
his courtship of another, is from Middleton,[75] and again Durfey's debt
remains at the superficial level of plot outline. As an anonymous critic
pointed out, Durfey's plagiarism was largely of a narcissistic sort: by the
1690s he was repeating plot elements with increasing frequency.[76] But
where in *Love for Money* Durfey reworks conventional materials to
achieve new effects, in *The Marriage-Hater Match'd* a traditional *mélange*
ends in ways that would not have surprised audiences a generation, or
even two, earlier.

The plot of *The Marriage-Hater Match'd* is a complex one, largely because there are so many characters involved in so little action. Unlike Middleton's Lactantio, Sir Philip tries to evade Phaebe because of an aversion to marriage developed when his first love chose his friend, Sir Solomon Subtle, over himself – a choice she made because she learned of his relationship with Phaebe. As the play opens, Sir Philip finds that Sir Solomon, now dead, has left him a considerable fortune that he must secure from Lady Subtle, also intended for Sir Philip by her late husband. The main plot, then, consists of Sir Philip's efforts, through trickery, to keep his money and his bachelorhood. The rest of the action revolves around the courtship of Sir Philip's friend, Captain Darewell, and Lady Subtle's sister, Berenice; Sir Lawrence Limber's attempt to wed his sons, Bias and Solon, to the sisters; Lieutenant Callow's design on Sir Lawrence's foolish daughter, Margery; and Lord Brainless's infatuation with La Pupsey. The play ends in a paroxysm of matrimony as seven couples are united, only two of them remotely suited to each other; the rest, like the fools in *Love in a Wood* or *The Old Batchelour*, are united in what simultaneously achieves the usual comic coda and punishment for folly.

Prefixed to the first quarto is a defence of the play by Charles Gildon, in the form of 'A Letter to Mr. D'Urfey Occasioned by his Play Called the Marriage-Hater Match'ed.' Gildon assumes the validity of traditional, Jonsonian comic theory, and uses it to advance Durfey's cause at the expense of his enemies, most notably Dryden. Since Durfey's enemies 'cannot arrive to the Excellence of the Old way of Writing,' Gildon argues, they 'would advance a new one of their own production, adapted to their *undesigning* Genius.' As a result, he continues, in language reminiscent of Shadwell's attacks on Dryden twenty years earlier, they would 'perswade us that a *Bundle of Dialogues* was all that was ever required to the framing a good *Play*.'[77] The key word for Gildon is his italicized *undesigning*, suggesting, as it did, a belief in the fundamental importance of careful plot construction for effective play-writing. 'Let the Moral or Instructive part be never so well writ, the Language never so fine, yet if the Action goes on without any Plot to divert us,' he concludes, 'we see through all at first sight, and grow weary before the Play is half done'.[78]

In *The Marriage-Hater Match'd*, as in *Love for Money*, Durfey worked hard to achieve unity in the material and efficient modes. Lady Subtle and Berenice are sisters who are courted by friends. Sir Lawrence Limber's family is involved, ultimately, in four marriages; his three children and his nephew, Van Grin, wed in the end. Lady Bumfiddle, the matchmaker, is Sir Lawrence's sister, and Phaebe, too, is his kinswoman. Callow is Sir

Philip's nephew. Van Grin, Bias, Solon, and Sir Philip are all rivals for the widow's hand and/or fortune. Lady Bumfiddle tries to involve herself in every intrigue, and the various characters all know one another, move in the same circle, and meet as a group frequently. But, again, Durfey's attention to his plot does not extend beyond the efficient mode. There are parallel love triangles involving the sisters – Lady Subtle-Sir Philip-Phaebe and Solon-Berenice-Darewell – but they seem no more pointed than the juxtaposition of the seven marriages at the end. Durfey's anonymous critic analyses the problem quite accurately in his parody of Gildon's praise: "'Tis true thy Play is altogether surprizing, and very unnatural; the several neat turns of a Play, I confess do keep the Minds of the Audience employed with Expectation, Hope and Desire, but I'm sure they don't end in Satisfaction; but let the instructive part be never so good, the Language never so fine (tho thine is mere *Billings-gate* Discourse, instead of Poetical Adornments in Conversation.) I must needs say, if the Action goes on without any Plot to divert us, we see through the whole at first sight.'[79] It is as if the critic perceived Gildon's confusion – perhaps deliberate – of the Aristotelian distinction between action and plot: Durfey's play is full of action, and much of it is well-constructed action for Durfey *is* a competent writer of scenes of farce,[80] but that action is not subordinated to a plot. Instead, the play consists of abundant comic business held together by an arbitrary, skeletal, unifying design to permit closure.

An Aristotelian plot is not, of course, required for either audience or critical approbation. *The Marriage-Hater Match'd* is evidence of the former, and could, as well, have been of the latter, had it offered alternative higher modes of organization. There is no point complaining of the 'absurdity' of the multiple weddings at the fifth-act masquerade;[81] those marriages are merely conveniences in a play that has little to do with love. Durfey's efforts in this play, like Shadwell's in most of his early plays, are in creating a multiplicity of new humours and turning them loose to expose their folly. Despite the Fletcherian, and even Shakespearian, echoes in the main plots – echoes of *The Scornful Lady, Rule a Wife, The Woman Hater, The Woman's Prize, The Taming of the Shrew, Twelfth Night* – it is Jonson who is Durfey's model here. The play, as Peter Holland observes, often presents 'the enacting of social set-piece scenes,' especially 'when the fools are allowed full rein.' So much time is given over to the presentation of humours that frequently 'the play, as plot, is held in stasis, while the play, as acting of character, is demonstrated.'[82]

The Marriage-Hater Match'd is Durfey's answer to *Every Man out of his Humour*. Holland cites Van Grin and Lady Bumfiddle as examples of the display of humour for its own sake. Other characters could as well be mentioned. A splendidly Jonsonian moment occurs when La Pupsey, characterized as 'an Impertinent Creature, always stuffing her Discourse with hard words, and perpetually kissing and talking to her Lapdog,'[83] so impresses the company with her exchanges of witty repartee with her dog, Adonis, that Mrs Bandy, a character Durfey probably introduced for just this reason and who is not included in 'The Names and Characters,' declares in a rhapsody of admiration: 'Well, I'vads I will have a Dog then, let my Mother say what she will; – I believe it teaches her to talk so, for I never heard such fine words in my life ... Well, I swear I could live and dye with this *La Pupsey*, if it were only to hear her talk' (3.2.pp30–1). But *The Marriage-Hater Match'd* is no 'comicall satyre' in that unlike the characters in *Every Man out of his Humour*, Durfey's humours, like most post-Restoration humours, are not to be driven from their follies. Instead, following the later Jonson, they are punished for them, providing easy victims for those more clever than they are. Sir Philip tricks the widow, and he, in turn, is tricked by Phaebe, who advises the widow to trick Van Grin. Berenice is so compulsive in her tormenting of honest Darewell that she almost loses him for a jest. Callow and Margery trick Sir Lawrence, his sons are tricked by the servant women, Comode and Pimpwell, and La Pupsey similarly tricks Lord Brainless. The intrigues finally culminate in the seven marriages in the fifth act.

The marriages themselves are hardly more than means to other ends. The intriguing is sometimes for its own sake, but most often in pursuit of money. In either case, Durfey shows himself working within the conventions of Jacobean city comedy: both the action and the characters fall within the well-worn conventions of Jonsonian punitive comedy. Durfey characterizes Sir Philip as 'a wild witty Gent. of the Town, who being Jilted by Lady *Subtle*, whom he Loved, professes himself a *Marriage Hater*,'[84] yet despite Mountfort's appearance in the role, the sense in which he is 'wild' and 'witty' is severely qualified by his marriage-hating humour. As Holland points out, he 'becomes a man whose wildness and wittiness are based on a desire for revenge and an avarice that is as obsessive as his dislike of marriage.' For Holland, Sir Philip is 'brutish and revengeful' to such an extent that he 'subverts the sympathetic attitude on which our acceptance of the freedom of action of the rake is founded.'[85]

Sir Philip is obsessive. Even after Phaebe has won Sir Solomon's bequest for him, tricked him out of it, and returned it once more, he finds himself unable to keep his promise of marriage:

Of what an odd kind of Composition is the Nature of Man: – If Consideration
now could take place in me, I have no reason to deny doing Justice, to this pretty
Creature, that is so kind, and can do me so much good; but on my Conscience,
my only cause of hating a Wife, is, because it is convenient for me; and Marriage
in those of my humour, is just like Devotion, Lov'd and Practic'd the less,
because it is Enjoyn'd us; besides, being out-witted by this little Devil has so
nettled me, that I cannot forbear putting one Trick more upon her, tho' 'tis
unreasonable.   (5.1.p43)

However obsessive they may seem, these are not the words of a rake. Durfey claims that he once loved Lady Subtle; the play reveals little sign of it.
We know that he has seduced and had a child by Phaebe, but we see little
interest in seduction or any other kind of sexual desire. What really
excites Sir Philip is a trick. Like Volpone, he is an obsessive trickster; his
warmest responses to Phaebe are like Volpone's to Mosca ('my wittie mis-
chiefe, Let me embrace thee'[86]), in response to her inventive contributions
to his intrigues. When Sir Philip's last trick backfires and he finds himself
indeed married to Phaebe, a genuine parson having been substituted for
his servant, he cheerfully accepts the dispensation of 'Providence'
(5.3.p54), and the play ends somewhat anticlimactically from the perspective of a Jonsonian study in character.

Wycherley used a similar structure of parallel intrigues to raise serious
questions about the issues and conventions of earlier comedy in *The
Plain-Dealer*. But by giving Sir Philip (Manly) the widow (Widow Black-
acre) for his adversary instead of Berenice (Olivia), who is matched
against Capt. Darewell (Freeman), and by compromising his characters to
accommodate the happy ending of the series of weddings, Durfey stays
well within the confines of the conventions Wycherley violated so effectively. *The Marriage-Hater Match'd* would have been a conservative play
in 1676. There is nothing sentimental about it in any sense of the vexa-
tious term – the women inhabit a world unknown to the likes of Mirtilla.
Yet *The Marriage-Hater Match'd* is by the same playwright as *Love for
Money*, and was first performed a year later. It offers an especially convincing warning against generalizing from a single play to an entire *oeu-
vre*, and against assuming that generic development, even within the work
of a single playwright, is linear.

In *The Marriage-Hater Match'd*, Durfey looks back several generations
for his comic conventions and structure; in *Love for Love*, Congreve, too,
looks back to the comedy of Fletcher and Jonson, as well as Shakespeare,
but he does it via the first generation of post-Restoration playwrights.

And if he 'waves the flag for hard comedy in the old Carolean tradition,'[87] he nonetheless writes a play very much of its time, one that proves seminal in both its plot and characters. The opening scene offers a good example of this double perspective of the 1690s.

As the curtain rises, the witty hero and his clever servant are revealed discussing their current situation: extravagance, especially in courtship, has reduced Valentine to a debt-induced form of house arrest. The stock situation of Jacobean comedy, a young man in want of money, recalls the likes of Young Loveless in *The Scornful Lady*, Dauphine in *Epicoene*, and Witgood in *A Trick to Catch the Old One* – even, perhaps, the reverse image of Valentine's prodigal namesake in *Wit without Money*. But as his situation emerges, Valentine more and more resembles the heroes of post-Restoration comedy, especially since money, for him, is merely the means to his ultimate end, love. William Archer's summary of his condition appears to be a valid one: 'Valentine Legend is deeply in love with an heiress named Angelica, who, out of sheer contrariety as it would seem, affects indifference toward him.'[88] The immediate perspective is thus more like that of the plays of Dryden, Shadwell, Etherege, and Wycherley. Congreve brings his two perspectives into single focus by making the required happy ending conditional upon Valentine's tricking his father out of his forfeited inheritance while simultaneously winning the witty but evasive heroine. As he applies his considerable wits to his tasks, Valentine emerges as a character with much in common with other heroes in comic plots of the 1690s. His poverty and his bastards testify to his past extravagance, but at the time the play opens, he has given up all pretence to his old habits in both word and deed. Not only is he no longer interested in other women, but his obsession with Angelica is such that Mrs Frail chastises him for breach of common social decency:

VALEN. Well Lady Galloper, how does *Angelica?*
MRS FRAIL. *Angelica?* Manners!
VALEN. What, you will allow an absent Lover –
MRS FRAIL. No, I'll allow a Lover present with his Mistress to be particular –
But otherwise I think his Passion ought to give place to his Manners.
VALEN. But what if he have more Passion than Manners?
MRS FRAIL. Then let him Marry and reform.[89]

The witty exchange continues, but Mrs Frail has made an important observation, for Valentine has already reformed, and all that remains to make him happy – he thinks – is to win Angelica in marriage.

Given the traditions and conventions of English comedy to date, the plot of *Love for Love* would seem to be straightforward and predictable: Valentine uses his wit to trick his father and win Angelica. In act 1, he agrees to his father's 'hard Conditions' in order to 'be at Liberty to see her' (1.1.673–4), but freedom does not bring expected rewards. Valentine's energies are soon consumed in battle with his father, largely in inventing ways to avoid signing the final papers to legitimize his disinheritance. It is not until the fourth act that he invents a trick to achieve both his goals at once – his pretended madness.

For three acts, Valentine's conventional approach to his problems seems appropriate. Sir Sampson is a splendid combination of avaricious miser and *senex*, and Angelica appears to be all one expects from a Restoration heroine. She possesses the sharp-tongued wit and independence of mind of the liveliest of her Carolean predecessors such as Dryden's Florimell, Wycherley's Alithea, and Etherege's Harriet. Her exchange with her uncle Foresight in act 2, her first appearance, establishes both these qualities as she ridicules his astrology and his relationship with his wife when he responds to her request for his coach with insult and denial. And in her initial exchanges with Valentine in acts 3 and 4, she seems to epitomize the master of what John Harrington Smith refers to as the 'love game':[90]

VALEN. You are not leaving me in this Uncertainty?
ANGEL. Wou'd any thing, but a Madman complain of Uncertainty? Uncertainty and Expectation are the Joys of Life. Security is an insipid thing, and the overtaking and possessing of a Wish, discovers the Folly of the Chase. Never let us know one another better; for the Pleasure of a Masquerade is done, when we come to shew Faces.   [4.1.784–90]

Yet despite her similarities to earlier comic heroines, Angelica differs from them in her ultimate expectations and, thence, in the means she would use to achieve them. Early in act 4, when Valentine's friend Scandal tells her of his madness, she responds openly: 'Mr. *Scandal*, you can't think me guilty of so much Inhumanity, as not to be concern'd for a Man I must own my self oblig'd to – pray tell me truth' (4.1.42–4). It is only when truth reveals a trick that she reverts to the gamesmanship she has displayed up until this point. And Smith must truncate the above quotation to show Angelica's continuity with earlier heroines. The passage ends with an enigmatic declaration: 'But I'll tell you two things before I leave you; I am not the Fool you take me for; and you are Mad and don't know it' (4.1.791–3), a second revelation of the real Angelica, though its import remains unclear until the final scene.

Only at the end of the play does it become clear that what she has been testing in Valentine is the sincerity of his love; she has had to 'play Trick for Trick' (4.1.66) because she has been unable to exchange 'Love for Love.' Smith recognizes the novelty of Angelica's attitude in the following perceptive analysis: 'In the first decade and a half of the love game, heroines had felt sincerity in heroes to be a secondary matter. One could make sincerity, not perhaps as fast as one pleased, but fast enough, even when the man was a Celadon or Dorimant. These heroes achieved Florimel and Harriet not because they were sincere, but because they were capable of inspiring love in the woman and had – in addition – wit, intelligence, and personal force. The ground of Angelica's choice shows the influence of her time; the love action of the play is a mixture.'[91] When Dorimant declares to Harriet that 'I will renounce all the joys I have in friendship and in Wine, sacrifice to you all the interest I have in other Women –,' she dismisses his rhapsodic protestations: 'Hold – Though I wish you devout, I would not have you turn Fanatick' (*The Man of Mode*, 5.2.143–7). It is precisely that kind of 'fanatical' gesture, but made with complete sincerity, that is required to win Angelica. When his assumed madness fails, and it seems that his father is to win both Angelica and his fortune, the disappointed Valentine makes the grand gesture she has been waiting for all along, saying: 'I have been disappointed of my only Hope; and he that loses hope may part with any thing. I never valu'd Fortune, but as it was subservient to my Pleasure; and my only Pleasure was to please this Lady: I have made many vain Attempts, and find at last, that nothing but my Ruine can effect it: Which, for that Reason, I will sign to – Give me the Paper' (5.1.543–9). Her response (aside), 'Generous *Valentine*!' (5.1.550), is but the prelude to a full explanation that she 'always lov'd' Valentine, though she was 'resolv'd to try him to the utmost' (5.1.572–4). Now that he has shown the proper 'Virtues,' she can acknowledge her love in the certainty that it is returned in kind.[92]

This is indeed a great change in the witty heroine; compare Angelica's values, for example, even with Belinda's in *The Old Batchelour*. It is a change that explains the impossibility of Valentine's initial situation. Before he met Angelica, he led the libertine life of the extravagant rake. But unlike Dorimant, he must do more than acknowledge his love in public before Angelica will accept him. Wit and trickery cannot possibly win Angelica; his scheme is doomed from the start. Though the intrigue against his father is largely successful, buying sufficient time for Sir

Sampson's inevitable disillusionment with his son Ben, the result is but a stalemate. It is only the active intervention of Angelica – paradoxically through her tricking of Sir Sampson – that resolves Valentine's almost irreconcilable dilemma of having at once to win both wife and fortune. Congreve's solution brilliantly fuses the traditions of the older comedy with the new, though the forces of their disparate elements continue to pull critics in different directions.[93]

It is not, however, the main plot of *Love for Love* that has traditionally received the large share of attention and admiration from critics. Rather, it is the humours. Like the majority among eighteenth-century audiences,[94] Samuel Johnson seems to have preferred *Love for Love* to Congreve's other comedies. His brief discussion of it cites only two noteworthy features, the characters of Foresight and Ben. For Colley Cibber 'no Author, and Actor could be more oblig'd to their mutual masterly Performances' than Congreve and the original Ben, Thomas Doggett. Bonamy Dobrée was convinced that the popularity of *Love for Love* was due to 'the return of a certain Jonsonian obviousness,' particularly in the humours. He suggests John Wilson's *The Cheats* and Wycherley's comedies as likely models. For Leech, *Love for Love* is Congreve's heartiest, most vigorous play and his first with characters who are genuinely 'vivid,' characters 'individually not outside Wycherley's scope.' The difference for Leech, and 'the secret of the play's popularity is the diversity of its humour.'[95]

Only recently have critics turned their attention to the love plot, most influentially Northrop Frye. In his discussion of the 'mythos of spring' or comedy, Frye singles out *Love for Love* to exemplify 'the third phase of comedy ... the normal one ... in which a *senex iratus* or other humor gives way to a young man's desires.' In *Love for Love*, he finds 'two Oedipus themes in counterpoint: the hero cheats his father out of the heroine, and his best friend violates the wife of an impotent old man who is the heroine's guardian.'[96] Others limit their attentions more exclusively to the main love intrigue, emphasizing only its romantic and sentimental elements. This tendency to overlook the once dominant humours elements causes Hume rightly to stress the 'beautifully interwoven' quality of the lines of action. Valentine and Angelica coexist in a plot in which there is also '(1) a cuckolding action ... (2) a trick marriage ... (3) satire on an astrological pretender ... [and] (4) the introduction of a country innocent.' All four of these 'hoary devices,' Hume adds, would 'be perfectly in place in *The Country-Wife*,' though not, he must add, without some important new twists. '1695 is not 1675.'[97] What transforms most of the minor plot elements in *Love for Love* is the same conception that required Angelica to expect sincerity in a lover.

Some of Congreve's predecessors, such as Shadwell and Mountfort, had already found it useful to balance their rakish gentlemen with an *honnête homme*. Congreve chooses to ignore their lead, instead adding a cynical libertine, Scandal, to Valentine's extravagant albeit reformed rake. It is Scandal, not Valentine, who is involved in the cuckolding action, and it is Scandal who is convincing in the role of the rake. His evaluation of the Foresight marriage readily uncovers the smooth and easy path to Mrs Foresight's bed. The twist comes only after his assignation, when Scandal indulges in the standard post-coital confidences of the successful rake:

SCANDAL. Hush, softly – the Pleasures of last Night, my Dear, too considerable to be forgot so soon
MRS FORE. Last Night! and what wou'd your Impudence infer from last night? last Night was like the Night before, I think.
SCANDAL. 'S' death do you make no difference between me and your Husband?
MRS FORE. Not much, – he's superstitious; and you are mad in my opinion.
SCANDAL. You make me mad – You are not serious – Pray recollect your self.
MRS FORE. O yes, now I remember, you were very impertinent and impudent, – and would have come to Bed to me.
SCANDAL. And did not?
MRS FORE. Did not! with that face can you ask the Question?
SCANDAL. This I have heard of before, but never believ'd. I have been told she had that admirable quality of forgetting to a man's face in the morning, that she had layn with him all night, and denying favours with more impudence, than she cou'd grant 'em.[98]   (4.1.316–37)

The rake's wounded pride forces him to recognize the value of his conquest, thus providing an important context for Scandal's final lines in the play. After the customary comedy-ending dance, called for by Scandal, he turns to Angelica and in an almost allegorical epilogue confesses: 'Well, Madam, You have done Exemplary Justice, in punishing an inhumane Father and rewarding a Faithful Lover: But there is a Third good Work, which I, in particular, must thank you for; I was an Infidel to your Sex; and you have converted me – For now I am convinc'd that all Women are not like Fortune, blind in bestowing Favours, either on those who do not merit, or who do not want 'em' (5.1.619–26).

There is a sense in which Scandal – and Congreve – here acknowledge the death knell of the Restoration rake. But the philosophical defeat of the libertine[99] in no way implies the introduction of 'sentimental slush.'[100] Scandal's recantation does not deny all validity to his earlier views: most

women in the play are not like Angelica. Mrs Foresight, like earlier Con-
grevean humours, remains unchanged at the end; Prue and Mrs Frail, too,
show no signs of potential improvement. The world has not changed.
Rather, Scandal has realized that it is possible, though difficult, to tran-
scend the cynical life of the rake in a world dominated by knaves and fools,
a theme Congreve explored more fully in *The Way of the World*.[101]

Trick marriages, like cuckoldings, are basic building blocks for the comic
playwright. Clodpate in *Epsom-Wells* and Heartwell in *The Old Batchelour* are victims of false trick marriages. Sir Mannerly Shallow in *The
Countrey Wit* marries Winnifred Rash by mistake, and Silvia and Betty
are passed off on Sir Joseph and Bluffe, also in *The Old Batchelour*, in an
action that clearly anticipates the union of Tattle and Mrs Frail in *Love for
Love*. In none of these cases, as I have indicated previously, is anything
like a genuine poetic justice imposed in determining the victims of trick
marriages. Rather, they are presented as either the appropriate fate for
fools or, when a rationale is invoked, as the necessary consequences of
maintaining the social code that provides the accepted values in most Carolean comedies – the code that proves inadequate for Valentine in his
courtship of Angelica.

Tattle and Mrs Frail are, throughout, characters on the make. Tattle
would like to be a successful libertine like Scandal, but his powers of
seduction limit him to the likes of the awkward and uncouth though eager
young country girl, Miss Prue. And even here, he does not quite succeed.
Mrs Frail diagnoses her own condition quite well: she has 'no great Stock
either of Fortune or Reputation' (2.1.490–1) and is therefore in need of a
rich husband. She is prepared to do anything to gain one. Tattle, too, feels
the want of fortune, and is also prepared to try to win one fraudulently. As
a result Mrs Frail chases first Ben, thenValentine; and Tattle, similarly,
pursues Angelica. When Scandal recognizes their designs, he immediately
formulates the appropriate response: 'I have discover'd something of *Tattle*, that is of a piece with Mrs. *Frail*. He courts *Angelica*, if we cou'd contrive to couple 'em together –' (4.1.597–9).

Valentine and Angelica match love for love. 'In neat contrast,' Harriett
Hawkins points out, 'the treacherous and mercenary schemes of Mrs. Frail
and Tattle appropriately boomerang, and they get trick for trick.'[102] The
comic analogue of poetic justice determines their fates, as the earlier more
purely social values are transformed into moral values. The careful attention Congreve provides to rationalizing what in earlier comedies required
no explanation points to the new concerns of the dramatists of the 1690s.

The Old Batchelour is an unusually diffuse comedy for the 1690s. Congreve never returned to a plot with so many disparate elements. Norman Holland describes *Love for Love* as 'surely [Congreve's] most neatly conceived and executed' play,[103] a judgment supported by its popularity as a stage piece. The characters are all from the same social group; most of them are members of two extended families, the Legends and the Foresights. Material unity, in other words, is so great that it necessitates efficient unity. *Love for Love* has received considerable attention for a post-Restoration comedy; it is not surprising that a great deal of that attention has been directed to considerations of the play's thematic unity: the play is 'about three different kinds of knowledge, three different ways of life – we might call them presocial, social, suprasocial'; 'there is hardly a character in the play who does not at one point trust and who is not at another point deceived'; 'the play's ethical center [is] its witty exploration of the traditional Christian paradox that worldly wisdom may actually be a form of folly or madness, and that some kinds of seeming madness or folly may be of the highest form of wisdom'; 'the central question which the play asks ... is whether either naturalness or any kind of honesty is often possible in human relationships given a world where people almost invariably behave inhumanly, unnaturally, dishonestly, and where interest is the dominant motive'; 'the thematic movement of William Congreve's intricate comedy, *Love for Love*, seems concerned with recognition of the worth of a woman's love as the ultimately sane action'; 'the madness, or at least the irrationality, of love is the central theme of the play.'[104] Though unresolved issues remain, the wealth and unusually fine quality of the thematic criticism of *Love for Love* testifies to the tightness and coherence of Congreve's play.

The formal unity of *Love for Love* recalls that of *The Country-Wife* in that it is built upon a series of direct contrasts, though here the contrasts are between a more or less exemplary couple, Valentine and Angelica, and a series of other couples who, for varying reasons, fail to measure up to their exemplary standard. The most interesting and important couples, of course, are Scandal and Mrs Foresight and Tattle and Mrs Frail. Through these contrasts, both libertine and mercenary bases for relationships are dismissed in favour of the sincere and genuine commitment evidenced by Valentine and Angelica. Possible matches between Mrs Frail and Ben, Mrs Frail and Valentine, Tattle and Prue, Ben and Prue, Sir Sampson and Angelica, and the existing match between the Foresights further emphasizes the isolated and special quality of the forthcoming marriage of Valentine and Angelica. (Congreve develops the same technique of contrasting couples to even greater effect in *The Way of the World*.)

Ben, though not properly a humours character by Congreve's own definition, since he is distinguished by 'habit' – that is, since most of his 'singularity' results from his profession and is shared by other members of it,[105] – is the only rounded character among the 'humours' in *Love for Love*, and even he is not allowed much in the way of sympathy. (In this sense, *Love for Love* is more traditional than *The Old Batchelour*.) Ben's candour and independence are somewhat admirable, but, as Holland indicates, he remains 'presocial,' a 'boorish but likable sailor.'[106] The only appropriate place for him in the end is back at sea; his departure from a society he cannot join is nothing to lament. Congreve puts great care into characterizing the remaining humours, but little sympathy. Novak considers Old Foresight 'Congreve's finest "humours" character, for his superstition dominates his entire life, whether as an astrologer or a cuckold,'[107] and Sir Sampson and Miss Prue are not far behind. But they are very much 'humours' of the old sort, figures primarily for ridicule or negative example. They also facilitate much of the farcical business Congreve includes – which again makes *Love for Love* a play of the 1690s – but farce is always kept subordinate to plot and character; Congreve does not allow it to take control in the way that Durfey so often does.

Norman Holland considers *The Plain-Dealer* 'the single most important influence on Congreve,' seeing 'the relation among Valentine, Scandal, and Tattle ... still faintly like that among Manly, Freeman, and Vernish; the thematic contrast is still between the two worlds of Manly-Valentine and Freeman-Scandal.' Birdsall extends the comparison: 'Like Fidelia's, Valentine's and Angelica's very names mark them as characters of romance; and if their fate is exemplary, it is also rare.'[108] The comparison is an interesting and telling one, but as much for the differences it reveals as for the similarities. Angelica is parallel to Olivia, not Fidelia, and she proves to be true without the ongoing protestations of either of Wycherley's characters. Valentine is anything but a plain dealer; much of the action is devoted to bringing him to the degree of sincerity he achieves at the end. And Scandal, the Freeman figure in *Love for Love*, is converted from the hard-nosed reality he believes in, unlike his predecessor, who is rewarded for his cynicism. *The Marriage-Hater Match'd* would have offered few surprises to the original audiences of *The Plain-Dealer*. *Love for Love*, though not a radical play for its time, certainly would have been so a generation earlier.

4

Six Representative Comedies,
1705–10

A mere eleven years separate *Love for Love* from George Farquhar's equally successful, post-Collier comedy, *The Recruiting Officer*. Though Congreve and Farquhar have often usefully been associated respectively with the old comedy and the new, the penultimate comedies by these young writers who dominated the London stage for consecutive and slightly overlapping decades also point to the similar problems each faced in coming to terms with their shared comic tradition. That Farquhar, like Congreve and Shadwell before him, gave serious thought to the relationship between the punitive and sympathetic elements in comedy is evident from 'A Discourse upon Comedy,' his most extensive theoretical consideration of his craft.

For Farquhar, 'in all Productions either Divine or Humane, the final Cause is the first Mover,' and to find the final cause of comedy, he looks back to its origin, which he finds in 'The Philosophical *Mythology* of the Ancients.' As a result 'old *Æsop* must wear the Bays as the first and original Author.' The fable, of course, was Aesop's chosen form, and it is the Aesopian fable that provides Farquhar with his conceptual model for comedy: '*Utile Dulci* was his Motto, and must be our Business.'[1] While it is difficult to find a playwright or critic who fails to subscribe to a version of Farquhar's Horatian commonplace, his emphasis on the moral efficacy of the fable aligns his theory with the views of Jonson, Shadwell, and especially Dennis. The vindication of stage comedy against the attacks of the Collierites results from reading its 'Veils and Figures' for the kind of instruction found in a biblical parable: '*Fondlewife* and his young Spouse are no more than the *Eagle* and *Cockle*; he wanted Teeth to break the Shell himself, so somebody else run away with the Meat, – The Fox in the Play, is the same with the Fox in the Fable, who stuft his Guts so full, that he cou'd not get out at the same Hole he came in; so both *Reynards* being Delinquents alike, come to be truss'd up together' (II 378).

Farquhar had sufficient experience as a man of the theatre not to neglect pleasure in his quest for instruction. If, unlike Dryden, he refused logical priority to 'divertisement and delight,' he nonetheless recognized that pleasure was the requisite means to his end: 'To make the moral Instructive, you must make the Story diverting; the Spleenatick Wit, the Beau Courtier, the heavy Citizen, the fine Lady, and her fine Footman, come all to be instructed, and therefore must all be diverted' (II 379).

It is within the context of these general assumptions about comedy that Farquhar develops the ideas about humour found in Congreve's 'Concerning Humour in Comedy.' Humour is particularly a characteristic of English life: *'we have the most unaccountable Medley of Humours among us of any Nation upon Earth.'* The implications of writing plays for a nation of humourists are clear to Farquhar:

An *English* Play is intended for the Use and Instruction of an *English* Audience; a People not only separated from the rest of the World by Situation, but different also from other Nations as well in the Complexion and Temperament of the Natural Body, as in the Constitution of our Body Politick: As we are a Mixture of many Nations, so we have the most unaccountable Medley of Humours among us of any People upon Earth; these Humours produce Variety of Follies, some of 'um unknown to former Ages; these new Distempers must have new Remedies, which are nothing but new Counsels and Instructions.   (II 378–9)

If the audience is made up of living humours, and if those humours result from the very nature of English society (making it pointless to try to change them), and if those humours must be pleased in order to be instructed, an alternative to the Jonsonian and Shadwellian approaches to humour becomes essential. At the same time, since Farquhar holds instruction to be the final cause of comedy, he cannot accept Dryden's relegation of it to an almost incidental result of malicious laughter any more than he can consider wit and raillery the noblest ornaments of comic art. Farquhar shares Dryden's sense of the importance of pleasing his audience (without Dryden's contempt for the resulting artistic compromises), but he takes his pedagogical responsibilities far more seriously. As a result, he is forced to rethink the theoretical principles of comedy he inherited from pre-Collier comic theorists – that is, he must reinterpret the place of the punitive and sympathetic elements in English comedy.

Critics have often pointed out that, like Jonson, Farquhar was as interested in representing character as in presenting action.[2] His nationalistic view of humours – one that continued to gain adherents throughout the eighteenth century – required that Farquhar soften his satiric treatment of humours. They became, as a result, far more three-dimensional than most of their predecessors – hence the frequent detection of 'Shakespearean' models. A gentler handling of humours, and in fact of most characters who fall short of the paradigm of the Restoration truewit – a very limited paradigm as the above discussions should have indicated – has implications, too, for Farquhar's comic heroes, the descendants of the various kinds of rakes, rogues, and wits of both sexes. They, too, must be tempered, since wit and raillery can no longer represent society's best and brightest. In this context, Pope's observation, 'What pert low Dialogue has Farqu'ar writ!' makes perfect sense.[3]

Pope's comment also points to Farquhar's treatment of the punitive elements of the plot. Like Durfey, he turned to farce in order to lighten the impact of the folly of his humours. Farquhar's humours can be as ridiculous as Jonson's but the stakes are never as high. Their folly, the folly of the good, solid, English middle class, cannot be condemned morally as it so often is in Jonson's plays. Nor can it be contemned as it had so often been by the previous two generations of comic playwrights.[4] Similar changes must also occur in the sympathetic strands of Farquhar's comic plots, plots generally dominated by a traditional love action. Here Farquhar's divergence from Fletcher's model is made overtly clear by *The Inconstant*, his 1702 revision of *The Wild-Goose Chase*. Fletcher, as I noted above, is interested in situation, not character. His plots are intricate, clever, and witty; like Dryden he devotes considerable energy to displaying balance and pattern in them. This is not the place to detail the particular changes Farquhar made in his adaptation but rather simply to take note of the consistent rejection of what Eric Rothstein calls 'formal arrangement' in favour of '"ideological" appeals' to moral sensibility. 'The formal arrangement receives its neat completion in the earlier play; the moral progression receives its in the later.'[5] Sympathetic and punitive elements of plot, character, and language are thus reintegrated by Farquhar in a mixed comedy much closer to the moral values of its audience – though not identical with them – than earlier mixed comedies had been. By the time Farquhar wrote *The Recruiting Officer*, he had mastered a 'humane' form of comedy that would hold the stage throughout the eighteenth and much of the nineteenth centuries, and continue to please audiences in the twentieth.[6]

Farquhar's transformation of traditional comic elements is particularly evident in the humours characters. His decision to set the play in Shrewsbury and to treat his country setting with respect has received the bulk of the critical attention given to *The Recruiting Officer*. It is a crucial decision, for in turning to a society in which an aging, humourous country justice is looked to as the arbiter of social and moral values, Farquhar has relocated his comic world in time as well as space. Justice Ballance dispenses justice with an eccentricity not unlike Jonson's Adam Overdo, but the events in *Bartholomew Fair* serve to reveal to Overdo his own limitations. As blocking father, Ballance must, of course, be overcome, but as representative of Her Majesty, he is vindicated despite his often cruel or arbitrary treatment of those who appear before him. The genial comedy with its occasional overlay of farce subsumes the more critical implications of much of the action. Shadwell's Clodpate is a typical late seventeenth-century country justice, and he remains a pure comic gull throughout. Significantly, Ballance and the other inhabitants of Shrewsbury no more share Clodpate's antagonism to London than the more sophisticated outsiders reveal their contempt for the country. In fact, for the people of Shrewsbury, *it* is the town; when Ballance learns that his son is fatally ill and wishes to separate Silvia from Plume, he requests that she 'go into the Country' (2.2.63).

Plume's rival recruiting officer, Captain Brazen, is another humours character remade by Farquhar. Created for Cibber, this combination of fop and *miles gloriosus*, the union of Congreve's Tattle and Captain Bluffe, escapes the treatment traditionally reserved for his prototypes. An ineffective officer of questionable courage, Brazen, like Bluffe, could have been exposed a coward and dismissed. His introduction follows the familiar formula for fops in the earlier plays: his character is presented by one of the male leads – in this case Worthy – just before his initial entrance: 'his Impudence were a Prodigy, were not Ignorance proportionable; he has the most universal Acquaintance of any Man living, for he won't be alone, and no body will keep him Company twice; then he's a *Cæsar* among the Women, *Veni, Vidi, Vici*, that's all. If he has but talk'd with the Maid, he swears he has lain with the Mistress; but the most surprizing part of his Character is his Memory, which is the most prodigious, and the most trifling in the World' (3.1.198–205). Brazen is, moreover, Worthy's rival for Melinda, and in his conceit, he thinks himself her favourite. He is thus easy prey for Melinda's scheming maid, Lucy, who intends to marry him disguised as her mistress. But unlike Tattle and Bluffe and countless other fops and cowards, Brazen is not punished with an undesirable marriage. Rather, like Heartwell, he is spared, in this case by the intervention, albeit undesigned, of Worthy. Then, when Plume is won away from the army by

Silvia, he turns over his hard-won recruits, complete with his gifted Ser-
jeant Kite, to his former rival. Brazen leaves Shrewsbury without Melinda
and her £20,000, but not without twenty new recruits; his stop has proved
quite successful indeed. And there is no sign whatsoever that he has
learned anything or that he will behave at all differently in the future.
Brazen is no better than his predecessors, but his folly is no longer simply
subjected to the malice of ridicule; instead, it has become the object of a
more generous-minded enjoyment.

As a result, similar alterations can be seen in the punitive action of the
play. This is especially clear in the most Jonsonian scene, act 4, scene 2,
when Kite sets up as the fortune-teller, Doctor Copernicus.[7] Kite, a combination of the rogue and witty servant in the tradition of Mosca and Face,
adopts his role as Copernicus in order to gull new recruits for Plume
through predictions of brilliant careers and to impress upon Melinda the
importance of accepting Worthy. He is fully triumphant, and, like Horner,
apparently in a position to continue to be so in the indefinite future. But
his world changes around him, and Kite is noticeably absent from the final
scene. There is really no place for him in the humane, genteel world of
Shrewsbury. The thought of abandoning him to Brazen does not seem satisfactory, but a happier alternative is difficult to imagine. Silence about his
future was no doubt best; audiences and critics seem not to notice. But
Kite's unclear status at the end of *The Recruiting Officer* points to the difficulty in trying to sustain a punitive action in the eighteenth century.

Farquhar's gentlemen-heroes also show signs of changing attitudes and
conventions. Like Horner, Plume has deliberately acquired a false reputation; his rakish facade, he tells the disguised Silvia, is a means to his pro-
fessional end: 'kiss the prettiest Country Wenches, and you are sure of
listing the lustiest Fellows.' When she expresses surprise at his apparent
preference for male company to female, he states his principles more
plainly: 'I am not the Rake that the World imagines, I have got an Air of
Freedom, which People mistake for Lewdness in me, as they mistake For-
mality in others for Religion; the World is all a Cheat, only I take mine
which is undesign'd to be more excusable than theirs, which is hypocritical; I hurt no body but my self, and they abuse all Mankind – –' (4.1.140–
1, 181–7). An extravagant rake like Crowne's Ramble apologized for his
womanizing as the product of uncontrollable appetite; Horner pursued his
appetites with more control and design. Mountfort's Young Reveller and
Congreve's Valentine had rakish pasts, but their behaviour was explained
in part as youthful folly to be abandoned. Silvia's father, Justice Ballance,
seems to have had just such a past, as he sees his younger self in Plume's

public manner: 'I was just such another Fellow at his Age; I never set my Heart upon any Woman so much as to make me uneasie at the Disappointment, but what was very surprising both to my self and Friends, I chang'd o'th' sudden from the most fickle Lover to be the most constant Husband in the World' (3.1.183–8). But while Ballance follows the earlier pattern, Plume, despite his many bastards and his extravagant manner, seems never to have been a rake at all. His constancy needs only be transferred from public to private life; little change will be required to enlarge him into a husband.

In order to have two pairs of lovers, Farquhar pairs Plume with Worthy, the *honnête homme* character in *The Recruiting Officer*. Less sententious than his namesake in *Greenwich-Park*, Farquhar's Worthy is nonetheless an earnest, decent, and straightforward young lover. And he, too, must suffer – comically, to be sure – for his attempt at keeping. Unlike Mountfort's Lord Worthy, Farquhar's Worthy is unsuccessful since the woman he intended to keep, Melinda, inherited a substantial fortune just before she was to accept his offer. Worthy clearly loved her all along and was going to keep her only because she lacked a proper fortune for a wife. Now that she has one, he explains to Plume, he has 'alter'd [his] Conduct, given [his] Addresses the obsequious and distant turn, and court[s] her now for a Wife.' The result has been as Plume anticipates: 'So, as you grew obsequious, she grew haughty, and because you approach'd her as a Goddess, she us'd you like a Dog' (1.1.204–9).

Plume again offers Worthy good, practical advice (he had earlier advised the offer of a settlement): combat pride with pride, strength with strength. Worthy takes his advice, and it works, but the result is that Melinda and Worthy are rarely on stage together. They say nothing to each other until late in the play (4.2.68–98) when a brief, heated exchange is ended abruptly by Melinda's cuffing of Brazen, a favour she had intended for Worthy. Soon after, Kite convinces her that she will lose Worthy forever if she doesn't come to terms with him immediately, and their final dialogue (5.3.1–56) resolves their difficulties happily. These lovers had little keeping them apart, and Farquhar found little to stage in their courtship. In her initial appearance with Silvia (1.2.1–98), Melinda seemed almost like Wycherley's Olivia in her affectation, hypocrisy, and malice, but this is merely her response to the 'barbarous' treatment she received from Worthy (5.3.39). Both Worthy and Melinda are basically good and decent, if rather dull. Farquhar necessarily must look elsewhere to keep his comedy lively and engaging.

Far more witty and entertaining are Farquhar's principal pair of lovers,

Silvia and Plume. But again, it is not in their dialogue with each other that they display their wit. *The Recruiting Officer* remains firmly in the Jonsonian tradition in its neglect of the wit game so much at the heart of the Restoration Fletcherian tradition. Silvia and Plume, too, have but two brief exchanges (2.1.53–94 and 5.7.65–97), and in theirs, too, little wit is displayed. Were it not for Plume's performance as recruiting officer and Silvia's as rake-turned-recruit, there would be little reason to single them out as the 'sprightly' (rather than the 'subdued') pair of lovers that they are.[8]

Silvia's sprightliness is entirely without affectation (her criticism of Melinda is earned), and so is her love. As a result it would be impossible for Farquhar to enter her into the earlier style of love-game without downright breaking her character. She is, by nature, 'unfashionably kind,' as her father describes her to Plume when he comes to understand what she has done (5.7.83). The audience and Plume have been aware of this since the first act, when Kite reported (to him and Worthy) that it was Silvia who provided ten guineas to support Plume's bastard. This generous gesture was followed by her summons of Kite to her:

KITE. ... I went; and upon hearing that you were come to Town, she gave me half a Guinea for the News, and order'd me to tell you, That Justice *Ballance* her Father, who is just come out of the Country, wou'd be glad to see you.
PLUME. There's a Girl for you, *Worthy* – Is there any thing of Woman in this? No, 'tis noble and generous, Manly Friendship, show me another Woman that wou'd lose an Inch of her Prerogative that way, without Tears, Fits, and Reproaches.

(1.1.290–8)

Silvia's honest and open generosity is matched, too, by her father. Unlike a traditional *senex* figure such as Congreve's Sir Sampson, Justice Ballance is genuinely concerned with his daughter's welfare. He is afraid that Plume will take advantage of her openness, and, after the report of his son's death, he wishes to match her with a social equal. His pact with her is an early version of what becomes the model for father-daughter relationships in the eighteenth century, perhaps best known through Goldsmith's Kate Hardcastle and her father:

BALL. ... I expect you will make me one solemn Promise.
SIL. Propose the thing, Sir.
BALL. That you will never dispose of your self to any Man, without my consent.
SIL. I promise.

BALL. Very well, and to be even with you, I promise, That I will never dispose of you without your own Consent.   (2.2.67–74)

And again anticipating Kate, Silvia stoops to conquer Plume, by taking on the identity of the young recruit Jack Wilfull (or Pinch, as she later calls herself) in order to trick her father into impressing her into Plume's service, literally disposing of her to Plume. The trick works, but finally proves unnecessary as the goodness of all the characters involved leads them to the same conclusion – that Silvia and Plume should marry. With this resolution, Farquhar contributed to the eighteenth-century transformation of the blocking father.

In *The Recruiting Officer* Farquhar continues the trend of the 1690s toward plays tightly unified at the material and efficient levels, though the inclusion of the soldiers and the rustics opens up the range of social classes. Melinda and Silvia are cousins, Worthy and Plume old friends who are also friends of Justice Ballance. Plume and Kite have recruited in Shrewsbury before, so they already have contacts and connections. And because of the Recruiting Acts of 1703–4, they share with Ballance the responsibility for raising recruits, and, necessarily, the need to do business with many of the townspeople of Shrewsbury.[9] The love plots and the recruiting plot are so thoroughly intertwined that they can scarcely be separated. Melinda's quarrel with Silvia results in Silvia being sent away, and her return in disguise makes her an object for recruiting. Plume and Brazen attempt to enlist Silvia; Plume vies with the disguised Silvia for Rose; Brazen is Worthy's rival for Melinda. Melinda and Lucy and the recruits all visit the disguised Kite (Copernicus); and Justice Ballance determines who is to be recruited and who is to be Silvia's husband.

Material and efficient unity provide a base for formal unity, again through the favoured device of a series of direct contrasts. The principal contrast builds on the metaphoric equivalence of love and war so that, for example, though Plume tries to recruit the disguised Silvia, it is Silvia, in the end, who recruits Plume: 'Madam, I resign my Freedom, and to your Beauty, my Ambition; greater in obeying at your Feet, than Commanding at the Head of an Army' (5.7.94–7).[10] Plume and Brazen, the two recruiting officers, provide alternative models for the army; Silvia and Melinda, both unexpected heiresses as well as cousins, provide contrasting approaches to love and courtship; and Plume and Worthy, as well as Worthy and Brazen, similarly provide alternative modes of love and courtship. So central is the dualism of love and war that there has been little critical debate about the thematic unity of the play.[11] And so effectively does Far-

quhar realize the potential of his plot that the inconsistencies so frequently noticed by critics are easily ignored by audiences and mere casual
readers.[12]

Farquhar's last and greatest play, *The Beaux Stratagem*, provides another
example of his new approach to the double tradition of Jonson and
Fletcher in comedy. Archer and Aimwell begin as traditional Jonsonian
rogue-heroes, donning their disguises as master and servant in order to
cheat an unsuspecting country family of its daughter and her fortune –
not necessarily in that order. Earlier love plots, of course, are not free from
trickery. But in most comedies, when marriage and money are the object,
the gull is the blocking parent-figure, not the prospective bride, and the
young woman at least acquiesces if she does not actively participate in her
suitor's schemes. Alternatively, in those cases where the young woman is
to be tricked along with her parent(s), she is herself a comic gull, like Vanbrugh's eponymous Hoyden in *The Relapse*. Aimwell and Archer have
much in common with Vanbrugh's Young Fashion: all are younger brothers who have wasted their limited fortunes and look to marriage to
remedy their desperate financial situations. But while Young Fashion is
sent to scrounge for a wife in the two-dimensional country world of Sir
Tunbelly Clumsy and his daughter, Archer and Aimwell try their luck in
the Lichfield of Lady Bountiful and Dorinda, innocents in their way, but
nonetheless singularly inappropriate victims for traditional punitive comedy, as Aimwell, too, ultimately concludes.

The play opens in Bonniface's inn where, over the course of the first act,
Archer and Aimwell reveal their strategem, while Bonniface and his
daughter, Cherry, try to infer it from their appearance and the little they
say. When they leave their box of £200 in Bonniface's care, their ostenta-
tious attempt to gain attention provokes speculation quite different from
what they had hoped for and later receive from the Bountiful household:

BON. Ay, Child, you must lay by this Box for the Gentleman, 'tis full of Money.
CHER. Money! all that Money! why, sure Father the Gentleman comes to be
chosen Parliament-man. Who is he?
BON. I don't know what to make of him, he talks of keeping his Horses ready
sadled, and of going perhaps at a minute's warning, or of staying perhaps till the
best part of this be spent.
CHER. Ay, ten to one, Father, he's a High-way-man.
BON. A High-way-man! upon my Life, Girl, you have hit it, and this Box is
some new purchased Booty.   (1.1.290–300)

Eric Rothstein has pointed out that Bonniface's inn is 'appropriate for the beaux, then, for he, like them, is a hypocritical user of beauty and bounty for his own ends.' It is not surprising that one rogue recognizes another. Rothstein also notes that 'Boniface serves not only as a comment on the beaux but also as an antithesis to Lady Bountiful – scenically as well as thematically, because his inn is the only other setting used besides her house.'[13] The members of Lady Bountiful's household are no less curious about Aimwell and Archer than Bonniface, but they are inclined to assume the best. The two settings offer a basic moral opposition; they also reveal the consequences of moving a punitive action from so natural a home as Bonniface's inn to the benevolent domain of Lady Bountiful. That move is emblematic of the change in punitive comedy in the early eighteenth century.

Charles Fifer sums up the standard ambivalent placement of *The Beaux Stratagem* as 'the last of the traditional comedies of manners, the destroyer of that tradition, or the first comedy of a new tradition' because, like most works recognized as transitional, it shares 'certain characteristics with the Restoration comedy of manners that preceded it and other characteristics with the chaster and more bland comedy that followed it.'[14] Aimwell and Archer offer another version of the almost formulaic pair of comic heroes, the rake and the *honnête homme*.[15] But they differ from most of their predecessors because of their involvement in Farquhar's more clearly punitive plot. It is the more generous, soft-hearted Aimwell who at first seems out of place: the mildest of benevolent world-views forces impossible constraints on the traditional Jonsonian rogue. Even the good-natured Plume could not afford to contemplate the likely fates of his recruit-victims. Archer is more clear-sighted about his goals, and what he is prepared to do to achieve them. The resulting tension emerges early in the play:

ARCH. ... For my part I can stick to my Bottle, while my Wine, my Company, and my Reason holds good; I can be charm'd with *Sappho's* singing without falling in Love with her Face; I love Hunting, but wou'd not, like *Acteon*, be eaten up by my own Dogs; I love a fine House, but let another keep it; and just so I love a fine Woman.
AIM. In that last particular you have the better of me.
ARCH. Ay, you're such an amorous Puppy, that I'm afraid you'll spoil our Sport; you can't counterfeit the Passion without feeling it.
AIM. Tho' the whining part be out of doors in Town, 'tis still in force with

the Country Ladies; – And let me tell you *Frank,* the Fool in that Passion shall outdoe the Knave at any time.   (1.1.226–39)

In his sympathetic love plots, Congreve could allow Valentine and Mirabell to attempt to win their mistresses through trickery without compromising their status as comic heroes since their intentions are genuinely honourable. Yet Congreve allows neither ultimately to succeed by trickery. In a punitive plot, however, the distance the comic hero maintains from his objects encourages greater freedoms. In *The Beaux Stratagem,* too, honesty wins out over trickery, but the result is far more problematic.[16] Archer is the more attractive of the male leads because he is the more active, witty, and vital – though his attractiveness diminishes as the play progresses. Archer's early exchanges with Cherry, especially 'Love's Catechism,' his later exchanges with Mrs Sullen, and his evasion of the attempts by Bonniface, Gibbet, and Scrub to determine his true identity far outshine anything Aimwell does in the play.

Aimwell is a second-rate rogue. And the plot does little to establish a more effective presence for him as a sympathetic lover. As Judith Milhous and Robert D. Hume point out, 'Farquhar's presentation of Aimwell and Dorinda is most unusual. Not until the finale do we hear the couple talk.'[17] This certainly distinguishes Farquhar's lovers from their best-known predecessors, but not to their advantage to be sure. (The punitive plot structure significantly mitigates the problem of lovers who remain apart on stage.) The best lines remain with Archer and his two prospective mistresses. Aimwell's honesty proves the best policy, but the ending lacks even the conviction of Congreve's in *Love for Love.* And the imposition of the sympathetic ending undermines the punitive plot by forcing the audience to consider Archer's behaviour from the point of view of a sympathetic comedy. When Congreve ended *Love for Love* with the triumph of honesty, he converted his most rogue-like character, Scandal, to Angelica's doctrine of sincerity. Archer is unrepentant to the end and thus must answer for those values that made him so splendid a rogue-hero in the first part of the play. It is not surprising that critics who read the play as if it were a sympathetic comedy throughout fail to appreciate Archer. F.S. Boas, for example, takes the Aimwell of act 5 as the play's exemplary figure. It follows, then, that 'Farquhar has throughout shown Archer of inferior quality.'[18]

In his introduction to the old Mermaid edition of Farquhar's plays, William Archer argues that Farquhar's characters differ from those of his Restoration predecessors in that they 'are not for ever feeling their own pulses, taking the social temperature, or noting the readings of the wit-barometer ... He is much less given to the elaborate portrayal of a Jonso-nian "humour" for its own sake.' When compared to early Jonson, Shad-well, or Durfey, Farquhar is indeed anything but self-indulgent in presenting his humours. Archer's observation, though, is part of his larger argument that in repeatedly passing up the opportunity to linger over a character sketch, even when introducing a character (the exception is Bra-zen), Farquhar is moving beyond the Jonsonian tradition so much a part of post-Restoration comedy, evidence that he is a more 'highly developed' dramatist than his contemporaries.[19]

Archer is surely right in noticing the absence of the more traditional humours characters in Farquhar's plays and the effect of their absence on the movement of the action. But Archer fails to see a relationship between the kind of humours characters Farquhar does create, based on the theory discussed above, and the humours characters of his predecessors. Like Congreve, Farquhar rounds his humours. He presents them sympatheti-cally, occasionally from within. Since he no longer needs to maintain dis-tance from his humours, Farquhar abandons the quick, two-dimensional character sketch so favoured by Jonson and Shadwell in favour of more complex, mixed – even amiable – humours.

Sullen provides a useful example. He is described in the 'Dramatis Per-sonae' as 'A Country Blockhead, brutal to his Wife.' As such, he is the ideal candidate for a truewit's cuckold. And as the obstacle to Mrs Sullen's happiness, he is also the waiting victim for a comic rogue. Since Archer plays both roles effectively and with style, it would have been easy for Farquhar to follow the conventions of his predecessors. Bonniface's description of Sullen to Aimwell in act 1 sets the audience's expectations in just that direction:

AIM. And marry'd, you say?
BON. Ay, and to a curious Woman, Sir, – But he's a – He wants it, here, Sir.
(*Pointing to his Forehead*).   (1.1.94–6)

Sullen may be a 'blockhead,' but Farquhar gives him some decent lines nonetheless, for example, his response to his wife and sister's criticism of his late-night drinking:

DOR. Stay, stay, Brother, you shan't get off so; you were very naught last
night, and must make your Wife Reparation; come, come, Brother, won't you
ask Pardon?

SULL. For what?
DOR. For being drunk last Night.
SULL. I can afford it, can't I?
MRS SULL. But I can't, Sir.
SULL. Then you may let it alone.   (2.1.93–100)

Unlike earlier cuckolded husbands, even those more 'brutal' to their wives, such as Pinchwife, Sullen is not possessive of his wife or unnaturally jealous of other men. The famous fifth-act reverse proviso scene reveals the extent to which Sullen, too, is unhappy in his marriage: Mrs Sullen married 'To support the Weakness of [her] Sex by the strength of his, and to enjoy the Pleasures of an agreeable Society.' Sullen married 'To get an Heir to [his] Estate.' Both have failed miserably in achieving their desires, and Sullen proves no less eager to separate than his wife, as his surprisingly gleeful response indicates:

SULL. ... Pray, Sir, who are you?
SIR CHAR. I am *Sir Charles Freeman*, come to take away your Wife.
SULL. And you, good Sir?
AIM. *Charles Viscount Aimwell*, come to take away your Sister.
SULL. And you pray, Sir?
ARCH. *Francis Archer*, Esq; come –
SULL. To take away my Mother, I hope – Gentlemen, you're heartily welcome,
I never met with three more obliging People since I was born –   (5.4.197–208)

Sullen is forced by trickery to part with his wife's fortune along with Mrs Sullen herself; as the play ends his 'Head akes consumedly.' But the final words in the play, spoken by Archer, point to the mixed treatment Sullen receives throughout: 'Twou'd be hard to guess which of these Parties is the better pleas'd, the Couple Join'd, or the Couple Parted?' (5.4.289–90). Few critics have found Sullen as attractive or sympathetic as his wife, but few, too, have dismissed him as a mere punitive comedy gull.

The same pattern of treatment is to be found in the play's many other humours characters – Count Bellair, Foigard, Gibbet, Hounslow, Bagshot, Bonniface, Scrub, Lady Bountiful, and Gipsey. Each can be traced to a line of earlier humours characters; many are the victims of punitive comic action. But none of these characters is entirely without charm or saving grace. Even such easy targets as French soldiers, Irish priests, and fathers willing to corrupt their innocent daughters are spared outright condemnation. The new attitudes toward humours are clearly in force in Farquhar's plays.

A more balanced treatment of traditional humours makes it difficult to display them at work – Archer's 'humour for its own sake.' Instead, their various traits must emerge from the action. But Archer is right, too, in suggesting that a change has also taken place in plot construction in plays like *The Recruiting Officer* and *The Beaux Stratagem*. Discussions of earlier comedies, especially those with three-level plots such as *Love in a Wood* and *The Old Batchelour*, require some effort and occasionally some ingenuity on the part of critics who wish to demonstrate their unifying principles. Where earlier playwrights use emblematic patterns and balances to hold together materials of a fairly disparate nature, Farquhar – and he is here representative of his contemporaries – contains his materials within what is essentially a single, coherent action.

The characters are related in fairly obvious ways: Lady Bountiful's household provides the centre of the action; Aimwell and Archer travel in the same social circles in London as Mrs Sullen's brother, Sir Charles Freeman; Bonniface is Sullen's tenant; and Lichfield is sufficiently small for anyone visiting – Count Belair, Foigard – to be known to Lady Bountiful and her family. Farquhar also provides causal connections among his characters as abundant as his material connections. Archer and Count Belair both show interest in Mrs Sullen, just as Scrub and Foigard both pursue the ladies' maid, Gipsey. Archer also dallies with Cherry, and he and Aimwell both have exchanges with Gibbet. Archer blackmails Foigard into placing him rather than the count in Mrs Sullen's closet, allowing him to be on hand when Bonniface's gang attempts to rob Lady Bountiful's house. And Cherry warns Aimwell when she is unable to find Archer. Sir Charles brings the news of the death of Aimwell's brother, while Archer liberates Mrs Sullen's portion from her husband. Additional connections proliferate, but they all seem so natural and obvious in Farquhar's late plays that such catalogues are of limited value. In the earlier comedies, these mechanical connections are crucial for holding together complex plots; Farquhar's plot is far simpler and requires few conceptual helps to hold the parts together. This is not, of course, to suggest that it is thin in action; on the contrary, there is more action in this simple plot than in many plays with far more complex plots.

Formal unity, too, is not wanting, and it, too, is easy to identify, though different critics stress different themes: 'The fundamental verity in the play is money; the fundamental metaphor involves commerce; the fundamental axiom is that poverty is nonexistence'; 'I think the play ... makes a very real comment on the difficulty, if not the impossibility, of committing oneself to one love, to one person'; 'Farquhar has something real to say about a world that believes more in appearance than in reality and in which the fine people are no better than the lowliest people on the social scale, and in some cases not as good'; 'Farquhar's concerns include a considerable attention paid to such concepts as freedom, particularly in its negative aspects'; 'the plot revolves around deception ... the play echoes Milton to the end, extolling divorce by mutual consent in the name of freedom.'[20] Interpretation of this thematic material, however, is no more straightforward or obvious than it was for earlier plays. This is in part because Farquhar treats large social issues with the complexity of thought they deserve, and in part because Farquhar never subordinates his plot to didactic ends.[21] With its increased amiability, 'robustness and energy,' and good-natured laughter pointing to altered modes of 'characterization, dialogue, and plot,' yet always retaining 'many of the traditional techniques and motifs of earlier comedy,' *The Beaux Stratagem* is perhaps the central text in the body of plays Shirley Strum Kenny has identified quite persuasively as the new and 'distinct mode' she calls 'humane comedy.' Few if any of Farquhar's component parts are entirely new, but the effect of the whole differs greatly from that of the plays of the 1670s. Kenny is probably right to suggest that the differences are responsible for 'the fact that a play like *The Beaux Stratagem* continues to be revived more often' than either its immediate predecessors – or successors.[22]

Less central but very much present among the writers of humane comedy is Sir John Vanbrugh. Vanbrugh's reputation as a playwright has always suffered from the difficulty most critics find in placing his comedies firmly in any single camp. John Palmer's influential judgment is, in this sense, typical: 'He is a dramatist of the fall. He accepted a tradition; and shattered it ... Vanbrugh made the breach whereby Farquhar entered in and destroyed the citadel.' Kenny makes a similar if less melodramatic point in maintaining that Vanbrugh was more 'strongly affected ... by the theatrical traditions of the 1670s, 1680s, and 1690s' than Farquhar.[23] Even Vanbrugh's critical views are difficult to place. Comedy, for Vanbrugh as for most of his traditional predecessors, is 'a Discouragement to Vice and Folly.'[24] Vanbrugh is as conservative as Dennis in his prescription for how comedy should affect its audience: 'The Business of Comedy is to shew People what they shou'd do, by representing them upon the Stage, doing what they shou'd not,' even to insisting upon the traditional comic mirror: 'The Stage is a Glass for the World to view itself in; People ought therefore to see themselves as they are; if it make their Faces too Fair, they won't know they are Dirty, and by consequence will neglect to wash 'em'

(I, 206). At the same time, Vanbrugh seems far less concerned with the place of the plot or fable in comedy than almost any post-Restoration critic to date, from Dryden to Shadwell, or from Dennis to Congreve. However much these critics disagreed on many issues, they would all have found extreme Vanbrugh's claim that 'I believe I cou'd shew, that the chief entertainment, as well as the Moral, lies much more in the characters and the Dialogue, than in the Business and the Event' (I 209). Four years later even Farquhar would ground his generally more radical theory of comedy in the Aesopian fable. Robert D. Hume confronts a similar mixture of old and new in Vanbrugh's original plays: 'In attitude, Vanbrugh is largely of the hard comedy persuasion, and most of his materials are in that tradition.' But Hume also finds a 'softening of the hard comedy' in Vanbrugh that 'may seem to betray the school of Wycherley to which Vanbrugh by direct descent belongs.' As a result, when he must choose between his categories of 'hard' and 'humane' comedy, Hume 'surprisingly' finds that Vanbrugh should be placed in the humane camp.[25]

The Confederacy, Vanbrugh's adaptation of Dancourt's *Les Bourgeoises à la Mode*, shares with his earlier comedies the ability to resist easy classification, as the elements of both sympathetic and punitive comedy are again rearranged in a way that produces new, but largely traditional results. The adaptation itself is reasonably close to the French original; Vanbrugh adds but two scenes and part of a third. But in translating Dancourt's play, Vanbrugh also makes it thoroughly English, and, in so doing, according to his critics, he makes a good play into a much better one. For Louis Kronenberger, *The Confederacy* is 'Vanbrugh's best piece of work'; for Kenneth Muir, it 'is probably his most successful play.'[26]

Structurally, the subplot has much in common with the plot of *The Beaux Stratagem*. Dick Amlet has assumed the identity of Colonel Shapely in order to marry Corinna Gripe and gain her fortune. He is aided by his old school friend, Brass, who acts as his servant. Dick's attempt to deceive the Gripes, then, places his story firmly in the same tradition of punitive comedy that Farquhar was to draw upon. But the differences are many and call attention to themselves the minute the punitive skeleton is fleshed out. Dick's comic gulls are far more traditional than Aimwell and Archer's – an old city husband with a daughter cast from the same mould as Miss Prue and Hoyden. But while Gripe remains the stereotypical city husband, Corinna is a more complex character than Prue or Hoyden. 'Nature works in her more powerfully' is how Hazlitt described the difference; for Bernard Harris, her importance derives from a 'shrewd revelation of the false innocence of the sixteen-year old.'[27] She reveals a knowledge of the world in general and of sexual desire in particular that surprises even her stepmother's worldly-wise maid, Flippanta, though that knowledge is yet inadequate to allow her to see through the trick being perpetrated on her. Flippanta alternates between very mild concern for Dick, who is 'like to have a rare Wife o'thee' (III 32; act 2, scene 1), and equally mild concern for Corinna: 'Poor Child! we may do what we will with her, as far as marrying her goes' (III 63; act 5, scene 1). In presenting her character, Vanbrugh maintains a delicate balance between allowing Corinna to be dismissed as a comic gull and allowing her to be pitied as an innocent, if comic, victim, a balance he maintains for many of the characters in *The Confederacy*. When Mrs Amlet reveals her son's identity in act 5 only to provoke a response far more violent than she intended, it is Corinna who quickly joins her in defending Dick as he is threatened with the cudgel and the pump: 'Look you, *Flippanta*, I can hold no longer, and I hate to see the young Man abus'd. And so, Sir, if you please, I'm your Friend and Servant, and what's mine is yours, and when our Estates are put together, I don't doubt but we shall do as well as the best of 'em' (III 72; act 5, scene 2). Corinna's romantic attachment to a soldier with an assumed identity who declares his passion in comic hyperbole – and its result – looks forward as much to Sheridan's Lydia Languish as it looks back to Congreve's Miss Prue.

Peter Lewis is right, I think, in arguing that 'Vanbrugh was intent on keeping alive the satirical mainstream of seventeenth-century comedy descending from Ben Jonson,'[28] but Vanbrugh's handling of that mainstream tradition noticeably alters its course in the process. Dick's scheme and Brass's place in it set up a framework that resembles Jonson's in *Volpone*. Most of the plotting we see is performed by Brass, and many of the best lines are his, too. And like Mosca, Brass suddenly confronts his master with unexpected demands at a crucial point in the plot when he has the chance to make or break Dick's fortune. First he reminds Dick of the many subservient roles he has played in furthering Dick's numerous crooked schemes. Terms follow:

BRASS. ... Look you, Sir, some Folks we mistrust, because we don't know 'em: Others we mistrust, because we do know 'em. And for one of these Reasons I desire there may be a Bargain beforehand: If not [*Raising his Voice*] look ye, *Dick Amlet* –
DICK. Soft, my dear Friend and Companion. The Dog will ruine me. (*Aside*) Say, what is't will content thee?
BRASS. O ho.

DICK. But how can'st thou be such a Barbarian?

BRASS. I learnt it at *Algier*.

DICK. Come, make thy *Turkish* demand then.

BRASS. You know you gave me a Bank-Bill this Morning to receive for you.

DICK. I did so, of Fifty Pounds, 'tis thine. So, now thou are satisfy'd; all's fixt.

BRASS. It is not indeed. There's a Diamond Necklace you rob'd your Mother of e'en now.

DICK. Ah you *Jew*.

BRASS. No words.

DICK. My dear *Brass*!

BRASS. I insist.

DICK. My old Friend.

BRASS. *Dick Amlet (Raising his Voice)* I insist.

DICK. Ah the Cormorant – Well, 'tis thine. But thou'lt never thrive with't.

BRASS. When I find it begins to do me Mischief, I'll give it you again. But I must have a Wedding-Suit.

DICK. Well.

BRASS. Some good Lace.

DICK. Thou sha't.

BRASS. A stock of Linnen.

DICK. Enough.

BRASS. Not yet – a silver Sword.

DICK. Well, thou sha't have that too. Now thou hast every thing.

BRASS. God forgive me, I forgot a Ring of Remembrance. I wou'd not forget all these Favours for the World: A sparkling Diamond will be always playing in my Eye; and put me in mind of 'em.

DICK. This unconscionable Rogue! (*Aside*) Well, I'll bespeak one for thee.

BRASS. Brillant.

DICK. It shall. But if the thing don't succeed after all? –

BRASS. I'm a Man of Honour, and restore.   (III, 49–51; act 3, scene 2)

Even if Vanbrugh had Mosca's demand for half of Volpone's fortune in mind when he enlarged Dancourt's version of this exchange, he did not recapture the spirit of his Jonsonian model any more than Farquhar was to do in presenting a similarly uneasy moment in the working relationship of Archer and Aimwell. Volpone refuses to accept Mosca's terms in part because they are not equals: everything that Mosca has become he owes to his master, a genuine Venetian Magnifico. Farquhar alters the nature of the relationship by making his protagonists Restoration wits and men about town of the same background, right down to identifying them both

as younger brothers. Vanbrugh follows his source in making both Dick
and Brass characters of a lower social class, aspirant to the middle-class
status and comfort of the city scriveners, Gripe and Moneytrap. The son
of a pedlar who is 'a Gamester' to boot and his 'Companion' who 'passes
for his *Valet de Chambre*' (III 12) but was in fact his 'School-fellow' and
'Fellow-Prentice' are necessarily going to be engaged in activities far different from those of members of the aristocracy – and their parasites – or
members of established, upper-middle-class families, just as their goals
and aspirations differ. The similarity to Jonson in spirit – as opposed to
structure – is to the Jonson of city comedy,[29] the Jonson of *Eastward Ho!*;
still more similar in spirit is the later city comedy of Jonson's 'sons,' such
as Fletcher and Brome.

Vanbrugh began with a play about the middle class and intensified its
class character: 'l'insistance de Vanbrugh souligne la stupide prétention de
sa bourgeoise et renforce l'impact satirique et comique.'[30] The principal
concerns of most of the characters focus on money and social status. And
in enlarging the roles of the servants, Vanbrugh extends his social commentary to reflect the more fluid nature of early eighteenth-century
English society. Dick and Brass are not the only characters attempting to
climb the social ladder. Mrs Amlet has saved ten thousand pounds in order
to make her son respectable. And in the main plot, the behaviour of the
city wives is determined by their pretensions to higher places. Clarissa, in
particular, affects the attitudes of her betters – as she understands them –
in order to try to make herself one of them:

CLAR. Fey: A Woman must indeed be of a mechanick Mold, who is either troubled
or pleas'd with any thing her Husband can do to her. Prithee mention him no
more; 'tis the dullest theme.   [III 19; act 1, scene 2]

...

CLAR. ... Quality always distinguishes it self; and therefore, as the Mechanick People buy things, because they have occasion for 'em, you see Women of Rank
always buy things, because they have no occasion for 'em. Now, there, *Flippanta*,
you see the difference between a Woman that has breeding, and one that has
none.   [III 27; act 2, scene 1]

...

CLAR. And as this kind of Life, so soft, so smooth, so agreeable, must needs invite
a vast deal of Company to partake of it, 'twill be necessary to have the decency
of a Porter at our Door, you know.
GRIPE. A Porter – a Scrivener have a Porter, Madam?
CLAR. Positively, a Porter.

GRIPE. Why no Scrivener since *Adam* ever had a Porter, Woman!
CLAR. You will therefore by renown'd in Story, for having the first, my Life.

[III 56–7; act 4, scene 1]

Critics continue to agree with Dobrée that Vanbrugh's version is 'more realistic and racy of urban life [sic],' and that he substitutes a 'burly volubility, which makes his characters live in the world of flesh and blood rather than in the imaginary self-contained world of French comedy' (III, 3–4). This is an accurate description of one crucial difference between Vanbrugh and Dancourt, but it also points to an important way in which Vanbrugh resembles Farquhar in creating a comedy that is perceived as more realistic than the comedy that preceded it – just as it is perceived as more realistic than the comedy of Dancourt. There is no need to question the many critics who share this perception about what they mean by 'realistic' or whether their perception is accurate; the very fact that they share it and that they tend to look back to the plays of Shakespeare and his contemporaries for antecedents is indicative of the change in comedy at the turn of the eighteenth century. (It remains curious that critics call 'more realistic' a play in which the son of a pedlar fails in his scheme to marry an heiress but is saved in the end by his mother's fortune; *The Beaux Stratagem* is another curious choice for realism since the resolution depends on the death of an elder brother, the unexpected appearance of a second brother, and a divorce-like arrangement impossible in law.)

Vanbrugh's characters in general, and his humours in particular, share the same tendency as Farquhar's to be relatively rounded and softened: the force of the play's satire is not directed at particular characters. Since there are neither the traditional wits – or even *honnêtes hommes* – of post-Restoration comedy nor the exemplary heroes and heroines of later eighteenth-century comedy, there can hardly be satiric targets who will stand out in a crowd. Vanbrugh's characters are more homogenized in their social and moral functions. Even the most traditional humours are modified by Vanbrugh, as he had done in his original plays in such characters as Lord Foppington and Sir John Brute. (In other words, Dancourt cannot be given full credit for provoking Vanbrugh's variations on stock character types.) Gripe and Moneytrap, the aging cits with young wives, are given less sympathetic treatment than Sir John or Lord Foppington. Neither is given the opportunity – say, in soliloquy – to develop individual character traits to win special understanding or sympathy; both remain two-dimensional tight-fisted citizen-husbands. But neither is cuckolded, and both, in fact, offer additional evidence in support of Vanbrugh's ongoing hypothesis that since marriage is difficult under the best conditions, most marriages are necessarily going to be troubled. By making each husband the admirer of the other's wife, Vanbrugh was able to achieve an effect similar to Dryden's in the comic plot of *Marriage À-la-Mode*. And by using city scriveners as his gallants, he defused more thoroughly the potential for unpleasant consequences. The audience knows all along that there will be no adultery in this play. Despite structural similarities, the world of *The Confederacy* is a long way from that of *Epsom-Wells* or Ravenscroft's *The London Cuckolds*.

Neither the city wives nor the servants are new character types, but they, too, reveal trends in early eighteenth-century comedy. Araminta and Clarissa are characterized as 'expensive, luxurious Wom[e]n' and 'great Admirer[s] of Quality' and thus share in the gentle satire on middle-class pretensions. Their energies are, indeed, devoted to money and status – and not sex. And in conspiring against their lecherous husbands, they assume the roles of rogues in punitive comedy, out to cheat their husbands of the money they think is theirs by right. Since they are active agents rather than objects of the sexual attentions of rakes or town gallants, their confederacy provides an interesting example of how a punitive plot could be incorporated into humane comedy. Brass and Flippanta, too, are new variations on standard comic types that go back to ancient new comedy. As witty servants, they animate the various plots and schemes more thoroughly than their counterparts in most post-Restoration comedy. Here they resemble Jonson's servants, though the immediate inspiration was no doubt from Dancourt and the French tradition in which servants play a more active role in plots. But in treating seriously the relationship between Brass and Flippanta, Vanbrugh follows such examples as Congreve, whose Waitwell and Foible in *The Way of the World* are to be rewarded with a small farm to grace their married life together. In giving many of the best lines to his servants, Vanbrugh points the way to plays like *The Conscious Lovers*; Steele's innovations were not as extraordinary as some of his critics have taken them to be.

The least traditional character in *The Confederacy* must surely be Dick's mother, that 'mighty useful Woman,' Mrs Amlet (III 65; act 5, scene 1). Working-class people, even those who have more or less climbed to middle-class status, rarely appear in post-Restoration comedy except to ply their various trades. In those rare cases where they are treated individually – Dorimant's orange woman, for example – they are clearly kept apart from and subservient to their betters. Mrs Amlet is sufficiently humble to know her place, but she is also immensely ambitious for the son she dotes on. And Vanbrugh allows her to realize her ambition when

Dick is established in a class higher than her own. Arthur Huseboe sees the other significant aspect of Mrs Amlet's character as 'something entirely new on the English stage – the fondly doting mother who is so much in love with her son's good looks – his shape, his nose, his cherry lip – that nothing matters but his success and her vicarious delight in it.'[31] Though nothing is entirely new on the stage, Mrs Amlet does seem to be an early example of the doting mother who pays for her fondness, which includes Goldsmith's still more memorable Mrs Hardcastle. Vanbrugh's sympathetic treatment both of Mrs Amlet and of her aspirations is a sign of the new openness to social mobility in early eighteenth-century comedy, even in a writer like Vanbrugh, many of whose attitudes are aristocratic, and even in a play where the satiric thrust of the plot is directed against the foibles of the bourgeoisie.

Huseboe is also right, I think, in considering *The Confederacy* Vanbrugh's 'most intricately plotted' play.[32] There are two distinct plots, but they are so intricately entwined that they almost create the illusion of one single plot. The play is so entirely set in the city that location alone provides a kind of unity extending far beyond the traditional meaning of the unity of place. Mrs Amlet is a frequent visitor to Clarissa, one of her better customers, and Dick has chosen the same household to provide his future bride. Clarissa and Araminta are 'very intimate' with each other, as neighbours and sister-sufferers of the lecherous brother-scriveners. Clarissa encourages Dick's addresses to her stepdaughter, Corinna, and she and Araminta find her maid, Flippanta, and Dick's servant, Brass, essential in their confederacy, as do their husbands in their respective seduction plans. Brass and Flippanta both help Dick in his pursuit of Corinna, and each, of course, anticipates the pleasure of establishing a more permanent, secure relationship with the other. An especially happy example of the tightly unified plot of *The Confederacy* is the use made of the diamond necklace. It is given to Mrs Amlet in pawn by Clarissa, stolen by Dick from his mother, promised by Dick to Brass, pawned by Brass to keep Dick's scheme afloat, brought by the goldsmith Clip to Gripe, where it reveals both the wives' confederacy and Dick's assumed identity. This is a fine piece of farcical plotting that Vanbrugh carried over from Dancourt. (Goldsmith, too, uses jewels this way in *She Stoops to Conquer*.)

As a good-natured, light-hearted exposure of the foibles of the middle class and those who aspire to that status, *The Confederacy* is also held together by common formal and thematic concerns. The love of money and the corruption it engenders informs both plots, along with the desire of most of the characters to better themselves socially; the main exceptions are Gripe and Moneytrap, who are held back by the fear that such improvement will prove too costly. Dobrée adds to this list the 'two things Vanbrugh most loved to dwell on, marital quarrels and low life, either as exhibited in the lives of valets and servants (those in *The Confederacy* as developed unrecognisably beyond Dancourt's), or as illustrated by the countryman or country gentleman of his time' (I, xxiv).

Both plots consist of the schemes and trickery of traditional punitive comedy; in both cases, Vanbrugh follows the lead of Congreve in *The Way of the World* and *Love for Love*, while anticipating Farquhar in not allowing his largely sympathetic characters to achieve their goals by trickery. The plots are resolved neatly together with the almost simultaneous exposures of both the wives' confederacy and Dick's identity. These rogues are not allowed an indefinite licence for success in cheating their gulls like several of their post-Restoration predecessors, but they are also not punished for their sins like most of Jonson's rogues. The small-time vice of this play is good, clean fun until its inevitable revelation. Vanbrugh here shares in the growing tendency to use farce to soften the impact of punitive comedy by keeping the stakes very low. Farce thus replaces punitive comedy in a theatre where sympathetic comedy becomes humane, exemplary, or sentimental.

Farce serves a similar function in the comedies of Colley Cibber, the playwright still frequently singled out for having 'ushered in the age of the sentimental.'[33] Cibber's reliance on farce, however, is in many ways less surprising than Vanbrugh's, in part because of his actor's approach to pleasing an audience, and in part because, like Farquhar, he considered the plot or fable – not the characters and the dialogue – as the 'Centre' of his plays 'towards which every Line ... ought to be drawn.' Cibber's reasons, like Farquhar's, are steeped in the best tradition:

If we can say of your finest Sentiments, This, or That might be left out, without maiming the Story you would tell us, depend upon it, that fine thing is said in a wrong Place; as though you may urge, that a bright Thought is not to be resisted, you will not be able to deny, that those very fine Lines would be much finer, if you could find a proper Occasion for them: Otherwise you will be thought to take less Advice from *Aristotle*, or *Horace*, than from the Poet *Bays* in the *Rehearsal*, who very smartly says – *What the Devil is the Plot good for, but to bring in fine things?*[34]

Again, as with Farquhar, Cibber's emphasis on plot and fable allowed him to justify his breaks with the practice of such playwrights as Dryden and Etherege on grounds of traditional comic theory.

Since its initial performance, *The Double Gallant* has provoked controversy among Cibber's critics over his use of sources. The issue was, from the first, the appropriateness of calling the play 'a New one.' Cibber defended himself at the time, and thirty-three years later still felt the need to defend himself:

[*The Double Gallant*] was a Play made up of what little was tolerable in two, or three others, that had no Success, and were laid aside, as so much Poetical Lumber; but by collecting and adapting the best Parts of 'em all, into one Play, the *Double Gallant* has had a place, every Winter, amongst the Publick Entertainments, these Thirty Years ... I have been often treated as a Plagiary on that Account: Not that I think I have any right to complain, of whatever would detract from the Merit of that sort of Labour; yet, a Cobler may be allow'd to be useful, though he is not famous: And I hope a Man is not blameable for doing a little Good, tho' he cannot do as much as another?[35]

Cibber's disingenuous attempt to circumvent the question of originality failed, and the issue remains an active one today. The three plays Cibber cobbled together, William Burnaby's *The Reform'd Wife* (1700) and *The Ladies Visiting Day* (1701) and Susanna Centlivre's *Love at a Venture* (1706), contribute considerably to his text. (Centlivre's source for her play, Thomas Corneille's *Le Galant double*, provided a title and perhaps the occasional phrase or line.) F.W. Bateson determined that the borrowing is so extensive that 'more than a quarter of *The Double Gallant* is taken over from Burnaby's two comedies, word for word'; he later concluded that this is one of the two plays by Cibber that 'deserve to be dismissed as plagiarisms.'[36]

Bateson's conclusion raises some difficult questions, especially as elaborated in his early article: 'Hazlitt, who is on the whole Cibber's most discriminating admirer, has given high praise to *The Double Gallant*. "The characters, he says, are well kept up: Atall and Lady Dainty are the two most prominent characters in this comedy, and those into which Cibber has put most of his own nature and genius. They are the essence of active impertinence and fashionable frivolity." The praise is not undeserved. But the credit for Atall and Lady Dainty is really due, not to Cibber, but to Mrs. Centlivre and Burnaby. Cibber was only their *impressario*.'[37] Cibber, no doubt, would not dispute his role as impressario; he might well, however, retain claim to much of the credit. His sources were failures; he had the good taste to recognize that there was much of value in Burnaby's plays, despite the audiences' neglect of them. And if Centlivre had little luck with a good French source play, Cibber profited from her attempt. The result seems to me no less original than *The Amorous Widow*, *The Countrey Wit*, *Amphitryon*, or *The Confederacy*. This does not make it 'original' in the sense that it sprang forth from Cibber's brain without assistance; nonetheless, Cibber performed his cobbler's role effectively enough to create a repertory mainstay from three forgotten failures.

Cibber does lift passages – even scenes – from Burnaby, but he is very careful in picking and choosing among his sources. His Lady Dainty, complete with her fashionable hypochondria and resistance to a worthy suitor, is taken directly from *The Reform'd Wife*, but the resolution of her courtship, her marriage to her lover disguised as a Muscovite prince, comes from *The Ladies Visiting Day*. The latter play also contributes Sir Testy Dolt (Cibber's Sir Solomon Sadlife), the wealthy cit who has moved to the fashionable 'end of the Town' where he tries to prevent his young wife from making him a cuckold while attempting to profit from the wedding of his niece. *The Ladies Visiting Day* also provides Lady Dainty with her secondary humour, a passion for exotic goods and fashions; Cibber transfers this trait from Burnaby's Lady Lovetoy to his Lady Dainty, and lifts a number of lines in the process. He also borrows almost verbatim Sir Testy's dismissal of his niece's three suitors. But in grafting Burnaby's plays together, and linking them to the main plot of Centlivre's in place of the subplots she appended to Corneille's, Cibber produced a play that is very much his own. The tone and ethos are closer to Centlivre than Burnaby, though the latter provided more plagiarized lines. But the particular combination of elements, finally, is more like Cibber, that is, more like his 'original' plays, than either of his sources.

Two examples should provide representative evidence. Burnaby's Sir Testy has allowed the suitor of his niece Fulvia, to be near her because he has been misled by Polidore into believing that he had been castrated in Italy by ruffians in a quarrel over an Italian noble's mistress. Fulvia ultimately gains her freedom by disguising herself as a young soldier and offering Sir Testy £1000 to marry his niece. When her offer is accepted, she challenges her 'rival,' Polidore, meets him for a duel, reveals her identity, and then agrees to marry without Sir Testy as intermediary. Cibber eliminates the Wycherleyan trickery – Wycherley is close in spirit to Burnaby but quite distant from Cibber – by transferring the courtship of the niece from Polidore to the *honnête homme*, Clerimont. And in the linking of this action to Centlivre's, Fulvia becomes Clarinda, the lively, proud, and imperious object of Atall's as well as Clerimont's attention. The grafting of the two plays is effected with considerable skill, and the result is true to none of its originals.

The main plot of *The Double Gallant*, from Corneille via Centlivre, is explained in the opening dialogue between Clerimont and the title character, his friend, Atall. In it, Atall explains how he has come to pursue two women under different false identities, while trying to avoid the marriage his father has arranged for him with an unknown third woman. Centlivre's Bellair (Atall) refers to one of his mistresses, Camilla (Silvia), as 'a perfect Venus.' Cibber develops her metaphor in Atall's explaining how he observed the newest object of his affections while returning from Greenwich:

By the most fortunate Misfortune sure that ever was: For as we were shooting the Bridge, her Boat, by the negligence of the Watermen running against the Piles, was over-set; out jumps the Footman to take care of a single Rogue, and down went the poor Lady to the bottom. My Boat being before her, the Stream drove her, by the help of her Cloaths, towards me; at sight of her I plung'd in, caught her in my Arms, and with much ado, supported her till my Waterman pull'd in to save us. But the charming Difficulty of her getting into the Boat, gave me a Transport that all the wide Water of the *Thames* had not the power to cool: For, Sir, while I was giving her a lift into the Boat, I found the floating of her Cloaths had left all her lovely Limbs beneath, as bare as new-born *Venus* rising from the Sea.   [1.1.52–64

Atall then contrasts Sylvia with his other new mistress, Clarinda: 'One's my *Juno*, all Pride, and Beauty; but this my *Venus*, all Life, Love, and Softness' (1.1.88–9). The development of both anecdote and metaphor, needless to say, is not from Centlivre, and they are representative of the liberties Cibber takes with his sources. When Atall next meets Clerimont, he again asks for help, having found that his Juno and his Venus are cousins, – whom he has met at the house of a third woman, Lady Sadlife, who has caught his eye. Clerimont agrees to help, concluding tentatively: 'For I dare swear thou doest not design to marry any one of 'em.' Atall's response, 'Shou'd my *Incognita*'s [Sylvia's] Birth prove equal to her Beauty, I tremble to tell thee what might become of me" (3.2.77–80). He thus assures the audience of his pure and honourable intentions. (In the opening scene, too, Atall insists, over Clerimont's sceptical response: 'I am honourably in Love; and if she proves the Woman I am sure she must, will positively marry her' (1.1.13–15)). The use of rakish language stripped of all consequences reproduces that observation of the letter of the moral law without regard for its spirit that Cibber boasts of so casually in the epilogue to *Love's Last Shift*, addressed to the 'Gallants':

> Now, Sirs, To you whose sole Religion's Drinking,
> Whoring, Roaring, without the Pain of Thinking,
> He fear's he's made a Fault you'll ne'er forgive,
> A Crime beyond the Hopes of a Reprieve:
> An honest Rake forego the Joys of Life!
> His Whores, and Wine! t'Embrace a dull chaste Wife.
> Such out-of-fashion Stuff! But then again,
> He's lew'd for above four Acts, Gentlemen![38]

Cibber's desire to please both rake and Collierite continues to infuriate critics today. Both the shape of the whole and the effect of many of its component parts are not to be found in Burnaby or Centlivre; *The Double Gallant* is Cibber's own.[39]

Hazlitt was clearly right in identifying Atall and Lady Dainty as 'the most prominent characters.'[40] Not surprisingly, Cibber wrote Atall for himself. Atall quickly establishes himself as a throwback to the extravagant rake of the early plays. Like Crowne's Ramble or Mountfort's Young Reveller, he has an insatiable, indiscriminate appetite for women. He explains his response to Lady Sadlife to his man, Finder, in language reminiscent of that of Etherege's Dorimant or Wycherley's Horner: 'Well, I find 'tis as ridiculous to propose pleasure in Love without variety of Mistresses, as to pretend to be a keen Sportsman without a good Stable of Horses: We may talk what we will, but I say we Love, as we Hunt, for Pleasure, and he's likeliest to see most of the Sport I'm sure, that has a good Lead Nag in the Field: How this Lady may prove I can't tell, but if she is not a Deedy Tit at the bottom, I'm no Jockey' (3.2.8–14).

Atall's omnivorous tastes and his apparent inability to match his talk with action make him more like Ramble and his predecessors than most subsequent young men with rakish dispositions. One antecedent Cibber must have had in mind while writing *The Double Gallant* was Dryden's Celadon from *Secret Love*, a role he had played earlier in 1707 in another of his cobbled plays, *The Comical Lovers*, an amalgam of the comic plots of *Secret Love* and *Marriage À-la-Mode*. Atall's pursuit of Sylvia and Clarinda, and especially the rivalry it provokes in the cousins, recalls Celadon's simultaneous courtship of Melissa's daughters, Sabina and Olinda, who are contrasting character types like Atall's 'Venus' and 'Juno'. But

Atall differs from his predecessors in having declared his honourable intentions in the first scene; his subsequent declarations are qualified by the knowledge that his greatest desire is to find that his 'Incognita' is an appropriate mate. Characters like Celadon or Etherege's Sir Frederick Frollick in *The Comical Revenge* – that is, the extravagant rakes of the 1660s – resemble such predecessors as Fletcher's Mirabel in the innocent exuberance of their relationships with women. Later plays rarely exhibit such innocence in their characters until well into the eighteenth century, even when the action is as pure as that of *The Double Gallant*. It is as if Atall is a Celadon with the sensibility of Mountfort's Young Reveller – though his actions are, of course, wildly different – that is, a comic hero reconstituted from the various characters, such as Celadon and Young Reveller, that Cibber inherited from Mountfort himself. Cibber generously expresses his admiration for Mountfort in his *Apology*, where he indicates the extent of his debt to him in the acting of many of Mountfort's former roles. He observes that 'the *agreeable* was so natural to him, that ev'en in that dissolute Character of the *Rover* he seem'd to wash off the guilt from Vice, and give it Charms and Merit. For tho' it may be a Reproach to the Poet, to draw such Characters, not only unpunish'd, but rewarded; the Actor may still be allow'd his due Praise in his excellent Performance.'[41] In Atall, Cibber seems to have attempted to retain the appeal of agreeable dissolution without having to undergo the reproach for rewarding genuine dissolution. The audience is safe to enjoy Atall's frenzied womanizing, secure in the knowledge that he will marry Sylvia; his other relationships will remain unconsummated.

When Cibber constructed his Lady Dainty from Burnaby's character of that name and his Lady Lovetoy, he was probably again echoing his recent encounter with Dryden in putting together *The Comical Lovers*; his combining her hypochondria with her passion for things exotic and subsuming both under the desire to appear a 'Woman of Quality' (3.1.252), recall Dryden's Melantha with her passion for all things French and persistent desire to be recognized at court. Cibber wrote the part for Anne Oldfield, who inherited most of the comic roles of Susanna Mountfort (later Verbruggen) after her death, and in some cases, after the retirement of Anne Bracegirdle. Susanna Mountfort, like her husband, made a lasting impression on Cibber, as the 'Mistress of more Variety of Humour, than I knew in any one Woman Actress,' and nowhere more profoundly than as Melantha:

Melantha is as finish'd an Impertinent, as ever flutter'd in a Drawing-Room,

and seems to contain the most compleat System of Female Foppery, that could
possibly be crowded into the tortur'd Form of a Fine Lady ... The first ridiculous
Airs that break from her, are, upon a Gallant, never seen before, who delivers
her a Letter from her Father, recommending him to her good Graces, as an
honourable Lover. Here now, one would think she might naturally shew a little of
the Sexe's decent Reserve, though never so slightly cover'd! No, Sir; not a Tittle of
it; Modesty is the Virtue of a poor-soul'd Country Gentlewoman; she is too
much a Court Lady, to be under so vulgar a Confusion ...[42]

Cibber's description extends another half page, lovingly detailing Mountfort's mannerisms as Melantha, his very relish revealing the new attitude
toward humours. This is one female fop it is impossible to dismiss without
sympathy – even affection. Her very folly disarms criticism by its charm.
Lady Dainty shares most of her character traits and provokes the same
response; there is no attempt to disguise her shortcomings or downplay
them, but they are so enjoyable that the traditional response of punitive
comedy no longer seems appropriate. Careless is able to trick her into
marrying him, but this is one trick marriage in which there are no victims;
the marriage seems in their mutual best interest. (Vanbrugh's Clarinda
offers an interesting contrast. She shares Lady Dainty's affected sense of
place in society, but she is firmly planted in the middle class of her scrivener husband. She is an amusing character not without charm, but though
less affected than Lady Dainty she is also less sympathetically portrayed.
Cibber's design is clearly less satirical than Vanbrugh's.)

Cibber's reluctance to condemn his characters extends even to such traditional comic butts as Sir Solomon and Lady Sadlife. Sir Solomon shares
with Farquhar's Justice Ballance the split response that results from serv-
ing two rather different functions, though the balance between sympathetic and punitive is reversed. He is largely the blocking father-figure,
trying to gain as much money as possible from the marriage of his niece.
In this role, he recalls the avaricious villains of Middleton and Massinger,
but money is never a serious issue in Cibber's play, and Sir Solomon
remains at best a pale copy of his more forceful predecessors; he is not
even up to the villainous standards of similar figures in the plays of Behn
or Durfey. Sir Solomon's potential as a villain is undercut by the two
scenes Cibber appropriated from Burnaby in which Sir Solomon effectively disposes of the only traditional punitive butts in the play, the three
additional suitors for Clarinda – the *miles glorious* Captain Strut, the city
miser Sir Squabble Splithair, and the family-proud but impoverished
Saunter. It is still more fully undercut by the third role Cibber adds to Sir

Solomon's character, that of an old husband worried about being cuck-olded by his young wife. Here he resembles characters like Congreve's Fondlewife, rightly jealous but nonetheless ready to believe the best. Like Burnaby, Cibber exaggerates his situation by turning to *The Country-Wife*, but rather than Sir Jaspar Fidget, Pinchwife provides the model for his action. When his wife pretends that Atall's letter is really addressed to her maid, Sir Solomon is so eager to embrace this sham that he assists his wife and Wishwell, the maid, in producing a very syrupy and very encouraging reply. But Sir Solomon's gullibility produces no horns. Atall's plans are frustrated by the traditional early return of the husband in time to interrupt the intended seduction. Sir Solomon is tricked out of his niece and a share of her portion, but nothing comes of his wife's desire for a lover. There is no reform on her part and no resolution of this part of the action. Much the same can be said of Cibber's source, but Burnaby makes it explicitly clear in the final scene of his play that Lady Dolt regrets not having consummated her affair with Polidore. Lady Sadlife is strangely silent as Cibber again softens traditional humours characters. Much of the uncertainty in characterization here comes from Cibber's sources, especially Burnaby, and from the use of a single character to fulfil so many plot requirements. The lack of resolution seems more the result of incoherence than design, but Cibber has, nonetheless, rounded these characters where possible in order to weaken the traditional satiric responses they inspire. Once again a turn-of-the-century dramatist inte-grates the traditions of Jonson and Fletcher at the cost of the more strongly punitive elements.

Like *The Confederacy, The Double Gallant* is a busy play, full of farcical action. And like Farquhar, Cibber exhibits humour, not wit, in his charac-ters. Nor does Cibber allow himself long passages of repartee. But he is more traditional than such contemporaries as Farquhar and Vanbrugh in maintaining a full plot with a number of semi-independent lines; his plun-dering of three plays rather than one or two demonstrates his agreement with Dryden that English audiences require great variety in their enter-tainments. And he is justifiably pleased with the craftsmanship of his cob-bling, though the unity he achieves is more at the material and efficient levels than the formal or final. Just as he minimized the punitive elements of Jonsonian comedy, he also downplayed the balance, pattern, and sym-metry of the Fletcherian plot. Atall pursues Sylvia, Clarinda, and Lady Sadlife simultaneously. He asks his friend Clerimont for assistance in his amours, without realizing that Clarinda is also the woman Clerimont loves. And Sir Solomon is both the jealous husband of one of Atall's mistresses and the uncle of another. Careless and Clerimont are friends; Lady Dainty is a friend of both Sylvia and Lady Sadlife. Sir Solomon is also a friend of Sylvia's father, Old Mr. Willful. The characters are from a single extended social circle, and there is remarkably little tension between old money and new. Sir Solomon has moved from the city to the fashionable part of town to please his wife, but aside from his reluctance to indulge her in her every desire, no problems arise. There is no question, in other words, of the kind of barrier to such a move that Vanbrugh clearly envisaged in ridiculing Clarissa's desire for a porter. It is interesting how quietly Cibber is able to effect the kind of middle-class melting pot Steele lobbied for so noisily in *The Conscious Lovers*.

Cibber follows his sources and many of his predecessors in balancing the lively Atall with the *honnête homme*, Clerimont, and the lively Clarinda with the less colorful Sylvia, in each case pairing a lively lover with a more proper one. But there seems to be little design in linking the title action with the Sadlifes' marital-discord action and still less in including Careless's courtship of Lady Dainty. It is as if Cibber is observing the traditional forms without recognizing their original significance. It is not surprising, then, that the more simple and straightforward plots of Farquhar and Vanbrugh come to prevail as the eighteenth century progresses. Cibber's 'original' plays are rarely constructed with so little attention to a sense of the whole. A.H. Scouten, following Bateson, has identified their central concern as 'the reconciliation of a married couple who have drifted apart.'[43] I find it particularly telling that in *The Double Gallant* the state of the Sadlife marriage is dropped without resolution as a dramatic issue barely halfway through the play.

Cibber's original plays usually have at least one very clear moral tacked on at the end, unselfconsciously (shamelessly, according to his critics) and without apology – as opposed to the more self-conscious clumsiness of, say, Mountfort in *Greenwich-Park*. But in *The Double Gallant*, Cibber seems almost systematically to avoid confrontations with serious issues. Marital discord is raised, but quickly dropped. Fortune-hunting, too, is a potential issue, but Careless's interest in Lady Dainty's fortune is merely the motive to justify the aging bachelor's acceptance of matrimony, and Atall's disguise as Colonel Standard, unlike Dick Amlet's Colonel Shapely, is taken on merely to enable him to avoid his father's notice. Greed and avarice, too, are raised as issues, but remain similarly of minor import. Most of the themes that dominate other contemporary comedies are to be found in *The Double Gallant*, but they remain undeveloped. It is difficult to disagree with Robert Hume's conclusion that 'Cibber does a slick job of piecing together standard elements: the results are good theatre entertainment but indifferent drama.'[44]

Like her friend George Farquhar, Susanna Centlivre was aware of the need to come to terms with the demands of post-Collier audiences in London. Like Farquhar, she speaks of the theatres as 'Schools of Divinity and Morality' where comedy ridicules 'Folly, Intemperance, and Debauchery' in order to encourage the pursuit of 'the opposite Virtues.' Again like Farquhar, whose 'Discourse upon Comedy' she must have known, she also recognized the need to entertain in order to instruct: 'The Design of this Piece [*The Gamester*] were to divert, without that Vicious Strain which usually attends the Comick Muse, and according to the first intent of Plays, recommend Morality.'[45] And recommending morality was no more a didactic endeavour for Centlivre than for Farquhar. Rather, it meant keeping the moral attitudes represented in her plays in line with the standards imposed by her audience, especially by sanitizing dramatic language to free it of the growing number of words and phrases that were no longer tolerated in the theatre.

Since Centlivre also shared Farquhar's view of humours, she could, contrary to the Jonsonian view above, minimize their satirical function; overt didacticism was once again out of the question. Instead, stage bustle and the display of amiable humourists dress a traditional comic plot in a way that pleased the English-speaking world for the next two hundred years; *The Busie Body* was 'the most frequently performed comedy at Covent Garden between 1747 and 1776,' and one of 'only four non-Shakespearean comedies written before 1750 ... still being performed regularly in Britain and America' by 1900.[46] The plot formula of *The Busie Body* provides a splendid textbook example of new comedy: two pairs of lovers must overcome the opposition of blocking parents in order to marry. (It would be hard to find a better play to exemplify Frye's 'mythos of spring.'[47]) Centlivre's play is unencumbered by the kinds of open-ended questions Farquhar raises in his last two plays. And there are few distractions from the basic love plots of *The Busie Body*, except, of course, for Marplot.

Few critics have doubted that the key to Centlivre's success in *The Busie Body* was the title character. Centlivre herself quickly confirmed the point by providing a sequel called *Marplot: or, The Second Part of the Busy Body* (1710), though like most sequels, it rightly was denied the long-term success of her earlier effort. Marplot has no real function in the plot structure of *The Busie Body*, except, perhaps, that of a would-be fifth

business who impedes rather than furthers the love plots. Marplot is typical of the new approach to humours characters favoured by the writers of
humane comedy. Marplot's instinct for interfering with an otherwise
well-conceived plot is in itself not unprecedented. Centlivre's likely inspiration, Dryden and the Duke of Newcastle's title character in *Sir Martin
Mar-all*, and their two sources, Quinault's Cleandre in *L'Amant Indiscret*
and Molière's Lélie in *L'Étourdi*, shares his tendency to undo clever love
schemes. Marplot is simple, impetuous, and slow-witted; in earlier comedies he would undergo a Jonsonian punishment or learning experience or
both. But Marplot's weaknesses, unlike Sir Martin's (though more like his
French sources) are not presented as deficiencies requiring correction. His
curiosity is tied to what Arthur Murphy described as 'his favourite passion for doing good,' the motivating factor that justifies all. Thus, when
Murphy summarizes Marplot's character, what emerges is anything but a
traditional humour: '[He is] under one and twenty, a gentleman, and of a
good fortune; keeps the best company; honest in his passions; of manners
not inelegant, at least not underbred; no swords-man, good-natur'd, and
ever eager for opportunities ... of proving his regard for his friends, and he
is ever officious in their service.'[48] A far cry, in other words, from Dryden's Sir Martin. F.W. Bateson captures the difference well in his discussion of Centlivre's use of sources: Marplot is no 'mere copy. He wears his
folly with a difference. He is absurd, but he is never, like Sir Martin, contemptible.'[49]

Centlivre helps ensure Marplot's amiability by two changes in his function in the plot. In Dryden's sources, Quinault's and Molière's blunderers
(to use Samuel Foote's translation of *l'étourdi*) pursue and are allowed to
win one of the heroines, despite repeated follies, through the aid of a witty
servant. Dryden rewards his servant-figure Warner with the heroine
rather than turn her over to a fool. Centlivre makes Marplot less tedious
by allowing him only three chances to interfere with his friends; repeti-
tion contributes to Sir Martin's contemptibility. And Centlivre also
removes Marplot from direct involvement in courtship. Neither Miranda
nor Isabinda must suffer his attentions or spend the rest of her life with
him. This latter change, in particular, facilitated the transformation of a
Restoration fool into a new and endearing character. The likeable Marplot
is the most memorable character in *The Busie Body* and the one who
attracted the skills of the best eighteenth-century comic actors. Without
him, it is unlikely the play would have enjoyed its considerable success.[50]

Though Marplot is, as Hazlitt calls him, 'the whimsical hero of the
piece,' *The Busie Body* remains a comedy of 'intrigue'[51] in which Marplot

is only a marginal character. (As early as 1719, Giles Jacob declared that Centlivre's 'Talent is comedy, particularly in the Contrivance of the Plots and Incidents.'[52]) The 'plots' here consist of the parallel courtships of Sir George Airy and Miranda, and of Charles and Isabinda. Each must overcome the objection of the father/guardian of the ladies, and, in Charles's case, of his father, too. Centlivre follows the pattern of other writers of humane comedy in maintaining a tightly unified plot at the material and efficient levels. The milieu of the play is especially uniform in that all the characters belong to the same segment of the middle class; even town and city values do not separate characters here. Sir Francis Gripe is Charles's father as well as the guardian of both Miranda and Marplot. His interest in Miranda makes him the rival of Sir George, Charles's close friend. Miranda and Isabinda, likewise, are close friends; Miranda sent Patch from her own household to become Isabinda's woman. Sir George and Charles help each other with their respective love plots, and Marplot interferes with both.

The two love plots are closely parallel; their juxtaposition provides much of the formal unity in the play by creating the 'uniform telos' of Centlivre's comic world: 'happiness through married love with financial security.'[53] Centlivre's values are assumed rather than argued; the full force of the traditional comic plot structure is her chief enforcer. Interest is maintained by the mechanics of the intrigues rather than by their outcome, which is always a foregone conclusion. For Bateson, the play is characterized by 'vitality and technical *finesse*' without 'intellectual or literary significance'; he considers it 'the most remarkable comedy of intrigue in English.' For Hume, its 'ultra- formulaic ... utterly representative' use of 'stock materials' is the source of its success, though he sees 'the form but not the spirit of Carolean social comedy ... [a] sterile intrigue comedy, with no sex, little passion, and little satire.'[54] Their disagreement is typical of the (limited) critical debate about Centlivre's comedies. What they are or how they work or what they mean is not the issue; instead, the value of the emerging formulaic humane comedy is the only genuine issue, as it is in the following pair of similarly opposed views: 'Mrs. Centlivre was one of those writers who have what is known as "a sense of the theatre" and little other sense at all ... *The Busy-Body* (1709) is an empty comedy of intrigue, without any reality of emotion whatsoever.' Alternatively, '*The Busie Body* is a much finer play [than Centlivre's earlier comedies], one of the masterpieces, indeed, of this type [intrigue comedy].'[55] *The Busie Body* is devoid of virtually any problematic or open-ended issue. Centlivre develops humane comedy, especially through intrigue and humour, in a direction that gradually leads to such better known and more highly regarded plays as *The Rivals* and *She Stoops to Conquer*. In formal outline, these plays are very similar indeed.

Richard Cumberland, in his notes to *The Busie Body*, suggests that *Love for Love* served as the source for the Miranda–Sir George Airy courtship.[56] If so, the borrowing is only of the most general sort, but a comparison is nonetheless instructive. Miranda's guardian, Sir Francis, motivated largely by self-serving greed, wishes to marry her himself in order to retain her £30,000. Miranda encourages his advances, and his trust along with them, to prepare for the trick that will win her her freedom with her money. Like Congreve's Angelica, she gains control of the necessary papers that allow her to marry the man of her choice. But where Angelica tested an already committed Valentine to the limit before accepting him, Miranda's testing of Sir George is perfunctory. She abandons her 'incognita' disguise, revealing her identity to him in act 4; she had long before assured the audience of her 'Choice' when she referred to him as such to Patch.[57] Sir George seems the less certain of the two, but only because he fails to realize that the two women who interest him are in fact one. In earlier intrigue plots, like several of Dryden's or *Greenwich-Park*, the heroine uses her disguise to test her lover's fidelity. If this is Miranda's purpose, she abandons it in act 1; the only thing she really tests in the play is his wit – and an impartial observer might well claim that he fails the test, though she is pleased with her find: 'Sir *George* is what I have try'd in Conversation, inquir'd into his Character, am satisfied in both' (4.4.p51). The result is the virtual elimination of the moral depth found in *Love for Love*.

Because Sir Francis is motivated more by greed than by dotage, and more by either than by the desire to have his way, he is closer in spirit to the Puritan aldermen of the earlier plays than to Sir Sampson Legend. His exchanges with Miranda, punctuated by the pet names 'Chargee' and 'Guardee,' recall Fondlewife and Laetitia ('Nykin' and 'Cocky') more than Sir Sampson and Angelica, but Sir Francis never shows signs of subordinating his interest to his love. His refusal to forgive and forget – 'Confound you all!' (5.4.p71) are his final words as he storms off at the end of the play – almost hints at the proto-melodramatic Sir Giles Overreach in Massinger's *A New Way to Pay Old Debts* as he came to be interpreted toward the end of the eighteenth century. Sir Francis' intransigence and the refusal of the servants to joint in wedlock are the only remotely shrill notes at the end of the play:

CHAR. Here's no Body but honest *Whisper* and Mrs. *Scentwell* to be provided
for now. It shall be left to their Choice to Marry, or keep their Services.
WHISP. Nay then, I'll stick to my Master.
SCENTW. Coxcomb! And I prefer my Lady before a Footman.
SIR JEAL. Hark, I hear Musick, the Fidlers smell a Wedding. What say you, young
Fellows, will ye have a Dance?   (5.4.p72)

Sir Jealous's call for a dance points to the thoroughly comic resolution
to the other, equally traditional plot. In it, Charles Gripe must not only
recover his own fortune but also win Isabinda against the wishes of her
father, Sir Jealous Traffick, who, because he 'had liv'd some time in Spain'
is so 'great' an 'Admirer of the Spanish Customs' that he plans to marry
Isabinda to a Spanish husband. His humour, as F.P. Lock has observed,
seems modeled on that of James Formal in Wycherley's *The Gentleman
Dancing-Master* (1672),[58] though it has been slightly softened. Charles
tricks Sir Jealous out of his daughter by disguising himself as her Spanish
intended. J.W. Bowyer thinks it possible that Centlivre used 'the disguise
of Courtine' in *The Ladies Visiting Day* or 'the disguise of Careless as
Prince Alexander' in *The Double Gallant* as her model for Charles's masquerade – 'if a source for masquerading in an intrigue drama is necessary.'[59] It is pleasing to think that Centlivre repaid Cibber in kind for his
appropriation of *Love at a Venture*, but the evidence is, alas, insufficient.

Charles is certainly a pale copy of most of his dramatic predecessors. A
young man at odds with his father over money, with a 'Liberal Education'
and a familiarity with the fashions and the town, he is nonetheless rarely
allowed more than a few general expressions of what would have been
called wit and is reduced to despair by the impending marriage of Isabinda
to Don Diego Babinetto before Patch suggests the masquerade. Isabinda is
similarly ineffective, unwilling to marry an unknown Spaniard but unable
to take effective action. And her inability to recognize Charles almost
undermines his masquerade. All of this makes for good stage comedy, as
the play's popularity indicates, and it makes no more sense to decry
Centlivre's play because it is not, say, *Love for Love* than to decry Congreve for not being Shakespeare. Centlivre uses the comic conventions of
the 1670s and 1690s, but creates from them a very different comedy from
what pleased audiences a generation or two earlier. As the subsequent criticism demonstrates, critics are divided in their appreciation of eighteenth-
century comedy – though rarely in their understanding of it. Centlivre is
one of the earliest playwrights of acknowledged importance on whose
works the effects of this critical shift can be seen.

This study began with the 1670s Jonsonian comedy of Thomas Shadwell. It ends, too, with a Shadwellian comedy, but his time by Thomas' son Charles, who, as Nicoll points out, 'on setting up as a dramatist, quite naturally embraced the Jonsonian style.'[60] But after nearly a generation of humane comedy, Thomas Shadwell's Jonsonian style is no longer recognizable even in the first play by his own son. 'I have taken care to show Vice in such a manner, as to make every body abhor it, and have used all my stock of Understanding to make Virtue shine out in full Glory,' Shadwell claims in the dedication to his collected plays.[61] The claim is, of course, one that was made by virtually every playwright in the seventeenth and eighteenth centuries, including Shadwell, Sr. But when made for *The Fair Quaker of Deal*, it is an honest and accurate claim, and one that points to a new development in punitive comedy that brings it full circle, at least in its operating principle.

Shadwell's play is subtitled *The Humours of the Navy*, and the first two characters listed in the Dramatis Personae are Commodore Flip, 'a most illiterate *Wappineer*-Tar' who 'hates the Gentlemen of the Navy, gets drunk with his Boats-Crew, and values himself upon the Brutish Management of the Navy' and Mizen, 'a finical Sea-Fop, a mighty Reformer of the Navy,' who 'keeps a Visiting-day, and is *Flip*'s Opposite.'[62] These deliberately contrasting extremes are the only developed humours in the play, Shadwell drawing on his personal experience to produce what John Loftis describes as 'the plays about military life which seem most authentic in circumstantial details.'[63] Shadwell's desire to represent a recognizable portrait of the Navy in Queen Anne's time in all its extremes is in line with the increased appreciation of English eccentricity as a manifestation of English liberty. Even Her Majesty's Navy reflects the national character and must tolerate the considerable variety of humours found within it.

What distinguishes *The Fair Quaker of Deal* from the other punitive comedies or plays with humours is the determined imposition of the reformation of vice and folly on the traditional characters and structures of English comedy. Thomas Shadwell did not expect to reform his humours; they provided negative examples for us to reject. And Congreve, especially in a character like sailor Ben, and Farquhar in, say, Captain Brazen, did not emphasize the moral deficiencies of their humours; hence, they did not have to worry about reforming them. But Charles Shadwell applies a rigid version of poetical justice to his comedy. Vice, as a result, is either punished or reformed or both.

'Beau' Mizen, as he is called, has the effrontery to pretend to the eponymous heroine, Dorcas Zeal, though she is the intended of his captain, the hero, Worthy. Worthy plots the standard revenge for Mizen's affront, a trick to marry him off to a whore disguised as Dorcas. But instead of allowing the marriage to take place, as Congreve did Tattle's to Mrs Frail, Shadwell instead follows Congreve's pattern in *The Old Batchelour*; Mizen, like Heartwell, is saved by a false ceremony, performed by a disguised Lieutenant Cribidge. By the end of the play, reform replaces revenge as Worthy's motivating principle:

WOR. No Murmurs, thou knowst how thou deserved'st it.
MIZ. Touch my past Shame no more, I'm a true Penitent.   (5.2.p60)

Flip's offence is not so personal as Mizen's, other than that of providing disagreeable company on the voyage the sailors have just completed. In earlier comedy, his brutishness would have been sufficient cause for punishment, another mock marriage to a whore. But Worthy again is more noble, more humane in his behaviour:

WOR. And for thee *Flip*, I knew thee such a Rake, that the least mad drunken fit would run thee headlong into irrevocable Shame and Ruin, and therefore even for they meer Preservation, I put this innocenter Cheat upon thee, only to stand a Warning Sea Mark to thee, against all future Shipwrecks on this Quick-sand.
FLIP. By *Neptune* and by *Mars* thou art a brave Fellow.   (5.2.p60)

And Shadwell is not content merely to correct his humours. Worthy's scheme was a more complete one that allowed for the reform not only of Mizen and Flip, but also of the whores, Jenny Private and Jiltup. In forcing Flip and Mizen to buy their way out of their marriages, Worthy equips the whores with the money they need to achieve a long-desired escape from a life of sin:

WOR. Well, tho' I have made your Purses smart a little, you see I have made you do some good in your Generation; put a helping hand to two poor Sinners Conversion.
FLIP. Ay, and my own Conversion too. Hence forward I'll keep such honest Fellows as thee Company; cast off my old dull rascally Conversation, and learn good Sense and Manners.
MIZ. Nay, dear *Worthy*, take one new Convert more; for from this Hour. I'll play the Effeminate Fool no more; but bare the Face of a Man like thee, strip my fop

Cabin of all my China Bawbles, Toys for Girls, and shew my self a true Hero for my Glorious Queen.

Wor. Nay now, dear Gentlemen, you'll make me proud of this Days happy Work.

(5.2.p61)

I quote at length to help convey the commitment on Shadwell's part to spell out his moral in full and witless detail. A comparison to the ending of *Epsom-Wells* shows the extraordinary difference between father and son. Even the more 'humane' Congreve frees Heartwell from Silvia with jokes rather than lectures, and provides Angelica's moral with enigmatic wit rather than ingenuous earnestness.

Given the development of humours theory from Ben Jonson to Farquhar, it is somewhat surprising to find Shadwell's basic acceptance of the humane and patriotic concept of humours in a plot that reforms those same humours to improve their morals. Either Shadwell's commitment to a conception of 'natural' naval humours was only superficial, or he failed to think through the implication of reformable humours for the new idea of national character: English eccentricity itself must only be skin deep if it is so readily reformed. Later in the century, Baker's untroubled confrontation of this problem suggests how its resolution could be accomplished without great difficulty by Shadwell's audience; his is an interesting near-contemporary view of *The Fair Quaker*, with the benefit of another generation's development of the amiable humourist: '[Though it has] no extraordinary merit in point of language; yet the plot of it is busy and entertaining, and the contrast between the rough brutish tar, and the still more disgustful sea-fop, in the characters of Commodore Flip and Beau Mizen, is far from being a bad picture of the manners of some of the sea-faring gentlemen even of this age; at the same time that their ready reformation, on being convinced of their errors, is a just compliment to the understanding of a set of men, who are the greatest glory of Britain, and the terror of all the rest of Europe.'[64]

It was not the humours, however, who were most responsible for the initial success of Shadwell's play. Rather, that credit must go to the title character as created by Hester Santlow. Cibber provides a fine, if condescending, firsthand account of the initial production of a play he himself had rejected – and then offered to 'alter' in order 'That it might pass for one of his.'[65] Cibber places Shadwell's triumph in the context of hard times for the theatres because of the competition for audiences provided by the Sacheverel trial. Because the 'better Rank of People' were at the trial, Shadwell's was just the right play for what audience remained:

This Play, having some low Strokes of natural Humour in it, was rightly calculated, for the Capacity of the Actors, who play'd it [Cibber, of course, did not], and
to the Taste of the Multitude, who were now, more dispos'd, and at leisure to see it:
But the most happy Incident, in its Fortune, was the Charm of the fair Quaker,
which was acted by Miss *Santlow,* (afterwards Mrs. *Booth*) whose person was then
in full Bloom of what Beauty she might pretend to: Before this, she had only been
admired as the most excellent Dancer ... The gentle Softness of her Voice, the com-
pos'd Innocence of her Aspect, the Modesty of her Dress, the reserv'd Decency of
her Gesture, and the Simplicity of the Sentiments, that naturally fell from her,
made her seem the amiable Maid she represented.[66]

Shadwell's initial success was no doubt due in part to the discovery of a
new star; his play made Santlow's career as an actor. But Cibber's description of her performance, of the qualities she conveyed, also points to a
new kind of comic heroine. Dorcas Zeal is sincere in her adherence to her
religion. She is not, like many of the heroines in plays written shortly
after the Restoration, forced to pretend to nonconformity by Puritan parents or guardians. Nor is she, like Fielding's Quakers, a hypocrite. Instead,
she embodies Quaker ideals of simplicity and directness in a way that
audiences accepted as charming or admirable.

Dorcas is as direct as Farquhar's Silvia, and more earnest. When she
learns of the return of her intended, like Silvia, she summons him. It is
her Anglican sister and rival who resorts to reprehensible deception in her
unsuccessful attempt to win Worthy for herself. Dorcas's early response
to her sister's selfish attempt to get her to abandon her interest in him is
to offer her hand to Worthy the first chance she gets:

DOR. Sister, to show thee that I think it is impossible for thee to debauch the
Principles of my Friend *Worthy;* I now commit myself into his Hands.
WOR. Which Blessing I receive with all the Joy imaginable. This is a Reward
indeed for all my Services.
DOR. Take to thy self my Hand, and thus I plight it with my Faith. Now Sister
your Threatning Words were vain, for all your Looks and Sighs can never
take him frome me.   (1.2.p12)

There is very little indeed in Worthy or Dorcas to recall the witty lovers of
the earlier comedy, even the lovers of Shadwell, Sr. What tension the love
plot offers results from Arabella's schemes to convince her gullible sister
that Worthy is unfaithful and thus not good enough for her. Since Dorcas
is a very open, trusting woman, she is taken in by schemes as lame and

conventional as forged documents and disguised suitors, schemes so obvious that they have no real chance of success. Their failure in act 5 leads to the easy reconciliation of Dorcas and Worthy; Arabella then accepts her long-standing suitor, Sir Charles Pleasant ('*Worthy*'s Lieutenant, a Man of Quality'), more a reward than a punishment for her attempt to deny the principals their happiness. But so benign is the comedy of Charles Shadwell that neither long-term suffering nor punishment is allowed. Not for Shadwell the unresolved tension of Centlivre's Sir Francis; poetical justice requires universal reformation and closure.

Shadwell's unusual attention to poetical justice only enhances his more representative use of a simple, easily unified plot structure. The society Shadwell portrays is homogeneous: Arabella and Dorcas are sisters and both friends of Belinda. The men are almost all in the Navy; the only important exception is Worthy's friend Rovewell, described in the 'Dramatis Personae' as 'a Gentleman of Fortune, and true Lover of the Officers of the Navy.' Rovewell and Belinda offer a couple similar to Worthy and Melinda in *The Recruiting Officer*, though Shadwell again removes the harder edges. Belinda is a 'Woman of Fortune' who has withstood two years of honourable courting merely out of good-natured contrariety. When Dorcas, Worthy, and Sir Charles shame her into accepting Rovewell, her exchange with Rovewell reveals how little genuine concern their prolonged courtship occasions:

BEL. Had *I* not some Inclinations, your Force and Threats should never do. Here, *Rovewell*, take my Hand; I hope for better usage from you than you have received from me.
ROVE. Oh my *Belinda!* one pleasing Look makes amends for all my Pains and Agonies.   (4.1.p41)

The play ends, then, with three easily accomplished matches, Worthy and Dorcas, Sir Charles and Arabella, and Rovewell and Belinda. But most of the play's energy comes not from its love plots but from the marriages that never take place and the machinations behind them: Flip, Mizen and their whores, and Worthy and Arabella. Since the lovers are almost all involved in the various punitive actions, too, Shadwell has no trouble keeping his play unified at the efficient as well as the material level. Formal unity is a more difficult problem, however. Strict poetical justice does not encourage more abstract thematic coherence; nor does the display of humours. Complex issues are either simplified or avoided. At the end of the play, after the dances, Dorcas gratuitously converts to the Established

Church with a logic less than compelling: 'Well, Dear *Worthy*, since I have heard the affected Sanctity, and friendly Cant; not only from my Sister *Arabella* but even from that carnal Vessel of Pollution; to make our Marriage Yoke more chearful still, from this blest Hour I'll join thy holy Worship' (5.2.p63). Shadwell does everything possible to ensure a soothing ending, one that will not cause undue distress or thought in his audience. *The Fair Quaker of Deal* manages to unite the Jonsonian with the Fletcherian in a manner so thoroughly amiable as to remove the traditional challenges and most of the rewards of both forms. The result points the way to many lighter, justly neglected eighteenth-century comedies. It is not a play – or form – without its rewards, as its long success on the stage affirms, but it does point to the kinds of changes that occur in even the most conservative of literary genres, stage comedy.

Conclusion

In a typically clear and succinct statement, Alastair Fowler summarizes the most frequently employed means of generic change: 'The processes by which genres change are the same as those that produce most literary change ... Those that stand out may be identified as: topical invention, combination, aggregation, change of scale, change of function, counter-statement, inclusion, selection, and generic mixture. No doubt there are others; but these would be enough in themselves to cover the main changes known to literary history.'[1] A fuller summary might consider the impact of what have often been considered extraliterary factors, such as, for Restoration comedy, the Popish Plot and Exclusion Crisis or the Collier controversy. As the chaos theory of the new physics makes clear, altered conditions in remote and unexpected places can affect otherwise stable and orderly systems in surprising and unpredictable ways. But even after opening the avenues of change to include all known possible agents, the inescapable conclusion from the evidence of the horizon offered by the plays is that generic change is not great in the fifty-year period after the Restoration.

This does not, of course, mean that there is no change in the drama, as a survey of Fowler's 'processes' makes clear. But the changes are on a reduced scale, either at the level of mode or subgenre.[2] Topical invention is a recurring favourite device of playwrights. Unhappy marriage, for example, is a traditional subject for comedy, largely through the exposure of the difficulties inherent in arranged marriages, especially of the January-May variety. The cuckolding of elderly city husbands with witty young wives by town rakes provided a standard topic that could be varied in an almost infinite number of ways without effecting major generic change. Husbands become more sympathetic (Fondlewife); wives repent their behaviour (Mrs Raison). Shadwell makes both members of the unhappy couple young and witty; Farquhar borrows substantial passages from Milton's divorce tracts to encourage social change. Even the limited selection of plays discussed in this study reveals the range of invention employed by comic writers without, nonetheless, their altering the fundamental nature or structure of English comedy.

The same pattern holds for Fowler's other processes. Combination 'is most obvious at the assembly stage,'[3] and stage comedy was assembled long before the Restoration. Other forms such as the novel and the essay are undergoing their processes of assembly; Fletcher and Jonson had already institutionalized mature comedy half a century earlier. Aggregation, like combination, had occurred before the Restoration. In fact, there is considerable impetus to purify rather than add to the aggregate. Three-level, hierarchical plots, still common in the 1660s, are narrowed by the end of the century. (Split-plot tragicomedies, too, become virtually extinct during the same period.) The result may well have impoverished the English stage by eliminating attractive and interesting options from the realms of possibility open to new playwrights, but elimination itself did not alter the nature of comedy.

Changes of scale and function are more prominent in the comedy of the period, but their effects, too, are not great. It is not until well into the eighteenth century that the introduction of short, heavily farcical plays (Otway's *The Cheats of Scapin*, Tate's *A Duke and No Duke*, Farquhar's *The Stage-Coach*) has a strong impact on the stage. And even they are unable to break down an institutional genre like comedy. Change of function can be seen in every play I have looked at here. It is difficult to find a play that does not partake of the 'gradual change of function [that] is probably perpetual.' It is, as Fowler argues, sometimes deliberate, sometimes not, but always there. He considers the seventeenth century one particularly drawn to 'an aesthetic preference for altering function.' But while such variations do have 'a cumulative effect in changing genres and loosening them,'[4] in the case of comedy, the institutional nature of the genre allowed for changes far more radical before they posed serious threats to its established structure. Counterstatement, too, is limited in this period, largely to burlesque (*The Rehearsal*), a form that 'exaggerates generic features to absurdity, or juxtaposes them with contraries.' Burlesque, unlike genuine anti-genres, depends upon a host form for its significance; it does not develop a generic life of its own.[5] Inclusion, the embedding of one work within another, is similarly limited. There are few play-within-plays or masques in post-Restoration plays, and still fewer (if any) that make major generic contributions. Most common is the inclusion of songs, used in an increasingly complex and effective way by Purcell and his contemporaries, but even the short-lived fashion for operatic accretions failed to undermine the dramatic structure of English comedy.

Finally, generic mixing and hybridization, frequently preached against in the criticism, is practiced less rather than more frequently as the century ends. Comedy is rarely as pure as critics like Rymer would have preferred, but it is also rarely as mixed as it had been at the time of Fletcher and Jonson. Hybridization, too, is limited to small effects: changing values in tragedy, most noticeably the change from heroic to pathetic, are echoed in comedy as comic villains, for example, pose more serious threats to heroes and heroines than earlier comedies had allowed,[6] but no new hybrid develops to take the place of the mixed-plot tragicomedy used so effectively by Dryden. Change abounds, then, in late seventeenth-century comedy, but the mature institutional genre is sufficiently resilient to incorporate that change at the level of mode and subgenre without allowing the major transformations these processes so often accomplish on other genres.

One of the stronger claims Jauss makes for constructing a horizon of expectations in order better to understand the nature of historical reception is that it enables the twentieth-century critic to measure the distance between a new work and the horizon at the time of its reception as evidenced in such responses as 'spontaneous success, rejection or shock, scattered approval, gradual or belated understanding.'[7] He is able to offer a convincing explanation for the sensational contemporary success of Feydeau's *Fanny*, a largely forgotten novel that appeared in the same year as Feydeau's friend Flaubert's *Madame Bovary* (1859).[8] It should be clear from this study that such dramatic examples are not to be found among late seventeenth-century comedies. It is difficult to name a single example of a work widely held in regard today that was rejected by its Restoration audience. *The Way of the World* (1700) was not the smashing success we think it should have been, but success it was by contemporary standards. It was not forgotten in the early years of the eighteenth century and by 1718 had been adopted for regular performance by Wilks (Mirabell), Booth (Fainall), Cibber (Witwoud), and Oldfield (Millamant); between 1721 and 1762 it was performed at least once every year. It is, of course, always possible that a neglected masterpiece will be discovered: Otway's *Friendship in Fashion* (1678), Lee's *The Princess of Cleve* (1680), and Southerne's *Sir Anthony Love* (1690) and *The Wives Excuse* (1691) seem the most likely candidates. But even they are most unlikely to equal *Madame Bovary* in belated reputation.

Spontaneous success is a routine occurrence in theatre history. All of the plays in this study enjoyed considerable success for many years. Others' successes were far more short-lived, such as Shadwell's *The Sullen Lovers* (1668), Ravenscroft's *Mamamouchi, or The Citizen Turn'd Gentleman* (1672), Steele's *The Lying Lover* (1703), and Centlivre's *Marplot* (1710). *Marplot* enjoyed the short-lived success of a hasty sequel that cashes in on a superior original. Other short-term successes such as the burlesque parodies of Thomas Duffet (*The Empress of Morocco* (1673), *The Mock-Tempest* (1674), and *Psyche Debauch'd* (1675)) depend on the popularity of another play for their interest. *The Sullen Lovers* quite probably owed its popularity to its send-up of Sir Robert Howard as Sir Positive At-all. Still others, perhaps *The Lying Lover* or Centlivre's *The Basset-Table* (1705), simply went the way of many a best seller, pleasing its audience but not holding their interest for long. There are, then, few sensations like *Fanny* and fewer victims of outraged rejection like *Madame Bovary*. Challenges to established beliefs or principles rarely exceed commonly tolerated limits, and most of those that do are quickly censored. Failure to please cost the playwright dearly, and few, it seems, were willing to take that risk. The horizon of expectations was always broad enough to absorb new plays without serious disturbance. The repertory system kept the most popular old plays in front of audiences and playwrights; managers had little incentive to take risks. What emerged was a very conservative institution, but one of almost limitless flexibility within its chosen boundaries.

English comedy, as a result, undergoes continuous change, but change so institutionalized, so systematized that it never challenges the large structure of comedy, however freely it experiments with topical subject matter and character types or modal forays into other literary realms. Large-scale change in comedy requires far more than fifty years. The tradition of Jonson and Fletcher proved sufficiently rich and challenging to maintain a prospering generic institution. The eighteen-play sample I have examined demonstrates the adaptability of that mixed tradition that allowed it to continue to flourish.

During the fifty-year period of this study, comic theory – as seen in the representative work of Shadwell, Congreve, and Farquhar – undergoes a nearly revolutionary change as the nature of both the parts (humour, wit, action, language) and the whole (affective and educative ends) respond to radical challenge. The subject matter of comedy alters both in focus and treatment. Plays based on a dominant social code, a comic equivalent to the code of honour of the heroic play, gradually yield to plays that look instead to the kind of moral values so greatly admired in Renaissance comedy. Among the most visible casualties are the Restoration rake, and, along with him, the standard victims of comedies of the 1670s. A willingness to treat the middle class more thoughtfully encourages the return to citizen comedy, though in a new way. These changes coincide with the loss in popularity of multiple plots – especially hierarchical plots – and the increasing use of what have always been seen as more 'realistic' lines of action. The triumph of the subgenre humane comedy most clearly signals the kinds of changes encouraged – and discouraged – in the comedy of the early eighteenth century. Plays like Farquhar's, in many ways the most representative humane comedies, are highly traditional: it is difficult to find an element in them not also found in the tradition of Jonson and Fletcher. When Kenny describes them, she does so (rightly) in relative terms. They are 'a distinct mode,' not a new genre. They are 'far broader, less subtle, less harshly satirical' and 'increasingly believable in characterization and dialogue.'[9] Rather than any single component part, it is the cumulative effect that produces the sense of change. Older comedies continued to be performed throughout the eighteenth century, but the plays of Congreve, Vanbrugh, Cibber, Farquhar, and Steele dominated English comedy until late in the century. They were always seen as comedies, but they were seen as comedies sufficiently different from their predecessors and rivals to alter the standards of comedy irreversibly. The fact that Congreve and Farquhar continue to hold pride of place on the stage among the comic writers of the period points to a difference still perceived by actors, directors, and audiences today.[10]

But the examination of comic horizons by cross-section that occupies most of this study points even more to continuity than to change. The repertory system, with its emphasis on revivals, served as a constant buffer against rapid or extreme change. And most playwrights then, as today, were content to work within existing structures. Genuine innovators are always few, and perhaps fewer when there is no premium placed on newness. The pressure for change tended instead to come from without, to bring comedy in line with ever-changing social values. Such change, with its concern for ideas and their manifestation in plot and character is subgeneric; form is not its concern so long as it can respond to changing ideas. The discussions of the eighteen plays in chapters 2, 3, and 4 should again affirm that change can be explained by a comic model based on an ongoing dialogue between Jonsonian and Fletcherian comic structures. If so, what emerges most clearly is the remarkable stability of a great, durable, and responsive institution, English stage comedy.

Notes

CHAPTER ONE

1 A.H. Scouten 'Notes toward a History of Restoration Comedy' *Philological Quarterly* 45 (1966) 62–70 and 'Plays and Playwrights' in *The Revels History of Drama in English* V *1660–1750* (London: Methuen 1976) 159–229; Robert D. Hume *The Development of English Drama in the Late Seventeenth Century* (Oxford: Clarendon Press 1976)

2 Claudio Guillén *Literature as System: Essays toward the Theory of Literary History* (Princeton NJ: Princeton Univ Press 1971) 130, 111

3 Firmat attempts to separate 'historical' from 'theoretical' genres. The study of the former looks at 'genres as they happen in history, as they are articulated in history.' A historical genre 'can be regarded as a set of norms that has governed the reading and writing of literature at some time in the past or present' ('The Novel as Genres' *Genre* 12 (1979) 279). I comment on Firmat's distinction more fully below.

4 Stephen Orgel 'Shakespeare and the Kinds of Drama' *Critical Inquiry* 6 (1979) 109

5 John Dryden et al *Notes and Observations on 'The Empress of Morocco'* (London 1674) rpt in *'The Empress of Morocco and Its Critics,'* intro Maximillian E. Novak (Los Angeles: Clark Library 1968) sig a1^{r}; Thomas Rymer *A Short View of Tragedy* in *The Critical Works of Thomas Rymer* ed Curt A. Zimansky (New Haven: Yale Univ Press 1956) 145

6 John Dryden 'An Essay of Dramatick Poesy' in *The Works of John Dryden* XVII ed Samuel Holt Monk et al (Berkeley: Univ of California Press 1971) 73. Q1 reading. Richard Elias suggests that Dryden altered the Q1 reading from 'blown upon' to 'us'd' in response to Buckingham's parody in *The Rehearsal*: 'I have a new [play], in my pocket, that I may say is a Virgin; 't has never yet

been blown upon' ('"Bayes" in Buckingham's *The Rehearsal*' *English Language Notes* 15 (1978) 178–81).

7 John Dryden 'Preface' *An Evening's Love* in *The Works of John Dryden* X ed Maximillian E. Novak and George Robert Guffey (Berkeley: Univ of California Press 1970) 205; Thomas Shadwell 'Preface' *The Humorists* in *The Complete Works of Thomas Shadwell* ed Montague Summers (London: Fortune Press 1927) I 187

8 Clayton Koelb 'The Problem of "Tragedy" as a Genre' *Genre* 8 (1975) 260, 262

9 R.S. Crane 'History versus Criticism in the Study of Literature' in *The Idea of the Humanities and Other Essays Critical and Historical* (Chicago: Univ of Chicago Press 1967) II 8

10 Firmat 279

11 Ibid 274–84

12 Robert D. Hume's discussions of the range of theories of comedy and tragedy in the late seventeenth century make this point emphatically. See *The Development of English Drama* chaps 2 and 4.

13 Paul Hernadi *Beyond Genre: New Directions in Literary Classification* (Ithaca NY: Cornell Univ Press 1972) 3–4. And Hernadi considers varying response only across time. I do not share his confidence in an 'Ideal Critic' even for a limited period.

14 Koelb 254–5

15 See Sheldon Sacks 'The Psychological Implications of Generic Distinctions' *Genre* 1 (1968) 106–15 and Ralph W. Rader 'The Literary Theoretical Contribution of Sheldon Sacks' *Critical Inquiry* 6 (1979) 189–90.

16 Alastair Fowler *Kinds of Literature: An Introduction to the Theory of Genres and Modes* (Cambridge MA: Harvard Univ Press 1982) 38

17 In one of the most influential treatments of genre, R.S. Crane defined literary forms as 'species of works, inductively known, and differentiated, more or less sharply, in terms of their peculiar artistic elements and principles of construction' ('Critical and Historical Principles of Literary History' in *The Idea of the Humanities* II 59). My ideas about literary forms are clearly indebted to Crane, and to this essay in particular. But I agree with a number of more recent critics who challenge Crane's outdated scientific model, a model that masks what Adena Rosmarin calls the 'ineluctably deductive' procedures of genre criticism, procedures she details in a discussion of Crane and Todorov in *The Power of Genre* (Minneapolis: Univ of Minnesota Press 1985) 29–33. My quotation is from 33.

18 Guillén 120–2. Or, as Fowler puts it, 'genre ... is a communication system for the use of writers in writing, and readers and critics in reading and interpreting' (256).

19 Elder Olson *The Theory of Comedy* (Bloomington: Indiana Univ Press 1968) 89

20 Guillén 121

21 Koelb 252

22 Fowler 111–18

23 I disagree, for example, with the position taken by Laura Brown that 'greater priority' should be given to 'major' works since 'the best works are more representative of their genre and of their period than minor or average works, because they come closer to fulfilling the potential of their form.' See *English Dramatic Form 1660–1760: An Essay in Generic History* (New Haven CT: Yale Univ Press 1981) xiv

24 Guillén 131; Fowler 255

25 Glynne Wickham, for example, claims that 'any careful reading of the evidence relating to English religious drama between the late tenth and the early sixteenth centuries reveals unmistakably that as drama existed to postulate and propagate Roman Catholic doctrine, so that drama inevitably drew its structure from doctrine; and granted a doctrine of redemption obtainable through repentance, this drama was thus, inescapably tragi-comic. And later comedy and tragedy must be regarded as grafts upon the native root-stock, imposed somewhat awkwardly, by a relatively small but very articulate and influential group of bookmen' (*Early English Stages 1300 to 1600* III *Plays and Their Makers to 1576* (London: Routledge and Kegan Paul 1981) 178

26 Henri Bergson 'Laughter' in *Comedy* ed and trans Wylie Sypher (Garden City NY: Doubleday 1956) 59–190; Sigmund Freud *Jokes and Their Relation to the Unconscious* trans James Strachey *The Standard Edition of the Complete Psychological Works of Sigmund Freud* ed James Strachey et al VIII (London: Hogarth Press 1960); Eric Bentley 'Farce' in *The Life of the Drama* (New York: Atheneum 1964) 219–56 and 'The Psychology of Farce' in *'Let's Get a Divorce' and Other Plays* (New York: Hill and Wang 1958) vii–xx; Paul Goodman *The Structure of Literature* (Chicago: Univ of Chicago Press 1954) 82; Bernard Shaw 'The Farcical Comedy Outbreak' in *Our Theatres in the Nineties* (London: Constable 1932) II 118–24

27 Northrop Frye 'The Argument of Comedy' in *English Institute Essays 1948* ed D.A. Robertson, Jr (New York: Columbia Univ Press 1949) 58–9; Langer *Feeling and Form* (New York: Scribner's 1953) 331; Sacks *Fiction and the Shape of Belief: A Study of Henry Fielding with Glances at Swift, Johnson, and Richardson* (Berkeley: Univ of California Press 1964) 21

28 Dryden *Works* X 206.

29 *The Posthumous Works of William Wycherley, Esq.; in Prose and Verse* (London 1728) 7–8

30 Thomas G. Winner 'Structural and Semiotic Genre Theory' in *Theories of Literary Genre* ed Joseph P. Strelka. *Yearbook of Comparative Criticism* 8 (1978) 264; Guillén 385

31 Hans Robert Jauss urges a similar method for overcoming the opposition between synchrony and diachrony in order to produce a more viable literary history: 'It must ... be possible to take a synchronic cross-section of a moment in the development, to arrange the heterogeneous multiplicity of contemporaneous works in equivalent, opposing, and hierarchical structures, and thereby to discover an overarching system of relationships in the literature of a historical moment. From this the principle of representation of a new literary history could be developed, if further cross-sections diachronically before and after were so arranged as to articulate historically the change in literary structures in its epoch-making moments' ('Literary History as a Challenge to Literary Theory' in *Toward an Aesthetic of Reception* trans Timothy Bahti (Minneapolis: Univ of Minnesota Press 1982) 36. For a valuable critique of Jauss, particularly in the context of genre criticism, see Rosmarin 33–7.

32 Performance records are drawn from the *Index to the London Stage 1660–1800* comp Ben Ross Schneider, Jr (Carbondale: Southern Illinois Univ Press 1979).

33 See Shirley Strum Kenny 'Perennial Favorites: Congreve, Vanbrugh, Cibber, Farquhar, and Steele' *Modern Philology* 73 (1976) S4–S11. I have not included those plays from this period that entered the repertory after 1710.

34 In *Ben Jonson* III ed C.H. Herford and Percy Simpson (1927; rpt Oxford: Clarendon Press 1966) Induction ll 105–9. All my quotations of Jonson are from this edition.

35 James D. Redwine, Jr *Ben Jonson's Literary Criticism* (Lincoln: Univ of Nebraska Press 1970) xxvii. Robert E. Knoll also argues that 'Jonson was concerned with actions and their moral implications, and he was never as interested in the individuality of persons as he was in ideas' (*Ben Jonson's Plays: An Introduction* (Lincoln: Univ of Nebraska Press 1964) 44).

36 See Jonas A. Barish *Ben Jonson and the Language of Prose Comedy* (Cambridge MA: Harvard Univ Press 1960) 129, 218.

37 *The Complete Works of Samuel Taylor Coleridge* ed W.G.T. Shedd (New York: Harper 1854) VI 426

38 Goodman 82. The following discussion of punitive comedy – a form Jonson did not, of course, invent – draws heavily on Goodman.

39 Ibid 101

40 Dryden *Works* XVII 56; H. Harington 'To the Incomparable Mr. Fletcher, upon his Excellent Play, *The Wild-Goose Chase*,' in Rota Herzberg Lister ed *A Critical Edition of John Fletcher's Comedy 'The Wild-Goose Chase'* (New York: Garland 1980) 9; intro to *The Wild-Goose Chase* ed Lister lxxii

41 John Harold Wilson *The Influence of Beaumont and Fletcher on Restoration Drama* (Columbus: Ohio State Univ Press 1928) 7; Leech *The John Fletcher Plays* (London: Chatto and Windus 1962) 75; Emmett L. Avery and Arthur H. Scouten, intro to *The London Stage 1660–1800* pt 1, ed William Van Lennep (Carbondale: Southern Illinois Univ Press 1965) cxxviii

42 Lister xx

43 Leech *The John Fletcher Plays* 57, 48, 58

44 Kathleen M. Lynch *The Social Mode of Restoration Comedy* (1926; rpt New York: Biblo and Tannen 1965) 21

45 Wilson 7

46 *Works* X 206. For a fuller treatment of the theoretical positions of Dryden and Shadwell and their consequences, see my 'Thomas Shadwell and the Jonsonian Comedy of the Restoration' in *From Renaissance to Restoration: Metamorphoses of the Drama* ed Robert Markley and Laurie Finke (Cleveland OH: Bellflower Press 1984) 127–52.

CHAPTER TWO

1 Thomas Shadwell *Complete Works* I 254

2 Jonas Barish 288

3 Shadwell *Complete Works* I xciii; Colley Cibber *An Apology for the Life of Colley Cibber* ed B.R.S. Fone (Ann Arbor: Univ of Michigan Press 1968) 89

4 Shadwell *Complete Works* II 110 (act 1, scene 1). All quotations from *Epsom-Wells* are from this edition.

5 Rev of *The Dramatic Works of Thomas Shadwell, Esq. in Four Volumes* (London 1720) in *The Retrospective Review and Historical and Antiquarian Magazine* ed Henry Southern and Nicholas Harris, 2nd ser, 2 (1828) 71. The anonymous reviewer also notes that 'it is so rare for people to form their own opinions, or to examine into the validity of prevailing notions, that we must not be surprised to find the success of Dryden in ridiculing the pretensions of Shadwell has continued up to the present day ... Our author had a fair reputation in his day, and it will astonish many to hear that he deserved it' (55–6).

6 Eugene M. Waith *The Pattern of Tragicomedy in Beaumont and Fletcher* (New Haven CT: Yale Univ Press 1952) 105

7 James Sutherland *English Literature of the Late Seventeenth Century* (Oxford: Clarendon Press 1969) 124

8 Shadwell *Complete Works* I 183; Michael Alssid *Thomas Shadwell* (New York: Twayne 1967) 55, 175 n1

9 Alssid 60–1

10 See Hume 296.

11 Richard Levin *The Multiple Plot in English Renaissance Drama* (Chicago: Univ of Chicago Press 1971). The following discussion is greatly indebted to Levin's, particularly his methodology. Levin's discussion of ways to unify dramatic plots is especially valuable because (1) it offers a precise system for identifying the various kinds of unifying devices, and (2) it refuses to equate artistic value with unity. Quotations of Levin in the text are from this edition.

12 Alssid 59

13 Scouten *The Revels History* 195

14 Hume 284

15 Scouten 178

16 Katharine M. Rogers *William Wycherley* (New York: Twayne 1972) 40. See also Norman N. Holland *The First Modern Comedies: The Significance of Etherege, Wycherley, and Congreve* (Cambridge MA: Harvard Univ Press 1959) 43 and, for a more detailed discussion, W.R. Chadwick *The Four Plays of William Wycherley: A Study in the Development of a Dramatist* (The Hague: Mouton 1975) 25–6.

17 See, eg, Chadwick 22, Hume 278.

18 Anne Righter 'William Wycherley' in *Restoration Theatre* ed John Russell Brown and Bernard Harris (London: Arnold 1965) 73

19 See John Loftis *The Spanish Plays of Neoclassical England* (New Haven CT: Yale Univ Press 1973) 121–5.

20 See eg, Rogers 37, Scouten 195.

21 William Wycherley *Love in a Wood* 5.1.421–3 in *The Plays of William Wycherley* ed Arthur Friedman (Oxford: Clarendon Press 1979). All quotations from Wycherley's plays are from this edition.

22 Loftis 125; see also Virginia Ogden Birdsall *Wild Civility: The English Comic Spirit on the Restoration Stage* (Bloomington: Indiana Univ Press 1970) 108; Scouten 196.

23 Rogers 39

24 Gerard Langbaine *An Account of the English Dramatick Poets* intro John Loftis (1691; rpt Los Angeles: Clark Library 1971) II 443–6, 514

25 Louis Kronenberger *The Thread of Laughter: Chapters on English Stage Comedy from Jonson to Maugham* (New York: Knopf 1952) 65–6. See also Marvin Mudrick 'Restoration Comedy and Later' in *English Stage Comedy: English Institute Essays 1954* ed W.K. Wimsatt, Jr (1955; rpt New York: AMS Press 1964) 104; Righter 'William Wycherley' 112; Ronald Berman 'The Ethic of *The Country Wife' Texas Studies in Literature and Language* 9 (1967) 54; David Cook and John Swannell, intro *The Country Wife* (Manchester: Manchester Univ Press 1975) I vii–I viii

26 Birdsall 135

27 Dryden *Works* XVII 57, 61

28 Ben Jonson *Epicoene, or The Silent Woman* in *Ben Jonson* V ed C.H. Herford
    and Percy Simpson (1937; rpt Oxford: Clarendon Press 1965) 4.1.133–45.
    All quotations from *Epicoene* are from this edition.

29 Sutherland 117

30 David M. Vieth 'Wycherley's *The Country Wife:* An Anatomy of Masculinity'
    Papers on Language and Literature 2 (1966) 335; T.W. Craik 'Some Aspects of
    Satire in Wycherley's Plays' *English Studies* 41 (1960) 169; Rogers 59; Rose A.
    Zimbardo *Wycherley's Drama: A Link in the Development of English Satire*
    (New Haven CT: Yale Univ Press 1965) 147; Chadwick 129–30; Cook and
    Swannell xxxvii

31 Holland 84; R. Edgley 'The Object of Literary Criticism' *Essays in Criticism* 14
    (1964) 233

32 For accounts of the recent stage history of *The Country-Wife*, see Cook and
    Swannell I xviii–I xix. My own experience in the audience for three different
    productions confirms this impression.

33 Hume 101; Righter 79

34 Hume 101

35 Chadwick 109. See also Rogers 69.

36 Holland, eg, argues that 'Alithea finally learns the difference between the
    superficial appearance of faith and real faith' (82). See also Rogers 69.

37 Rogers 61

38 For discussions of Buckingham's original targets, see Peter Lewis '*The
    Rehearsal*: A Study of Its Satirical Methods' *Durham University Journal* 31
    (1970) 96–133, and George McFadden 'Political Satire in *The Rehearsal*'
    Yearbook of English Studies 4 (1974) 120–8. For Cibber, see Philip H. Highfill
    et al *A Biographical Dictionary of Actors, Actresses, Musicians, Dancers,
    Managers & Other Stage Personnel in London, 1660–1800* III (Carbondale:
    Southern Illinois Univ Press 1975) 223. For Garrick, see George Winchester
    Stone, Jr and George M. Kahrl *David Garrick: A Critical Biography* (Carbon-
    dale: Southern Illinois Univ Press 1979) 476–80.

39 Sheridan Baker 'Buckingham's Permanent *Rehearsal*' *Michigan Quarterly
    Review* 12 (1973) 160

40 Baker 162; George Villiers, Duke of Buckingham *The Rehearsal* ed D.E.L.
    Crane (Durham: Univ of Durham 1976) 2.1.1–2. All quotations from *The
    Rehearsal* are from this edition. For the applicability of 'mad authorial ego-
    tism' to Dryden, see 242 n6 above.

41 Baker 160, 164

42 John Wilcox *The Relation of Molière to Restoration Comedy* (New York:
    Columbia Univ Press 1938) 58–9

43 Ibid 68

44 See John Harrington Smith 'Thomas Corneille to Betterton to Congreve' *Journal of English and Germanic Philology* 45 (1946) 209–13.

45 Molière *George Dandin* in *Oeuvres complètes* ed Maurice Rat (Paris: Gallimard 1951) II 289 (act 1, scene 1). All my quotations from *George Dandin* are from this edition.

46 Thomas Betterton *The Amorous Widow* in Charles Gildon *The Life of Mr. Thomas Betterton, the Late Eminent Tragedian* (London 1710; rpt New York: Augustus M. Kelley 1970) 31 (act 2, scene 1). All my quotations from *The Amorous Widow* are from this edition.

47 Lionel Gossman *Men and Masks: A Study of Molière* (Baltimore MD: Johns Hopkins Univ Press 1963) 150–2

48 Ibid 151

49 Scouten 166

50 Joan Crow 'Reflections on *George Dandin*' in *Molière: Stage and Study. Essays in Honour of W.G. Moore* ed W.D. Howarth and Merlin Thomas (Oxford: Clarendon Press 1973) 9

51 Ibid. Crow points to W.G. Moore *French Classical Literature: An Essay* (London: Oxford Univ Press 1961) 99 and René Bray *Molière, homme de théâtre* (Paris: Mercure de France 1954) 312, 255 as examples of those who take Dandin's suicide seriously (ibid 8).

52 Brian Gibbons *Jacobean City Comedy* 2nd ed (London: Methuen 1980) 9

53 Ibid 11

54 There are, as always, exceptions. Hume points to John Wilson's *The Cheats* (1663) as an example of an 'old-fashioned ... enjoyable boisterous, Middletonian city comedy' (243).

55 Alexander Leggatt *Citizen Comedy in the Age of Shakespeare* (Toronto: Univ of Toronto Press 1973) 13, 3–4

56 Smith 'Thomas Corneille' 209

57 Thomas Corneille *Le Baron d'Albikrac* in *Théâtre complet* ed Édouard Thierry (Paris: Laplace, Sanchez 1881) 431 (act 1, scene 9)

58 John Harrington Smith *The Gay Couple in Restoration Comedy* Cambridge MA: Harvard Univ Press 1948) 85. See also Allardyce Nicoll *A History of English Drama, 1660–1900* I *Restoration Drama 1660–1700* 4th ed (Cambridge: Cambridge Univ Press 1961) 281, and Hume 90 where the play is described as 'the first real comedy of sex and cuckoldry,' and its appeal seen as largely in 'titillation.'

59 Hume 337

60 John Crowne *The Countrey Wit*, 2.1.227–36, in *The Comedies of John Crowne: A Critical Edition* ed B.J. McMullin (New York: Garland 1984). All my quotations from *The Countrey Wit* are from this edition. For the appropri-

ate lines in Rochester, see David M. Vieth ed *The Complete Poems of John Wilmot, Earl of Rochester* (New Haven CT: Yale Univ Press 1968) p 98, ll. 98–111. Vieth dates Rochester's poem 'before 23 March 1675/6' (94); Hume dates *The Countrey Wit* 'March 1675?' (307).

61 Hume 307

62 For a fuller treatment of possible borrowings from Molière, see Arthur Franklin White *John Crowne: His Life and Dramatic Works* (Cleveland OH: Western Reserve Univ Press 1922) 87–90, and McMullin 3–5.

63 Robert Jordan 'The Extravagant Rake in Restoration Comedy' in *Restoration Literature: Critical Approaches* ed Harold Love (London: Methuen 1972) 70, 86. Smith, in a footnote, refers to Ramble as 'an amusing scapegrace who talks more libertinism than he is permitted to display' (106 n7). The extravagant rake is also treated by Hume in his survey of Restoration rakes, 'The Myth of the Rake in "Restoration Comedy"' in *The Rakish Stage: Studies in English Drama, 1660–1800* (Carbondale: Southern Illinois Univ Press 1983) 138–75. See especially 155–8.

64 Etherege *The Man of Mode* in *Dramatic Works* II 278–9 (5.2.144–7)

65 Jordan 87–8

66 Dennis *Critical Works* I 284. Cited by Jordan 81

67 White points to the similarity between Lady Faddle and Wycherley's Lady Flippant, both in their shared hypocritic railing against marriage and in their common pursuit of a picture from men they are after (Dapperwit in Lady Flippant's case). He also cites the similarity in 'the gushing exchange of compliments between Sir Thomas Rash and Lady Faddle in which each tries to outdo the other' and the 'similar exchange of sarcastic flattery between Alderman Gripe and Mrs. Joyner' (90–1). He sees *She wou'd if she cou'd* as Crowne's other major English source.

CHAPTER THREE

1 Samuel Johnson 'Congreve' in *Lives of the English Poets* ed George Birkbeck Hill (Oxford: Clarendon Press 1905) II 216; 'Thomas Southerne on Congreve' in John C. Hodges ed *William Congreve: Letters and Documents* (London: Macmillan 1964) 151. More recent critics also concur, none more articulately than John Wilcox: 'Young Congreve produced a suave synthesis of dramatic stereotypes ... Obviously the author has assimilated the comic tradition of England and reproduced its matter and manner without significant change. Congreve has gone to school with a vengeance' (*The Relation of Molière to Restoration Comedy* 155–6). Brian Gibbons considers Southerne's account little more than a 'pleasant fiction' because he thinks Southerne is trying to take credit for extensive revision. But Southerne's contributions need not have extended beyond the 'minor suggestions' Gibbons sees as all that could have

been added to Congreve's playscript. I think Gibbons is right to insist upon the presence of but 'one hand' in *The Old Batchelour*; it remains, however, the hand of an apprentice – albeit a brilliant one ('Congreve's *The Old Batchelour* and Jonsonian Comedy' in Brian Morris ed *William Congreve* (London: Benn 1972) 8).

2 Dryden *Works* XVII 60–1

3 John Dennis 'John Dennis to William Congreve' in Hodges ed *Letters and Documents* 175

4 William Congreve 'Congreve to John Dennis' in Hodges 182, 185. For Temple's views, see 'Of Poetry' in *Essays on Ancient & Modern Learning and On Poetry* ed J.E. Spingarn (Oxford: Clarendon Press 1909) 73–7.

5 Stuart M. Tave *The Amiable Humorist: A Study in the Comic Theory and Criticism of the Eighteenth and Early Nineteenth Centuries* (Chicago: Univ of Chicago Press 1960) 100. My understanding of the development of comic theory is greatly indebted to Tave's study.

6 Congreve's transitional status is treated by Clifford Leech in his important, pioneering 'Congreve and the Century's End' *Philological Quarterly* 41 (1962) 275–93.

7 Dryden *Works* X 206–9

8 For a more extensive discussion of Congreve's theoretical position with an application to Congreve's play of this period not covered here, see my 'The Mixed Way of Comedy: Congreve's *The Double-Dealer*' *Modern Philology* 71 (1974) 356–65.

9 Malcolm Elwin *The Playgoer's Handbook to Restoration Drama* (London: Cape 1928) 168

10 Montague Summers ed *The Complete Works of William Congreve* (London: Nonesuch 1923) I 157. Many critics have pointed to the similarity of these characters; Summers' discussion is, I believe, the first of Heartwell to tie them together. Thomas Davies, who argued that 'Congreve formed himself on Wycherly,' was one of the earliest critics to see Heartwell's similarity to Pinchwife (*Dramatic Miscellanies* (Dublin: S. Price 1784) III 185–8).

11 William Congreve *The Old Batchelour* 1.1.302–5 in *The Complete Plays of William Congreve* ed Herbert Davis (Chicago: Univ of Chicago Press 1967). All my quotations from Congreve's plays are from this edition.

12 Gibbons 'Congreve's *The Old Batchelour*' 12; Aubrey Williams *An Approach to Congreve* (New Haven CT: Yale Univ Press 1979) 114

13 Maximillian E. Novak *William Congreve* (New York: Twayne 1971) 84

14 It seems likely that Congreve borrowed the business of Laetitia hanging upon Fondlewife's neck and kissing him while Bellmour kisses her hand behind his back (4.4.240) from *The Amorous Widow* (4.1.p51).

15 Novak 85. Novak also points to the parallel surrenders of Heartwell and Fondlewife when confronted by the tears of Silvia and Laetitia.

16 Harold Love *Congreve* (Totowa NJ: Rowman and Littlefield 1975) 29 argues that Bellmour, the more 'extravagant' of the wits, is 'on a lower rung than the terser and more guarded' Vainlove. I would consider Bellmour (to maintain Jordan's terminology) a 'more normal rakish gentleman' (Jordan 83), but a rakish gentleman of a distinctly later generation. I would agree with Love, however, in seeing the diminished place of extravagant values in Congreve's comedies.

17 Kenneth Muir *The Comedy of Manners* (London: Hutchinson 1970) 100

18 *The Old Batchelour* 'Dramatis Personae' 36

19 Love *Congreve* 29

20 Williams 116

21 Thomas H. Fujimura *The Restoration Comedy of Wit* (Princeton NJ: Princeton Univ Press 1952) 169 is reminded 'a little of the honorable couples in the first plays of Etherege and Wycherley' by Araminta and Vainlove.

22 Davies *Dramatic Miscellanies* III 187

23 Elwin 167; Muir 102

24 Novak 86; Holland 138; Williams 109; Love 34; John King McComb 'Congreve's *The Old Batchelour*: A Satiric Anatomy,' *Studies in English Literature* 17 (1977) 361

25 Leech 'Congreve and the Century's End' 287

26 See the Commentary on *Amphitryon* in *Works* XV ed Earl Miner et al (Berkeley: Univ of California Press 1976) 460–72. For a detailed comparison of Dryden, Molière, and Plautus, see Alexander L. Bondurant 'The *Amphitruo* of Platus, Molière's *Amphitryon*, and the *Amphitryon* of Dryden.' *Sewanee Review* 33 (1925) 455–68 and Thomas E. Barden 'Dryden's Arms in *Amphitryon*' *Costerus* 9 (1973) 1–8. For the most thorough discussion of Dryden's use of his sources, see Ned Bliss Allen *The Sources of John Dryden's Comedies* (Ann Arbor: Univ of Michigan Press 1935) 225–39 and 273–81, and for Heywood's contribution, see Margaret Kober Mezbach 'The Third Source of Dryden's *Amphitryon*' *Anglia* 73 (1955) 213–14.

27 Langbaine I 131; I 151; II Appendix, sig. Ool^V. *Amphitryon* also earned the praise of another of Dryden's sometime enemies, Luke Milbourne. For Milbourne's text, see *The Works of John Dryden* ed Sir Walter Scott (18 vols, 1808); rev by George Saintsbury (Edinburgh: William Patterson 1882–93) VIII 3–4.

28 *Works* XV 472. Scott also recognized the excellence of *Amphitryon*, 'in which Dryden displays his comic powers to more advantage than anywhere, excepting in the "Spanish Friar"' (*The Life of John Dryden* ed Bernard Kreissman (Lincoln: Univ of Nebraska Press 1963) 305).

29 Frank Harper Moore *The Nobler Pleasure: Dryden's Comedy in Theory and Practice* (Chapel Hill: Univ of North Carolina Press 1963) 208

30 Preface to *Secret Love* in *Works* IX ed John Loftis and Vinton A. Dearing (Berkeley: Univ of California Press 1966) 117

31 John Loftis 'Dryden's Comedies' in *John Dryden* ed Earl Miner (London: Bell 1972) 55

32 Allen 227

33 Bondurant 468

34 *Amphitryon* 1.2.160–2 in *Works* XV 244. All my quotations from the play are from this edition.

35 Miner in *Works* XV 468; Miner 'On Reading Dryden' in *John Dryden* ed Miner 17–18; Loftis, 'Dryden's Comedies' 53. (Dryden's interest in 'common folk' is perhaps overstated; there is nothing common about Jupiter's main victims, Amphitryon and Alcmena.)

36 Dryden's version was surely the source of Setter's '*Mercury* was a pimp too' in *The Old Batchelour*, 5.1.335.

37 *Works* XV 470. James D. Garrison's exploration of the political implications of *Amphitryon* also points to a tragic dimension. See 'Dryden and the Birth of Hercules' *Studies in Philosophy* 77 (1980) 180–201.

38 William Mountfort *Greenwich-Park* in *The Plays of William Mountfort* intro Paul W. Miller (Delmar NY: Scholars' Facsimiles and Reprints 1977) sig A3^v. All my quotations from the play are from this edition.

39 Nathaniel Lee *The Princess of Cleve* in *The Works of Nathaniel Lee* ed Thomas B. Stroup and Arthur L. Cooke (New Brunswick NJ: Scarecrow Press 1955) II 178 (2.3.7–9). If Martin W. Walsh is correct in ascribing Young Reveller's reference to the decline in society 'since *Strephon* the wise, the witty, and the gay and the Prince of all Company, as well as all hearts, forsook us' (1.2.p4) to a nostalgia for the 'Golden Days' (as Lord Worthy calls them) of the Earl of Rochester, the comparison between Lee's play and Mountfort's gains additional significance, for 'Nemours's whole character can very plausibly be read as a mixed but profoundly hostile depiction of that noble rake' (Hume 356). See 'The Significance of William Mountfort's *Greenwich-Park*' *Restoration and 18th Century Theatre Research* 12 (1973) 39. Mountfort's allusion would suggest just how remote the period of the 'court wits' seemed to a playwright who was still a teenager when Rochester died.

40 Nemours is given prominent treatment by Hume in 'The Myth of the Rake' 46–7.

41 See my 'Interpreting and Misinterpreting *The Man of Mode*' *Papers on Language and Literature* 13 (1977) 46–7.

42 For the stage history of *Greenwich-Park*, see Albert S. Borgman *The Life and Death of William Mountfort* (Cambridge MA: Harvard Univ Press 1935) 192–5.

43 Hume 'The Myth of the Rake' 41

44 Dryden, Dedication to *Mr. Limberham* in *Works* ed Scott and Saintsbury VI 9

45 Hume 85

46 Walsh 35

47 Paul W. Miller intro to *The Plays of William Mountfort* xxv

48 Walsh 37

49 Ibid 36

50 [Charles Gildon] *The Lives and Characters of the English Dramatick Poets* (London (1699); rpt New York: AMS 1976) 25

51 Walsh notes that in describing Raison and Sasaphras as 'jolly Citizens,' Mountfort uses 'an epithet rarely used since the days of Dekker and Heywood' (36).

52 Hume 396

53 Sutherland 151

54 Thomas Durfey *Love for Money, or, The Boarding School* (London: A. Roper and E. Wilkinson 1691) 1 (act 1, scene 1). All my quotations from the play are from this edition.

55 'Dramatis Personae' sig A1^{v}

56 Ibid

57 Smith 'Shadwell, The Ladies, and the Change in Comedy' *Modern Philology* 46 (1948) 31

58 Lynch 'Thomas D'Urfey's Contribution to Sentimental Comedy' *Philological Quarterly* 9 (1930) 250–9

59 Robert Stanley Forsythe *A Study of the Plays of Thomas D'Urfey* (Cleveland OH: Western Reserve Univ Press 1916–17) I 69. Betty Jiltall might be added to this list as a comic anticipation of Lillo's Millwood.

60 Sutherland 139

61 C.B. Graham 'The Jonsonian Tradition in the Comedies of Thomas D'Urfey' *Modern Language Quarterly* 8 (1947) 47–52

62 *Wit for Money: or, Poet Stutter* (London: S. Burgis 1691) 14. For a discussion of Behn's sources, see Marston Stevens Balch *Thomas Middleton's 'A Trick to Catch the Old One,' 'A Mad World, My Masters,' and Aphra Behn's 'City Heiress'* (Salzburg: Institut für Anglistik und Amerikanistik Universität Salzburg 1981).

63 Thomas Middleton *A Trick to Catch the Old One* ed G.J. Watson (London: Benn 1968) xvii

64 Aphra Behn *The City Heiress; or, Sir Timothy Treat-all* in *The Works of Aphra Behn* ed Montague Summers (London: Heinemann 1915) II 205 (act 1, scene 1)
65 'Dramatis Personae' sig A1^v
66 Ibid
67 Ibid
68 Ibid
69 Ibid
70 Ibid
71 Forsythe 69. Smith *The Gay Couple* 131 corrects Forsythe's misreading.
72 Nicoll *Restoration Drama* 276
73 Sutherland 137
74 Durfey 'Prologue' to *A Fond Husband; or, The Plotting Sisters* in *Two Comedies by Thomas D'Urfey* ed Jack A. Vaughn (Rutherford NJ: Farleigh Dickinson Univ Press 1976) 157. For a useful discussion of the 'Prologue' and Durfey's other contributions to comic theory, see Harold Love 'Dryden, Durfey, and the Standard of Comedy' *Studies in English Literature* 13 (1973) 422–36.
75 Durfey's source this time is *More Dissemblers besides Women*; see Forsythe 86.
76 *Poeta Infamis, or a Poet not worth Hanging* (London: B.C. 1692) 12
77 Thomas Durfey *The Marriage-Hater Match'd* (London: Richard Parker and Sam. Briscoe 1692) sig A4^r. All my quotations from the play are from this edition. Harold Love places Gildon's argument firmly in its context in 'Dryden, Durfey, and the Standard of Comedy,' especially 428–30.
78 Ibid sig a1^r
79 *Poeta Infamis* [4]
80 Gildon's later view of Durfey is a more accurate one: 'I have laught heartily at his Plays, which is one end of Comedy, or Farce at least; and if the Criticks will deny him to be a good Writer of Comedy, they must allow him to be a Master of Farce.' See his revision of Langbaine *The Lives and Characters of the English Dramatick Poets* 48. Gildon admits here that his letter is not 'free from Flattery; and we may conclude that Friendship, or some other Motive blinded his Eyes very much, when he made so large an Encomium of it' (52).
81 Forsythe 86
82 Peter Holland *The Ornament of Action: Text and Performance in Restoration Comedy* (Cambridge: Cambridge Univ Press 1979) 150
83 *The Marriage-Hater Match'd* 'The Names and Characters' sig A2^v
84 Ibid

86 Ben Jonson *Volpone, or The Fox* in *Ben Jonson* V 5.2.102–3. All my quotations
   from the play are from this edition.
87 Hume 411. Earlier, Hume refers to *Love for Love* as 'a verbally polished cross
   between Fletcher and Jonson' (106). Harold Love sees *Love for Love* in a tradition of courtship plays in which the women must teach the men about love
   before they can marry. He traces the tradition back to *Love's Labour's Lost*,
   Shirley's *The Lady of Pleasure*, and Fletcher's *The Elder Brother* (a likely
   source for the title phrase). See Love *Congreve* 61.
88 William Archer ed *William Congreve* (New York: American Book Company
   1912) 27
89 William Congreve *Love for Love* in *The Complete Plays* 1.1.552–9. All my
   quotations from the play are from this edition.
90 Smith *The Gay Couple* 157
91 Ibid 158
92 Two studies of Congreve's use of allusion in constructing the imagery of *Love
   for Love* testify to the care he took in emphasizing the particulars of Valentine's education. Shakespeare, Jonson, Horace, and Epictetus all contribute
   reinforcement of Angelica's lesson. See Arthur W. Hoffman 'Allusions and the
   Definition of Themes in Congreve's *Love for Love*' in Louis L. Martz and
   Aubrey Williams eds *The Author in His Work: Essays on a Problem in Criticism* (New Haven CT: Yale Univ Press 1978) 283–96, and James Thompson
   'Reading and Acting in *Love for Love*' *Essays in Literature* 7 (1980) 21–30.
93 For a good account of the critical debate, see Hume 104–11.
94 Schneider lists 485 performances of *Love for Love*, 343 of *The Old Batchelour*,
   168 of *The Double-Dealer*, and 297 of *The Way of theWorld*.
95 Samuel Johnson 'Congreve' II 218; Cibber *An Apology* 268; Bonamy Dobrée
   Restoration Comedy: 1660–1720 (Oxford: Clarendon Press 1925) 132; Leech
   'Congreve and the Century's End' 289
96 Northrop Frye *Anatomy of Criticism: Four Essays* (Princeton NJ: Princeton
   Univ Press 1957) 180–1. Foresight, of course, lacks a guardian's legal control
   over his niece.
97 Hume 106–8
98 Peter Holland *The Ornament of Action* 228 points to the special appropriateness of Mrs Foresight's lines when spoken by Elizabeth Barry, citing Tom
   Brown's report that 'Should you lie with her all Night, She would not know
   you next Morning, unless you had another five Pound at her Service' As I
   indicate below, such allusion does not preclude the inclusion of this intrigue as
   part of a more internal, central design. The two, in fact, are remarkably harmo-
   nious, given, as well, the contemporary reputation of Anne Bracegirdle.

99 It is worth recalling Scandal's earlier proverbial commonplaces, such as 'He only is Secret who never was trusted; ... As she is chaste, who was never ask'd the Question' (3.1.125–8) and the song he requests (3.1.200–8), a veritable rake's credo.
100 Hume 111, summarizing the views of Leech and Rose A. Zimbardo
101 See my 'The Way of the World and Morally Serious Comedy' Univ of Toronto Quarterly 44 (1975) 199–212.
102 Harriett Hawkins Likenesses of Truth in Elizabethan and Restoration Drama (Oxford: Clarendon Press 1972) 110
103 Holland The First Modern Comedies 161
104 Ibid; Love Congreve 70; Williams An Approach to Congreve 169; Birdsall Wild Civility 215; Charles R. Lyons 'Congreve's Miracle of Love' Criticism 6 (1964) 337; Novak William Congreve 118–19
105 Hodges ed Letters and Documents 179
106 Holland 165
107 Novak 114
108 Holland 173; Birdsall 226

CHAPTER FOUR

1 George Farquhar 'A Discourse upon Comedy' in The Works of George Farquhar ed Shirley Strum Kenny, 2 vols (Oxford: Clarendon Press 1988) II 376–7. All my quotations from Farquhar are from this edition.
2 Two remarks by Peter Dixon in his 'Revels Plays' edition of The Recruiting Officer (Manchester: Manchester Univ Press 1986) provide a typical, recent example: 'Farquhar has endowed his characters with remarkable lifelike language, expressive of a wide range of personalities ...; Not that Farquhar's scenes, for all their seeming unpredictability, are ever less than carefully moulded, with a very sure and practised eye for theatrical effect' (11, 13).
3 Alexander Pope 'The First Epistle of the Second Book of Horace' in Imitations of Horace ed John Butt vol 4 of Twickenham Edition of the Poems of Alexander Pope (London: Methuen 1939) l.288
4 By setting The Recruiting Officer in the country, Farquhar more easily overcame the greatest obstacle to the new middle-class comedy of humours, the tradition of the urban bourgeois as comic gull. The character closest to the earlier money-hungry cit is the corrupt constable, and his greed leads to impressment.
5 Eric Rothstein George Farquhar (New York: Twayne 1967) 86
6 For a discussion of Farquhar's popularity in the eighteenth century, see Shirley Strum Kenny 'Perennial Favorites: Congreve, Vanbrugh, Cibber, Farquhar, and

Steele'; for the fullest discussion of humane comedy, see her 'Humane Comedy' *Modern Philology* 75 (1977) 29–43. For stage history, see Kenny ed
Works II 7–12; John Ross ed *The Recruiting Officer* (London: Benn 1977) xxxi–
xxxxiii; Dixon 23–32; and, for an inside account of the most important recent
production, see Kenneth Tynan ed *The Recruiting Officer: The National Theatre Production* (London: Rupert Hart-Davis 1965).

7 Willard Connely *Young George Farquhar: The Restoration Drama at Twilight*
(London: Cassell 1949) 244 suggests a partial source in Jonson's *Volpone*;
Rothstein sees *The Alchemist* as a more likely model. Both, I think, are right to
emphasize the Jonsonian character of the scene; Kite, in his aims and methods,
seems to me closer to Subtle than to Scoto of Mantua. Peter Dixon also notes
the Jonsonian character of *The Recruiting Officer*, citing *Bartholomew Fair* as
being especially close in spirit. Dixon, following Rothstein, begins his discussion of the play by pointing to the frontispiece of Lintot's 1708 edition of Farquhar's plays, which shows Farquhar being presented to Apollo by Ben Jonson.
Jonson carries a copy of *Bartholomew Fair*. See Dixon 9–10 and Rothstein 160.

8 Rothstein 129

9 For a full discussion of the military background to *The Recruiting Officer*, see
Eugene Nelson James *The Development of George Farquhar as a Comic
Dramatist* (The Hague: Mouton 1972) 231–53. Nelson James provides considerable information in making a case for the play as a bitter anti-war satire, 'an
eighteenth-century *What Price Glory*' (p 237). Nelson James's description,
however, more accurately conveys the message of Brecht's adaptation, *Pauken
und Trompeten* (see Albert Wertheim 'Bertolt Brecht and George Farquhar's
The Recruiting Officer' *Comparative Drama* 7 (1973) 179–190). Farquhar's
presentation of recruiting and of the military in general is sufficiently balanced
to support Rothstein's antithetical case for *The Recruiting Officer* as 'a pro-
war play, characterized by the same dry-eyed militarism that appears in Farquhar's other plays, and in poems like "General Schomberg" and "Barcellona"'
(132). Peter Dixon 19 argues – against Nelson James and his eighteenth-century predecessor, Arthur Bedford, in particular – for a more balanced view on
Farquhar's part: 'Farquhar walks delicately between the pitfalls of jingoistic
complacency and militaristic propaganda on one side, and of cynical contempt
for recruiters and their gullible victims on the other.' I find Dixon's view per-
suasive.

10 Rothstein 132ff, Ross xx, and Wertheim 180, to name but three, make similar
observations about the basic structure of *The Recruiting Officer*.

11 Some of the themes most frequently cited are 'the disguises men put on to
hide themselves from the world (Nelson James 221); a 'view of heroism .. as
skeptical as our own' in a play whose 'invisible protagonist is war' (William

Gaskill 'Historical Note' and 'Production Preface' in Tynan ed *The Recruiting Officer* 11, 8; and 'the interrelation of loving and fighting' (Ross xx). There remains disagreement about Farquhar's attitude toward war in the play (see n9 above).

12 For the earliest comment on these inconsistencies, see Robert L. Hough 'An Error in "The Recruiting Officer"' *Notes and Queries* 198 (1953) 340–1, and 'Farquhar: "The Recruiting Officer,"' *Notes and Queries* 199 (1954) 474.

13 Rothstein 154. The dialectic between robbery and courtship is similar to one between recruiting and courtship in *The Recruiting Officer* (see Dixon 14–19).

14 Charles Fifer ed *The Beaux' Stratagem* (Lincoln: Univ of Nebraska Press 1977) xxv–xxvi

15 This line of 'twin heroes' is traced by William W. Appleton in 'The Double Gallant in Eighteenth-Century Comedy' in *English Writers of the Eighteenth Century* ed John H. Middendorf (New York: Columbia Univ Press 1971) 145–57.

16 Fifer xxvi notes that 'the bride is ultimately won not by wit or stratagem, but by honesty – the result of true love,' but he sees this as evidence of Farquhar's difference from Etherege, Wycherley, and Congreve.

17 *Producible Interpretation: Eight English Plays, 1675–1707* (Carbondale: Southern Illinois Univ Press 1985) 302. The similarity to Worthy and Melinda is, however, noteworthy.

18 Frederick S. Boas *An Introduction to Eighteenth-Century Drama, 1700–1780* (Oxford: Clarendon Press 1953) 60

19 *George Farquhar* (London: T. Fisher Unwin (1906)) 26–7. Archer argues that the humours tradition in his sense was taken over by the eighteenth-century essayists.

20 Ronald Berman 'The Comedy of Reason' *Texas Studies in Literature and Language* 7 (1965) 166; William L. Sharp 'Restoration Comedy: An Approach to Modern Production' *Drama Survey* 7 (1968–9) 85; Nelson James 276; Fifer xxxi; A. Norman Jeffares ed *The Beaux Stratagem* (Edinburgh: Oliver & Boyd 1972) 6, 8

21 Berman 168 points to an example of the complexity of *The Beaux Stratagem*: 'The Play has stated that nothing is durable but money, and we can see that money is not durable. It then offers the statement that nothing is necessary but passion, and we already have a sense of how far that is durable.' Milhous and Hume 316 credit Farquhar with 'a satire subtle enough not to offend those members of the audience determined to take the happy ending straight.' They maintain that a modern production would be equally valid as either 'romp or satire' (310–16).

22 'Humane Comedy' 30, 43

23 *The Comedy of Manners* (London: Bell 1913) 241; 'Humane Comedy' 30

24 Sir John Vanbrugh *A Short Vindication of the 'Relapse' and the 'Provok'd Wife,' from Immorality and Prophaneness* in *The Complete Works of Sir John Vanbrugh* ed Bonamy Dobrée and Geoffrey Webb (London: Nonesuch Press 1927) I 195. All my quotations from Vanbrugh are from this edition. Citations from Vanbrugh's plays are to volume and page, then act and scene.

25 *The Development* 414–15, 382

26 *The Thread of Laughter* 162; *The Comedy of Manners* (London: Hutchinson University Library 1970) 139. Dobrée discusses Vanbrugh's additions to and alterations of Dancourt's text (III 3–5). Some typical responses: 'There is not a scene in the play which [Vanbrugh] has left unimproved, and the improvements are uniformly conceived in his most felicitous vein' (W.C. Ward ed *Sir John Vanbrugh* 2 vols (London: Lawrence and Bullen 1893) I liv); 'the outstanding example [of Vanbrugh's translations] is *The Confederacy*, a superb adaptation of Dancourt's *Les Bourgeoises à la Mode*, itself a lively and witty comedy that Vanbrugh, by transferring the action from Paris to London, nevertheless succeeds in enhancing from beginning to end' (Peter Lewis 'Sir John Vanbrugh' in Arthur H. Scouten ed *Restoration and 18th Century Drama* (New York: St. Martin's 1980) 141)

27 William Hazlitt *Lectures on the English Comic Writers* in *The Collected Works* ed A.R. Waller and Arnold Glover (London: Dent 1903) VIII 82; Bernard Harris *Sir John Vanbrugh* (London: Longmans, Green 1967) 30

28 'Sir John Vanbrugh,' 140

29 Muir describes *The Confederacy* as 'closer to Jacobean City Comedy than to the comedy of manners' (*The Comedy of Manners* 139); Kronenberger, too, notes that 'we are closer to the Jacobean stage, and not simply because the economic motive is more pronounced, but because the social milieu is less exalted' (*The Thread of Laughter* 163). For a discussion of city comedy see above 41–2 and 146 n55.

30 Marie-Louise Fluchère *L'Œuvre Dramatique de Sir John Vanbrugh* (Paris: Ophrys 1980) 596

31 Arthur R. Huseboe *Sir John Vanbrugh* (Boston: Twayne 1976) 128

32 Ibid 125

33 Helene Koon *Colley Cibber: A Biography* (Lexington: Univ Press of Kentucky 1986) 27

34 *Apology* 189

35 *The Double Gallant: or, the Sick Lady's Cure: A Critical Old-Spelling Edition* ed John Whitley Bruton (New York: Garland 1987). All my citations from the play are from this edition; *Apology* 182–3

36 'The Double Gallant of Colley Cibber' *Review of English Studies* 1 (1925) 346; *English Comic Drama: 1700–1750* (Oxford: Clarendon Press 1929) 19

37 'The Double Gallant of Colley Cibber' 346

38 Colley Cibber *Three Sentimental Comedies* ed Maureen Sullivan (New Haven CT: Yale Univ Press 1973) 84 (ll. 9–16)

39 To treat the play as Cibber's is not, however, to take a moral position on his plagiarism, an issue as contentious today as it was in his time; witness the storm over such works as D.M. Thomas' *The White Hotel*. It is merely to say that his plagiarism is that of parts, not of the whole.

40 *Collected Works* VIII 162

41 *Apology* 75

42 *Apology* 94–5; 96. Tony Aston, for one, claims that 'the late Mrs. Oldfield borrowed something of her manner in free Comedy' (*A Brief Supplement to Colley Cibber, Esq. his Lives of the Famous Actors and Actresses* in Cibber *Apology* ed Robert W. Lowe (London: Nimmo 1889) II 313.

43 *The Revels History* 220

44 *Development* 472

45 Dedication to *The Basset-Table* (1705); Dedication to *The Gamester* (1705). Both cited in F.P. Lock *Susanna Centlivre* (Boston: Twayne 1979) 26

46 Richard Bevis *The Laughing Tradition: Stage Comedy in Garrick's Day* (Athens: Univ of Georgia Press 1980) 8. Centlivre's *The Wonder* was one of the other three.

47 See 87.

48 Arthur Murphy 'The Theatre' *London Chronicle* 4 (December 7–9, 1758) 559

49 *English Comic Drama: 1700–1750* 71

50 Baker recounts the shaky early history of *The Busie Body*, 'which all the players had decried before its appearance, in which Mr. Wilks had even for a time absolutely refused to play, and which the audience came prejudiced against, roused their attention in despite of that prejudice, and forced a run of thirteen nights' (*Biographia Dramatica* I 99).

51 *Collected Works* VIII 156,155

52 Giles Jacob *The Poetical Register* (London: E. Curll 1719) 32

53 Richard C. Frushell 'Marriage and Marrying in Susanna Centlivre's Plays' *Papers on Language and Literature* 22 (1986) 18

54 Bateson 64; Hume 116, 485, 490

55 Bonamy Dobrée *English Literature in the Early Eighteenth Century: 1700–1740* (Oxford: Clarendon Press 1959) 236; Nicoll II 167

56 Richard Cumberland 'Critique on *The Busy Body*' in *The British Drama* (London: C. Cooke 1817) X vi

57 Susanna Centlivre *The Busie Body* (London: Bernard Lintott 1709); rpt intro Jess Byrd (Los Angeles: Clark Library 1949) act 1, scene 1 p9. All my citations from the play are from this edition and are identified in the text by act, scene, and page.

58 Lock 65

59 John Wilson Bowyer *The Celebrated Mrs. Centlivre* (Durham NC: Duke Univ Press 1952) 100

60 Nicoll II 176. Dobrée's brief remarks on *The Fair Quaker of Deal* share a similar focus. He characterizes Shadwell's play as 'something different' because 'though vapid in sentiment and absurd as regards plot and denouement, [it] introduced naval types treated on hereditary Shadwell lines' (237).

61 *The Works of Mr. Charles Shadwell* 2 vols. (Dublin: George Risk and Joseph Leathley 1720) I v

62 Charles Shadwell *The Fair Quaker of Deal, or, the Humours of the Navy* (London: James Knapton, Bernard Lintott, and Egbert Sanger 1710) sig b4^v. All my citations from the play are from this edition and are identified in the text by act, scene, and page.

63 John Loftis *The Politics of Drama in Augustan England* (Oxford: Clarendon Press 1963) 38

64 Baker II 213

65 Shadwell's preface b1. I accept the standard view that Cibber is the unnamed 'famous Comedian belonging to the *Haymarket* Play-House' of Shadwell's account.

66 Cibber *Apology* 230

CONCLUSION

1 Fowler 170

2 'The terms for kinds [genres] ... can always be put in noun form ... whereas modal terms tend to be adjectival ... Modal extension can be either local or comprehensive ... Any kind might be extended as a mode ... Division of kinds into subgenres normally goes by subject matter or motifs. In fact, they are formed in just the opposite way from that which produces modes: subgenres have the common features of the kind – external forms and all – and over and above these, add special substantive features' (Fowler 106–8, 112)

3 Ibid 171

4 Ibid 174

5 Ibid 175

6 See, for example, my discussion of Fainall in '*The Way of the World* and Morally Serious Comedy' *Univ of Toronto Quarterly* 44 (1975) 202–3, 207–11.

7 Jauss 25

8 Ibid 27–8

9 Kenny 'Humane Comedy' 43–4

10 See Kenny 'Perennial Favorites' for a more detailed account.

Index